CARNIVORE

CARNIVORE

A MEMOIR BY ONE OF THE DEADLIEST AMERICAN SOLDIERS OF ALL TIME

DILLARD JOHNSON
AND JAMES TARR

WM
WILLIAM MORROW
An Imprint of HarperCollins*Publishers*

Map of Iraq on p. ix courtesy of the UN Cartographic Section.

All photographs are courtesy of the author.

HarperCollins books may be purchased for educational, business, or sales promotional use. For information please write: Special Markets Department, HarperCollins Publishers, 10 East 53rd Street, New York, NY 10022.

FIRST EDITION

Designed by Jamie Lynn Kerner

Library of Congress Cataloging-in-Publication Data has been applied for.

ISBN 978-0-06-228841-7

13 14 15 16 17 OV/RRD 10 9 8 7 6 5 4 3 2 1

THIS BOOK IS DEDICATED TO

My loving wife, Amy, for the support, understanding, and sacrifices she has made.

My children, Daniel, Janise, Jaycob, and Max, for understanding when I was gone and for the sacrifices they had to make because I wasn't home.

The Big Three group, David Fortier, and James Tarr for pushing me to write this book.

The best Commanders anyone could ask for, Captains McCoy, Bair, and Burgoyne.

First Sergeant Roy Grigges, SFC Jason Christner, and Lieutenant Garrett McAdams for their leadership and support.

CSM Tony Broadhead for his never-ending support, and for always saving my ass when I bit off more than I could chew. Without Tony Broadhead there would be no Crazy J or Carnivore—Bradley *or* book.

The crew of the Carnivore: Soprano, Sperry, Sully, and Patten, for putting up with all my crap and being the finest fighting crew in history.

My wingmen: Geary, Carter, Wallace, Williams, Miller, Sowby, and Kennedy, and to the Crazy Horse troopers of 3rd Squadron, 7th Cavalry, past and present, the finest fighting force ever trained.

And finally, the lost warriors of 3rd Squadron, 7th Cavalry: SFC Parson, SSG Mitchell, and SPC Williams.

Dillard (CJ) Johnson
February 2013

CONTENTS

Map of Iraq   ix

Prelude   xi

1. Bosnian D-Day   1

2. Junior Jackassery   7

3. No Such Thing as Friendly Fire   12

4. Raindrops Keep Falling on My Head   22

5. Love and Marriage, Army Style   28

6. Eight Ball and the Lipstick Lizards   41

7. Deathtrap   56

8. First Contact   70

9. Carnivore, Camel Toe, and Circus Freaks   81

10. Steel Beast   91

11. Ambush Alley   107

12. Junkyard Dogs   121

13. Line in the Sand   131

14. Every Truck in the Country   141

15. Repo Men   149

CONTENTS

16. The Great Baghdad Tank Battle . . . Sort Of   161

17. Iraqi Bullfighting   172

18. The Mafia Hit   188

19. Stage 3   202

20. Exchanging RPGs for IEDs   215

21. Sniping Is as Sniping Does   236

22. The Lion's Mouth   255

23. Syria vs. Kentucky   272

24. Blood, Sweat, and Tears   281

Acknowledgments   295

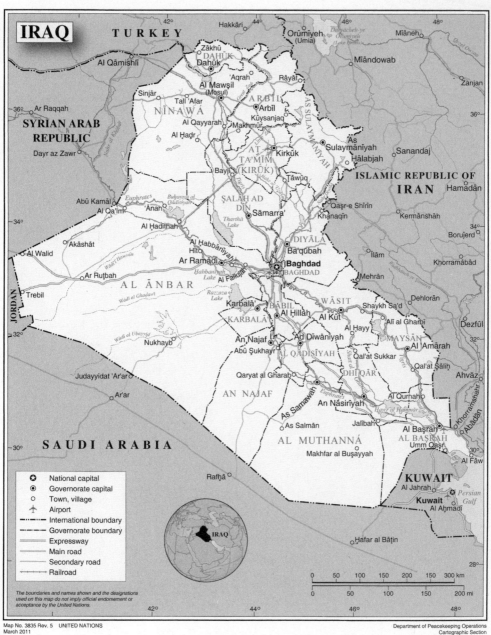

IRAQ

TURKEY

Hakkâri
Orūmīyeh (Umia)
Daryâcheh-ye Orūmīyeh (Lake Urmia)
Mīāneh
Qezel Owzan

Zākhū
DAHŪK
Dahūk
Mīāndowab

Al Qāmishlī

'Aqrah
Rāyāt

Zanjan

Al Mawşil (Mosul)
Sinjār
Tall 'Afar
ARBĪL
Arbīl

SYRIAN ARAB REPUBLIC

NĪNAWÁ
Al Qayyarah
Makhmūr
Kūysanjaq
AS SULAYMĀNĪYAH
As Sulaymānīyah
Sanandaj

Dayr az Zawr
Al Ḩaḑr
Kirkūk
Ḩālabjah

Nahr al Khābūr

AT TA'MĪM (KIRKŪK)
Bayjī
Tāwūq

ISLAMIC REPUBLIC OF IRAN
Hamadān

Abū Kamāl
Al Qā'im
'Ānah
Euphrates
Buḩayrat al Qādisīyah
ŞALĀḨ AD DĪN
Sāmarrā'
Qaşr-e Shīrīn
Khānaqīn
Kermānshāh

Al Hadīthah
Tharthā Lake

Borūjerd

Akāshāt
Al Ḩabbānīyah
DIYĀLÁ
Ba'qūbah
Īlām
Khorramābād

Al Walid
Wādī Ḩawrān
Ar Ramādī
Al Fallūjah
Baghdad
BAGHDAD
Mehrān

JORDAN
Ar Ruţbah
AL ĀNBAR
Habbānīyah Lake
Razzaza Lake
Karbalā'
BĀBIL
Al Hillah
WĀSIT
Shaykh Sa'd
'Alī al Gharbī
Dehlorān
Dezfūl

Trebil
Wādī al Ghadaf
KARBALĀ'
Al Kūt
Al Hayy
MAYSĀN
Al 'Amārah
Ahvāz

Nukhayb
Wādī al Ubayyiḍ
An Najaf
AL QĀDISĪYAH
Ad Dīwānīyah
Qal'at Sukkar
Qal'at Şālih

Judayyidat 'Ar'ar
Abū Şukhayr
Qaryat al Gharab
DHĪ QĀR
Al Qurnah
Khorramshahr
Ābādān

Ar'ar
AN NAJAF
As Samāwah
Euphrates
An Nāşirīyah
Shaṭṭ al 'Arab

SAUDI ARABIA
As Salmān
Jalībah
AL MUTHANNÁ
Makhfar al Buşayyah
AL BAŞRAH
Al Başrah
Umm Qaşr
Al Fāw

Rafḩā'
KUWAIT
Al Jahrah
Persian Gulf

Kuwait
Al Aḩmadī

Ḩafar al Bāţin

IRAQ

0   50 100 150 200 250 300 km
0   50   100   150   200 mi

Map No. 3835 Rev. 5   UNITED NATIONS
March 2011

Department of Peacekeeping Operations
Cartographic Section

PRELUDE

March 27, 2003
Outside An Najaf, Iraq

Emerging from the Commander's hatch of my Bradley Fighting Vehicle, the Carnivore, I stared out through my goggles and saw hell. A monstrous sandstorm swirled around us, and in the haze the flames from the dozens of destroyed vehicles that had charged our position cast a devilish glow on the terrain. Their steel carcasses stretched over a mile across the plain before us, but right then I could only view the few that had made it to within shouting distance of our little canal bridge: tanks, cars, trucks, a bomb-laden bus that had tried to ram us, and the tanker truck that had been burning for two days.

The sandstorm seemed as if it had been going on forever, like we'd been inside a vortex of dust the entire war, and it was only getting worse. Visibility was down to ten feet. The thick sand made the dancing flames even more orange, and the whole area was bathed in eerie light. The glow from the flames was enough to screw up our thermal and night sights, but not sufficiently bright for us to actually see what we needed to, namely the Iraqis we knew were out there. Luckily, that meant they couldn't find us, either; so in between troop trucks charging our position on the canal bridge we only had to contend with random, inaccurate AK fire.

Crazy Horse Troop, 3/7 Cav, had seen so much action in the first two days of the war that the Commander had decided to give us a break. He'd put us in the rear of the column on the march north, guarding the 100 or so thin-skinned vehicles that made up our headquarters and medical and support elements. Those 100 vehicles were stretched out three-quarters of a mile behind me all the way to the bridge we'd crossed over the Euphrates River and made one hell of a tempting target. Especially since we were no longer advancing and had been told to hold both bridges. I was at one end of the convoy in the Carnivore and Sergeant John Williams was at the other, guarding the bridge over the Euphrates in his Bradley, the Casanova.

"Stay alert," I told Sperry, my driver, but I was talking as much to myself as I was to him. *How long had we all been awake?* Four days of near-constant combat, most of two days crossing the desert before that, and three days in Kuwait to start it off, when they'd been afraid of the troop getting hit by rockets, so we'd been on the move almost nonstop. How many days was that in a row? With only snatches of sleep here and there. I couldn't count the days. I could barely think. The concussion didn't help. The pain from all the mortar shrapnel in my arms and shoulders and the bullet in my leg wasn't keeping me alert anymore. Everything was just a dull ache.

Lieutenant McAdams was behind us on the road in his Bradley. Sergeant Wallace was to our right in his Bradley, off the side of the road by the canal where he could get a different angle on any oncoming vehicles. The sandstorm roared and hissed, and the engines of the Bradleys were loud anyway, so we couldn't hear any vehicles approaching. I watched and waited.

A truckload of Iraqis rolled up right on us—to the far side of the canal bridge, 40 damn feet away—before we even spotted them. And they had their fucking headlights on! Wallace got on his gun quicker than we did and killed everybody in the truck with a short burst from his machine gun.

"I'm getting down!" I called to my crew.

Visibility was bad enough without headlights shining in our faces, so I jumped down to turn off the lights of the truck. My knees were so stiff from standing in the hatch, I could barely walk. When I reached the ground and started limping toward the truck, I looked over and saw an Iraqi soldier on foot just 10 feet away from me with an RPG launcher on his shoulder. Before I could react, he fired at the Carnivore. The rocket hit the driver's hatch, flipped up in the air, and exploded over the bridge.

I drew and fired my Beretta, hitting him in the arm and chest, then the pistol jammed. AGAIN. That pistol was trying to kill me. There was an AK-47 on the seat of the truck, and I dove for it. As I went down, I was spattered with gore as the man's head exploded all over me.

Over my shoulder I saw Soprano, my gunner, less than two feet away, holding an AK of his own. He grinned, held it out, and said, "Here you go. It shoots a little high." Smartass.

Soprano had gotten off the Bradley to back me up and had moved to my right to avoid the lights of the truck. He had one of the more than 100 AK-47s we'd picked up the day before that we hadn't gotten around to dumping in the canal. We'd been too busy keeping one another alive, which meant we'd done an extraordinary amount of killing.

Soprano headed back toward the Carnivore. As I turned off the lights of the truck, two more dark shapes appeared on the road about 200 meters out. McAdams and his gunner, Sergeant Mulholland, had picked up the movement and were watching to see if the trucks that were rolling closer were troop transporters or some clueless farmers. When they stopped, the swirling sand was thin enough for us to see they were troop trucks, and the enemy soldiers started jumping out. I ducked down behind the Iraqi truck. I knew what was coming.

Mulholland opened up with 25 mm HE (high-explosive) rounds on full auto, shooting right past me, and the Iraqis scattered like cockroaches when the light hits them. Most of the dismounts ran toward us, firing their AKs, but a few smart ones ran for cover.

Thirty soldiers charged our position, and I had AK bullets whipping past me in one direction while Mulholland fired the Bradley's main gun in the other. Looking up at the winking muzzle of that gun as Mulholland worked it back and forth was an unsettling experience—now I knew how the enemy felt. Mulholland was able to kill two-thirds of the soldiers before they'd gotten within 100 meters of the bridge. The rest of them were determined and kept working their way toward us. AKs are a poor match for 25 mm HE, however, and Mulholland was able to pick them all off in a few minutes.

I got up from behind the truck where I'd been crouching and headed back to the Bradley, which I never should have left. Remember the line from *Apocalypse Now,* "Never get off the boat"? Note to self—*Never get off the Bradley, dumbass.*

As I climbed back up on top of my Bradley, I checked the driver's hatch for damage from the RPG round that had slammed it. Sperry opened the hatch and looked at me with his baby face.

"What the hell hit my hatch?" he asked me.

Oh, nothing, just a rocket that should have killed you. Hell, Sperry, Soprano, my loader Sully—we all should have died a dozen times over the past few days, and yet somehow we kept battling. They were still just kids, and there they were, fighting a war. Not just fighting, but kicking ass and taking a whole bunch of names.

I was old and angry and liked to fight, but this *Butch Cassidy and the Sundance Kid* last-stand bullshit wasn't exactly what they signed up for. As much as we were killing dismounts and destroying vehicles, we just couldn't seem to stop them.

Captain Jeff McCoy, the Troop Commander, had already given us the bad news—in between rare breaks in the sandstorm, JSTARS, our eye in the sky, had spotted 44 tanks heading toward the rear of our column, right at Sergeant Williams sitting on the Euphrates bridge. If that wasn't bad enough, they'd then radioed there were 1,000 troop trucks—not troops, mind you, but troop trucks, each one of which could hold at least 20 soldiers—bearing down on our position. Potentially 20,000 troops. The sporadic trucks we'd seen so far were just the disorganized advance troops, random drops ahead of the oncoming tidal wave. We didn't have enough ammunition, enough time, enough visibility, and they just kept coming.

What we didn't know then was that Saddam Hussein himself was personally moving these pieces around the board. He knew he had a U.S. cavalry squadron surrounded and was going to destroy it to get his victory over the Americans. Whatever it took, he was going to wipe us out, and he sent all the assets he had at that early stage in the war, which was most of the Medina Division. We had an entire enemy tank battalion coming at our rear and a whole infantry brigade advancing toward us from the front. Coming straight at our little canal bridge. Destroying Crazy Horse and all the assets we were protecting could alter the course of the war, and Saddam Hussein knew it.

Korea is known as the Forgotten War. Iraq isn't a forgotten war; everybody knows someone with a relative who served there, but it was a war. People forget that before it devolved into snipings and improvised explosive devices (IEDs) on the evening news, it was a real war, where thousands of American troops lined up against thousands of Iraqis—the fourth-largest army in the world—and despite bragging claims to the contrary, nobody knew for sure quite what would happen.

This is the story of the Iraq War you never heard about in the media. First and foremost, this was a war fought by and between armor—M1 tanks and Bradleys against top-of-the-line Soviet T-72s, APCs, anything and everything the Iraqis could throw at us. The Special Forces operators are the darlings of the media, but the regular army always does the heavy lifting, and in Iraq things were no different. Armor wins wars.

I was lucky enough to ride at the front of the American war effort and serve with some of the finest soldiers and men you'd ever want to meet. Crazy Horse Troop, 3/7 Cavalry, 3rd Infantry Division, was the tip of the spear throughout the war, and this is their story as much as it is mine.

This book should have been written long ago, but I've been too busy. After recovering from cancer caused by firing all those depleted uranium rounds on my first tour, I did a second combat tour with Crazy Horse, then spent six years as a private contractor. I've retired from that life, though. In addition to being able to spend time with my wife and kids, I now have the opportunity to pass on what I've seen and learned. Not just that—I have a duty.

After all the close calls I have had in my life, I thought my purpose was to tell everyone this story. A tale of the young men and women of the cavalry making a charge into history, where a young soldier in a supply truck without armor raced to the front lines under a hail of bullets to resupply a Bradley under heavy fire. The supply soldier was black, the Bradley crew was a mix of Italians, a Korean, one white rapper, and an old hillbilly. There is no race or sex when you are fighting for your life: there are only the fellow soldiers around you. I was willing to give my life to save them, just as they were ready to do the same for me.

But why did I wait? I was afraid that if I ever did tell this story my life's purpose would be completed. As I am writing this, my body is again fighting cancer from the depleted uranium rounds that saved my life so many times. Every soldier who fought in Iraq has had to face his or her own demons, and I'm no different; my demon just happens to be cancer.

God bless the Cav, the 3rd Infantry Division, and the United States of America!

PUBLISHER'S NOTE

This book was submitted to the Department of Defense Office of Security Review, which cleared it for publication as originally written.

CARNIVORE

CHAPTER 1

BOSNIAN D-DAY

On 9/11 I was in Bosnia with the 3rd Infantry Division. We went over in 2000 as peacekeepers, part of the United Nations forces.

Our area of responsibility, of operations, was to the north, a town called Brcko ("Birchko"). We were right across from Croatia, and the entire situation was sad and horrible. Imagine being in post–World War II Germany. Everybody was starving, and a lot of people were wearing little more than rags. The city was in shambles and everything was falling apart. Most people were just trying to find food. The Russian mafia was there in force taking advantage of the chaos, and that meant a lot of human trafficking was going on, as well as pirating of videos and God knows what else. It was a free-for-all of exploitation.

That was an eye-opening experience for me, seeing a country in that shape. An impoverished country. Not a poor country, but a nation whose people have just been devastated by war. Whether they were Muslims or Christians, Serbs or Croats, I started really feeling what they were going through. It stuck with me. They looked like us, like Americans. The places we were, some of them looked like Anytown, U.S.A.

We did what we could, keeping the Croats on their side of the river. Our forces were based at Camp McGovern, which was in the Zone of Separation (we called it "zoss"). McGovern was right where the border had been before the whole conflict started. They built the camp outside the town, and there were minefields on both sides of us. Every day it was an adventure going out on patrol or trying to do anything. If you didn't stay right on the road, you'd hit a land mine. It was nothing to be driving down the road and see land mines right on the shoulder of the road.

When the countryside flooded, land mines actually floated up against our fences. So there'd be a land mine. You'd sit and watch it because you knew they were all using the Soviet land mines, and with the Soviet stuff, you just never knew. They weren't exactly reliable. We'd watch them float by, see them in a line like little wooden docks.

As far as action, actual combat, we had snipers firing at us every once in a while. They weren't really that big an issue, but you did have to watch out. We'd drive through and rounds would bounce off the turrets or whatever else, but they weren't really focusing on us. We were right on the border between Croatia and Bosnia, and the two sides were more concerned with each other.

Our duties involved frequent meetings with the Serbs. Many times we were going to disarm them, and they had big warehouses where we had to inventory their weapons. There had to be parity—if we went into Croatia and counted out 89 rifles in this country, then we would go to Bosnia and count out 89 rifles in that country. Everything had to be exactly the same.

On one of our trips I did get to meet one of the Serbian tank commanders, which was very interesting. He had something like 50 tank kills, 50 Soviet T-72s, which is what the Croatians were using. I wish I'd been able to take pictures of his tank. It had been hit by sabot rounds on the sides of the turret. They weren't direct hits but grazes, where the rounds just caught on the side. It looked as if somebody had taken a big knife and ripped through the side of the tank. The damage had happened when he'd taken on four tanks at once.

Fifty is an amazing number of tank kills. The Serbian tank commander would set up inside a building and wait for the Croats to drive down the street past him. When they rolled by he would shoot them in the ass (the most vulnerable side on any tank), but as soon as he took them out he would get out of there and set up somewhere else. They would send more tanks to try to find whoever had taken out the first one, and he would get more of them. It was guerrilla warfare with a tank. He was quite effective. I don't think there are very many people, even American Iraq War heroes, who have as many confirmed tank kills as that. I know in World War II the Germans had a lot, but this guy—one tank gunner, he'd just sit back and blast 'em. And I got to get in that tank and spin the turret around and work the gun, which was pretty cool.

There's another thing that sticks with me. I found a Tommy Gun, a Thompson submachine gun, in one of the warehouses. It was supposed to be destroyed. The weapon was engraved with a name, Sergeant Wilson, and it had D-DAY 1944 and JUNE 7TH carved in it with a knife. Talk about holding a piece of history in your hands—that was one of the machine guns actually used on D-Day. I hope it served Sergeant Wilson well. (Yes, *I* know D-Day was June 6, but I'm guessing Sergeant Wilson was a little too busy to keep track of his calendar.)

We attempted to get that Thompson sent back to the States for the division, but it had to be destroyed due to the United Nations mandate. There were lots and lots of guns like that in their armories, but the Tommy was the one I'll never forget.

On 9/11, we were out on patrol, and I actually had the V Corps Commander, Lieutenant General William Wallace, in my formation. He had flown in from Germany and was up looking at some of our areas because they fell under V Corps jurisdiction. We had his vehicle inside our formation, escorting him while on patrol, when we heard across the radio, "You are authorized to go Red Direct on weapons."

Usually we carried our weapons Green Clear, which basically means we had the ammunition lying on the feed tray, but we didn't have our weapons charged. Red Direct means to lock, load, and place the weapons on Safe.

We were also told to get our personnel immediately to Camp Eagle, which was in Tuzla, down at the airport. We were instructed, "Use extreme caution and get there immediately." Even the General didn't have any idea what was going on, but we did as we were ordered and rolled through the town ASAP. When we arrived at the U.S. airfield, the gates were closed.

The airfield was outside the town, and the Air Force was running security at the gate. It didn't move as we rolled up. I was lead vehicle, so I said, "Hey, you gonna open the gate and let us in or what? You need to open the gate and let us get in there."

The skinny, baby-faced guard at the gate told me, "We can't. The place is locked down. Nobody can get in or out."

So I got out and walked up to him. "What the fuck are we supposed to do?" I asked him. "Camp out here on the side of the road? You see our IDs. We're U.S. forces. We need to get in the damn base." I told him, "We've got a very important person with us. We need to get inside the base."

He said, "You can't come in here. I got my orders."

Admittedly, I have a short temper and very little tolerance for idiots. I said, "I got my orders, too. You need to open the gate up or I'm gonna run over it."

The guard looked at me and said, "If you do, I will use deadly force."

I looked at him, then at the column behind me, then back at him. I told him, "I've got four .50-cals. You've got a pistol. What the fuck are you gonna do?"

He opened the gate.

Why didn't I tell him to call his Commanding Officer or try another tack? Well, for starters, he threatened me with his pistol first. And you have to understand, nothing in the military is as simple as calling your Commanding Officer and getting it done. Especially with the base locked down. It's just plain stupid to lock U.S. forces outside when there's a possible hostile element out there. Whenever you can, let them inside the base. It's the checkpoint, for God's sake. You've got all the procedures, you searched the vehicle. Do what you need to do. Get us on the base. We've got ID cards. We're U.S. military. He could see we were who we said we were.

Once this dumb airman decided to let us in, he said something like, "Okay, we'll open it up, but I'm gonna call . . . I'm gonna call my . . . my guy." Yeah, whatever.

Once we were through the gate, and he realized we had the Corps Commander with us, the gate guard realized he'd been an idiot and decided that things might go better for him if he didn't call anyone.

On post we dropped the General. We had drills all the time,

and none of us knew that anything in particular had happened to cause the alert, so we decided to head to the PX.

We walked inside and there were no cashiers. The PX was open, but everybody was off in the back where the TVs were. We walked toward the crowd, and they told us, "Hey, a plane hit one of the World Trade Center towers."

And then, just right there, we watched the second plane impact, and I thought to myself, You've got to be fucking kidding me.

We knew what it was. There was a terrorist attack, and we realized, We need to go NOW. We need to get back to base. So we, I, everybody, dropped all the shit we were going to buy at the PX and hurried back to our vehicles.

Our base camp was a good three hours away, so before we headed out, we topped off our vehicles before heading to the gate. We pulled up there, and the same guard said to us, "Nobody in or out."

I walked up to him and said, "Really? Are we having this conversation again?" And he opened the gate and let us go.

So, I spent 9/11 doing peacekeeping missions in Bosnia. I still remember that day, of course. My parents' generation, everybody remembers where they were, what they were doing, when they heard Kennedy got shot. For us, it's 9/11, when the second plane hit the towers. *This means war.*

CHAPTER 2

JUNIOR JACKASSERY

Everybody says, "Things were different when I was growing up," and while that sounds old-fashioned, the fact of the matter is that it's true. I was born in the rolling hills of Kentucky and didn't live around very many other people until I was 10 or maybe 12 years old. It was pretty remote: western Kentucky, north of Bowling Green and south of Evansville, Indiana.

Island, Kentucky, is a tiny little town. It was originally called Worthington Station, named after Edward Worthington, who was a veteran of the American Revolution, pioneer, surveyor, and explorer of Kentucky and the Ohio River valley. Sometime in the 1800s, when the train came through, the town was renamed Island. The story I heard was that at some point all the rivers backed up and flooded the whole area, but this town stood out and was a little island above the waters. The name stuck.

I had a normal childhood. My dad worked all the time, and my mom off and on. I had two sisters and one brother, all older than me. They were all caught up in that whole 1970s hippie revolution or whatever you want to call it. I didn't really see or hang out with them much.

I don't know if Kentucky is far enough south for us to be officially called rednecks, but I'm sure no cosmopolitan Ivy League graduate. Hell, my name is Dillard, and my father is Harlan Johnson. If anyone called Harlan *or* Dillard has graduated from Harvard in the last fifty years I'll lose a bet. Like most people in this country, we weren't poor, but we weren't rich.

A lot of days after school or in the summertime I was out roaming around with my .22 rifle or pistol through the old strip mines or hiking through the hills. Shooting my gun and spending time out in the woods was great. Back then, you really didn't have to worry about the safety of your kids every second, especially in the small community that I grew up in. It wasn't like it is now.

Boys are naturally stupid, or prone to do stupid things, and I was no different. The list of idiotic things I've done could fill a book in itself, and it's a wonder I stayed alive long enough to make it into the Army.

While Kentucky's not too far north, it does get cold in the winter. Wandering around in the woods with some friends once, we found an old oil tanker. The bottom was rusted out, so we kicked our way inside. There was tar or congealed oil or something all over the ceiling of the tanker. Since we were cold, we built a fire. Thinking we were smart, we built the fire at the entrance so the smoke could get out, and it was really smoky because the fuel we used for the fire was plastic bottles.

So there we were, at the back end of the tanker, with the fire at the entrance to keep us warm, and we went to sleep. Three hours into the night we woke up and had dripping fire on us—not just fire, dripping fire. The tar or whatever it was on the ceiling had caught fire. We managed to get out, but did I learn or wise up? Nope.

One time I was at the barber shop with my dad and stuck my hand in the barber pole and felt what I thought was fur. I found out the hard way it was a beehive. I was stung so many times my dad had to take me to the hospital. I had more than 500 bee stings all over my body. I was red, blotchy, and so swollen my eyes couldn't open all the way. There was so much toxin in my body, I don't know how I didn't die.

A few more stories. My neighbor had a Yamaha 80 motorcycle, and there was an old lady in the area who had raked up a big pile of leaves. Our plan was to ride through it so fast she wouldn't even see who we were. We woke up in the road all cut up and bleeding, with what was now a useless Yamaha. Turns out the pile was only partly leaves: the rest of it was fire hydrant.

Motorcycles have always seemed to bring out something in me. I remember I had a Honda four-cylinder with flat tires. I had a brilliant idea, and a friend of mine helped me take the tires and tubes off of it and ride it on the rims. Well, when you're riding just on the rims and try to take a turn at about 30 miles an hour, you realize pretty quickly that you no longer have any traction.

I have a permanent scar in a very private place due to an incident involving a motorcycle, a patch of carpet, a long piece of rope, and an anchor made out of a piece of rebar.

This seems as good a spot as any to mention the time I shot my muzzle-loader into a five-gallon bucket. The bucket had a layer of lead on the bottom of it, and I felt sure I'd be able to knock a hole in the bottom. I turned it sideways and from about 10 feet took the shot. Half an hour later I woke up.

My maxiball hit the layer of lead, ricocheted right back, and hit me in the forehead. I had a knot sticking out of my head so far I looked like a unicorn. Did being thick skulled save my life? Maybe if I hadn't been hardheaded I wouldn't have shot into the bucket in the first place.

Like most kids I worked off and on during high school. We were out in the middle of farm country, so a lot of the work was agricultural—picking tobacco, driving a tractor, whatever needed doing. I didn't necessarily like it, but it was work—and it paid.

My father was in the labor union and worked construction, and after high school I fell into the construction thing with my dad. We labored on a lot of the big power plants in the area, doing concrete pours, building power plants and roads, or helping when there were power outages.

Why did I go into the Army? Well, some boys want to be astronauts, or fire fighters, or cops, but ever since I was a little boy, I wanted to be a platoon sergeant in the U.S. Army. Go ahead and laugh, but I wanted to be Sergeant Rock. I had *Sergeant Rock* and *Sergeant Fury* comic books—that's who I always wanted to be. Sergeant Rock and Easy Company, I can still remember that from the comics. Hell, I still have the comics as a matter of fact. In high school, I joined ROTC.

Doing construction with my dad was work, but it wasn't how I wanted to spend a career. Unfortunately, there weren't a whole lot of other jobs in the area. Finally I decided to pull the trigger. I went to a military med station and got my physical right after I took the ASVAB (Armed Services Vocational Aptitude Battery) test. Three days later I was at Fort Knox, Kentucky. I went into the Army on March 6, 1986. I was in the Army for more than seventeen years before I saw any serious combat—Desert Storm notwithstanding—but when I did, I was at the tip of the spear with the 3/7 Cavalry in Iraq.

I've gotten a lot of attention for what I did in Iraq. Bits and pieces of my story have appeared in books and magazines, and I even found myself on the cover of *Soldier of Fortune*. What I had to do for me and my men to survive was brutal, but I didn't do any of it without a conscience. I've killed a lot of people—some say my KIA total is near the record for an American soldier—but for every life I took, there were a hundred I *could* have ended. Either they gave me a reason to kill them or there was a reason that they needed to be killed. I did exactly what was called for, and I don't apologize for it. It was war.

This book is just about a guy who was in the wrong place at all the right times. Unfortunately for the enemy, I was ready for what came my way.

CHAPTER 3

No Such Thing as
Friendly Fire

The first time I was ever under fire was in Germany.

If that's got some of you scratching your heads, trying to figure out how an Iraq War veteran is old enough to have fought in Germany, let me explain.

When I first joined the Army, I was assigned to the 11th ACR (Armored Cavalry Regiment) in West Germany. We were positioned in the Fulda Gap, back during the Cold War when the Soviets were Public Enemy Number One. If you've never heard of the Fulda Gap, here's a little context: if the Cold War had ever turned into a land war in Europe, because of geography, it was a good bet the Soviet tanks would pour through the Fulda Gap in Germany. The Fulda Gap is actually two lowland corridors between East Germany and Frankfurt. They go around the Vogelsberg Mountains and are very strategically important.

When the 11th ACR came back from Vietnam it took over the Gap from the 14th ACR, which had been in place since 1951. The job was patrolling the area, providing reconnaissance, and spotting any pre-attack Soviet movement. In war our job would be to delay a Soviet attack until other units of V Corps could be mobilized.

Because I was in ROTC during high school, they made me an E3 (Private First Class—PFC) as soon as I got out of basic training. About four months after I graduated Basic and OSUT (One Station Unit Training), they sent me to Grafenwoehr, Germany. I was in 1st Squadron in the Black Horse Regiment and came in as a 113 Scout. I was basically a dismount, which is what we in the cavalry call someone who actually is supposed to, at some point or for some reason, get off the vehicle and walk. I was originally assigned to an M113 APC (armored personnel carrier).

I like the 113s. For APCs, they are small, quiet, and have lots of room. They are such a good design that they're still being produced today, even though they were introduced in 1960. The 113 is a tracked vehicle, basically a bullet-resistant maneuverable box designed to get soldiers into or out of trouble spots. The typical crew is seven men, and the 113 is armed with an M2 Browning .50-caliber machine gun. Compared to the M2—"Ma Deuce"— the 113 was a brand-new design.

John Browning originally designed the M2 machine gun in 1918, and it has been in service with the U.S. military since 1933. Browning was a genius when it came to designing guns, and nowhere is that more evident than in the M2—after almost 90 years in service, nobody has yet to come up with a better heavy-caliber belt-fed machine gun. They served us well in World War II and Vietnam, and in Iraq we mounted them on 113s, Humvees, and M1 Abrams tanks.

However, in the early 1980s the Bradley Fighting Vehicle came out, and many of the 113 crews transitioned over. I soon found myself transferred over to the Bradleys. The Bradley could be considered the halfway point between an APC and a main battle tank (MBT). It is tracked and has a small turret like a tank and a large compartment in back for troops.

The U.S. Army's main battle tank, the M1 Abrams, weighs 60 tons yet can do upwards of 60 miles per hour. It has a 120 mm main gun, with an M2 .50 machine gun for backup. The Bradley had just a 25 mm (25 mm = 1-inch diameter) main gun, and while it only weighed half what the Abrams did, an Abrams could easily outrun a Bradley. The adoption of the Bradley was a long and tortured process, and many people thought the end result was a complete dog—it was undergunned, either too big or too slow, and so on. To be honest, nobody knew how well the Bradleys would fare in actual combat, and it wasn't until the 2003 invasion of Iraq that they were really put to the test.

The first Bradley I was ever assigned to had a driver, a gunner, and a Bradley Commander. Back then I didn't even know how to drive the Bradley, because I'd come up on the M113s and M1 tanks, but when the Bradleys started coming in, quite a few tank crews transferred over. Our squadron had gone through a transition, but I hadn't done the driver training yet, so I was just the dismount/ loader in the rear of the vehicle.

One day I was sitting in the back of our moving Bradley. The gunner, Sergeant Carter, was sitting on the vehicle's steps, where you climb up from the outside to gain access. It was cold and he was sitting half in the turret with his feet hanging out, looking back and talking to me. We were having a conversation and then all of a sudden he disappeared, everything but his feet. Then he popped back up real quick. I was looking at him, trying to figure out what was going on, and then he completely vanished.

I thought, What the hell just happened? Then the Bradley stopped. I had my helmet on, but I didn't have a CVC (combat vehicle crewman) helmet with built-in radio, so I couldn't hear what was going on. The vehicle stopped, they dropped the back ramp of the Bradley, and everybody came rushing over. I couldn't hear what was going on or see what they were looking at.

The Bradley Commander had been inside the turret and hadn't been paying attention to where his gunner was. He thought Sergeant Carter was sitting in his seat and didn't realize he was only half in the vehicle. The Commander traversed the turret, Sergeant Carter got pinched between the wall and the turret hole, and the turret stopped.

The Commander thought something on the outside of the Bradley was sticking, maybe a tree limb or something else underneath the turret. So, still without checking to see where the gunner was, he moved the turret back over to the 12 o'clock position and then hit the Slew button. He slewed it again to the 3 o'clock or to the 9 o'clock position. There are two speeds for the turret—Traverse is the slower one, and Slew is the faster one. The Bradley has the fastest rotating turret in the world, or it did at that time.

When the Commander did that, it just raked Carter and dragged him around inside the hole. There's a little bit of room inside; there's a heater back there and part of a shelf, but the Commander dragged him right over the top of that stuff. We'd been at Grafenwoehr for all of two days. The Commander got relieved for cause. Carter was all broken up, and I don't mean his feelings were hurt: he had a broken pelvis and dislocated collarbone.

One of the things that a crew was required to do when they got to Grafenwoehr was qualify at the range with their Bradley, and now we didn't have a crew to do that. Ludville was our driver at the time, and we got a new guy as a replacement Commander, Sergeant Thompson. He didn't really have any experience with the Bradley either.

My Platoon Sergeant was Sergeant Green, and Green was a big black guy who was a Korean War veteran. Sergeant Green said, "Hey, let's let Johnson shoot, give him an opportunity to gun the vehicle. He can't do any worse than us not shooting at all. If he doesn't qualify, we'll just say that it's a crew in training. At least we can have six crews shoot for our platoon." He got approval from higher up.

Thompson told me, "Look, I'm never going to touch the gun. You're gonna shoot everything. I'll read the fire commands off and all you have to do is yell 'Identified' and 'Fire.'"

What could I say other than "Okay"?

We headed to the range and shot in Table 8, which is individual crew gunnery qualification. There is a daytime and a nighttime qualification. During the daytime qualification I pulled a perfect 700. The scoring went off a point system then, and you had a specific amount of time to engage a target. You also had a swing task, in which you could have six engagements in the daytime and four at night or seven in the daytime and three at night.

One of the swing tasks we had during the nighttime qualification was a moving engagement. I shot a perfect 300 at night, so I shot a perfect 1,000 points total, and out of the four squadrons that came down and shot there, ours was the only one to get a perfect 1,000 points. And I had found my calling.

I can't take too much credit. Thompson was right on with all his fire commands. He was reading them off cue cards. Ludville was really good too. He got us in and out of the positions quickly so I was able to engage all the targets and destroy them in the time allotted.

My job, after hearing the fire commands, was to say "Identified" and "Fire." When the first round hits, you zero the reticle and then use Kentucky windage for subsequent rounds. With the Bradley, you use a one-two-three system: fire one round to see where it hits, adjust, then fire two rounds to see if you're on the target, and then fire the next three to destroy it. You've got an exact number of rounds to do the job, and for whatever reason it was easy for me. Maybe because that was how I'd always shot growing up. If I was using a rifle with a scope, I'd never adjust the scope, I'd just see where it was hitting and then adjust my aim accordingly.

However, at that time the regiment had a policy requiring the gunner on a vehicle to be an NCO. After the Table 8 was done, all the crews who shot "Distinguished" (900 and above) were drinking champagne with Colonel Snodgrass, the Squadron Commander. Our crew went up there to meet with the Colonel face-to-face, and he found himself looking at a Specialist, an E6, and a PFC.

"Well, who's the gunner?" Colonel Snodgrass asked.

Sergeant Thompson said, "Sir, PFC Johnson is."

The Squadron Commander immediately looked over at the Troop Commander and said, "Hey, what's our policy on NCOs being in the gunner position?"

My Troop Commander said, "Well, sir, Johnson is an excellent gunner, he just doesn't have the time that we needed in there yet without getting a waiver for him to get . . ." And he was just pulling some stuff out of his ass, saying how great I was, hoping his brain would catch up to his mouth.

The Squadron Commander looked at the Sergeant Major and said, "Hey, tell the S3 to get me some Corporal stripes. We'll promote this guy now." So, *bam,* I got Corporal just like that. Really quick. At that point, after going through OSUT, I'd been in about 18 months, so I'd been in for barely enough time to get that promotion.

One day we were sitting at OP (Observation Post) Alpha in the Fulda Gap, and word came across the radio that there were some

VIPs in the area, touring various military installations. It turned out to be CBS News anchor Dan Rather. *Okay, yeah, whatever.* We didn't care—until we got the word that Rather was coming up to OP Alpha and wanted to take a look inside *our* Bradley, because he'd never been in one before. Uh-oh.

We lived in our Bradley. When we were up at OP-A, we were inside our Brad 24/7 for days at a time, if not longer, only leaving to hit the latrine. This was an era before iPods and portable video game systems, and we were normal guys, so a large portion of our entertainment dollars was spent on porn. We had Miss Aprils and Miss Junes, boobs and beaver shots taped up everywhere, magazines lying around all over the place in the back of the Brad. And let me tell you, German porn magazines, at least at that time, were the best in the world, because you could find anything you wanted. If you wanted a porn magazine featuring two chickens and a nun getting it on, you could probably find it. We were still scrambling to sterilize our vehicle when Dan Rather came rolling up. We got it cleaned up just in time, and Rather was none the wiser.

We spent the next couple of months at Fulda, then went back down to Grafenwoehr again to do a CALFEX (combined arms live fire exercise). Bradleys and tanks roll up and shoot at the same time, the mortar platoon engages the targets, and then we have our artillery company take their turn. We had an artillery battery with us, and after they'd shoot we would have A-10 Warthogs and Cobras come in and engage targets. It's a huge combined arms finale, all done with live ammo.

We were the last troop to fire on that particular CALFEX. It had been a long training rotation for us and I can remember the squadron XO, a Major, and the S3 Major bragging about how the range had run so smoothly. Things were already getting packed up, and the next morning we'd be prepping and putting stuff on the train to go back to home station.

With two engagements left to be done, we were down in our far defilade in front of the tanks. The tanks were behind us, but off to our left by about 400 meters, and we were waiting for the targets to pop up.

The tanks had their own targets, and we had ours. Each target array was in a fan. Ours were off to the right and theirs were off to the left. Well, the tank squadron had a supply Sergeant who, while he was officially a "tanker," had never shot an M1 before. They were trying to get him to the E5 promotion board, but the Sergeant Major's policy was that if you weren't working your MOS (military occupational specialty), you couldn't get promoted. So they went ahead and stuck him in this tank so he could get some trigger time and be eligible for promotion. He slewed his turret to the right, picked up a hot spot in his thermal sight, and engaged it.

The tanks were loaded with tungsten armor-piercing training ammo. Most military armor-piercing ammunition is saboted, meaning the projectiles themselves are narrower than the barrel they're being shot from and enclosed in a plastic sleeve or sabot (which is French for "shoe"). Being narrower and lighter than a standard round, these tungsten rounds fly out very fast, and it is this velocity, combined with their hardness, that allows them to penetrate armor. Even though it was a "training" round, it really didn't lack any lethality.

Problem was, the Sergeant behind the trigger slewed his turret too far and engaged my wingman, Bradley 34. The first round hit the periscope, punched through it, hit the driver between his shoulder blades, then stuck in the transmission. That was Jerry Westmoreland, and the first round killed him.

I was in our Bradley, Bradley 35, gunning for Sergeant Thompson again, and he announced, "They're engaging."

I was watching downrange and said, "I don't see anything."

Then the Platoon Sergeant in 34 came over the radio, yelling, "Incoming! Incoming! Incoming!"

We were trying to figure out what the hell he was talking about. We were between 34 and 36, and all of a sudden 36, right next to us, exploded and caught fire.

I yelled at Sergeant Thompson, "Hey, they got hit!" and started out of the turret.

Sergeant Thompson said, "What are you doing?"

"We gotta help those guys. We can't leave 'em there."

I jumped out of the back of the Bradley and ran over to 36. When I kicked open the hatch the driver, Williams, was inside screaming. I grabbed him and helped him out, but as I did so, his skin was coming off in my hands.

I got him out and behind his Bradley. Sergeant Chase, Bradley 36's Commander, reached down through flames to grab his gunner, Sergeant Hope. Chase grabbed Hope by the back of his fly suit and pulled him out. Hope was just limp, but Chase got him on the ground.

Once I saw all those guys were out of their vehicle I ran over to Westmoreland's track, Bradley 34. I reached in and grabbed Jerry. His hatch was open and he had transmission fluid all over him. The kid probably weighed 165 pounds, but it was like pulling four tons. It was just dead body weight. When I got him up to about shoulder level, I could tell that he was missing parts.

I put him back inside the vehicle and pulled the field cutoff to shut it down. I got behind the Bradley and started to help unload the other guys. By this time, Bradley 36 had rounds cooking off inside it. The 25 mm was cycling, the coax was going full auto, the whole vehicle was basically burning and blowing up. We got every-body out, though. The medevac was there really quick and I helped get those guys loaded.

Squadron did everything it could to cover its ass, saying they had the right people in the tower, but I don't blame them. It was just one of those training accidents that happen throughout the Army. Trucks roll over, helicopters crash. This was a kid killed on the range because of a stupid mistake.

I talked to everybody, trying to get Sergeant Chase the Soldier's Medal. He could have gotten away easily, but he reached in through the flames and pulled Sergeant Hope out of the vehicle. And they pretty much just pushed it underneath the carpet. He didn't get a medal or anything else.

That incident had a lasting effect on many careers. Westmore-land's Platoon Sergeant, as far as I could tell, he just jumped out of his vehicle and got behind the berm, but he didn't try to help anybody. He didn't get relieved, but he got sent away to another unit. Both Sergeant Hope and Sergeant Chase had some emotional problems dealing with what happened, and Williams and the other guys, they got out of the Army. It was a traumatic event that was completely unanticipated. It was the Cold War, when nobody expected anything to actually happen. The Army was a career, we weren't going to be fighting anybody, and then this happened.

That was my first test under fire. I don't know why my first reaction was *I need to get over there and get those guys out of the vehicle.* Most everybody else—they just weren't doing anything. I ran toward the fire. That was the point when I realized that apparently I was a little different from everybody else.

CHAPTER 4

RAINDROPS KEEP FALLING
ON MY HEAD

The 48th National Guard Infantry was supposed to head out for Desert Storm in 1990, but there was a problem. They never scored well enough in NTC (National Training Center) or RTAP (Reserve Transition Assistance Program) training to actually be deployed. That was a big issue, a really big issue. They couldn't be deployed.

In 1991 I was with the 197th Infantry Brigade(Mechanized) (Separate). We were part of the 18th Airborne Corps. The Division Commander for the 24th Infantry Division was General Barry McCaffrey. General McCaffrey needed another brigade to replace the 48th NG, so he snatched the 197th. We were a training brigade, and McCaffrey had a pretty good saying about us. He said we were "without a doubt the best training infantry brigade in the United States Army" at that time. And we were. We did all sorts of training, tons of dismounted stuff, lots of fire and maneuver exercises.

We went to NTC three times. We were a separate brigade and a lot of the other units wanted us to work with them, so we were constantly training and on the move, either at Fort Benning or NTC or Fort Polk. We were one trained-up unit.

Once General McCaffrey snatched us up, he made us his 3rd Brigade. That's why now you have the 1st and 2nd Brigade of the 3rd Infantry Division at Fort Stewart, but the 3rd Brigade is at Fort Benning. The 197th never went back to being an independent brigade, they continue to belong to the 24th Infantry Division.

We had M113 APCs. My 113 was a Vietnam-era vehicle that actually had patches on it from where it was shot up in Vietnam. It had been refurbished several times, that's how old it was. The .50-caliber machine gun was a relic, too. The serial number on it had a bunch of Xs in it where they had coded it out and brought it back into service again.

When people ask me how many soldiers you can fit in the back of a 113, my response is, "Comfortably?" You can always fit one more, like when kids used to see how many of their friends they could fit into a phone booth. Our 113 had a crew of seven.

We shipped out to Saudi Arabia in late August 1990. We repositioned several times, then finally headed way out west in preparation for the invasion, almost to the border. I think the closest town in Iraq was As Salman, and we were due south of it. We had the 101st with us, and the French coalition troops were part of our flank as well.

The plan was for the 2nd ACR and VII Corps from Germany to charge from Saudi, around Kuwait, and punch up and hit the Iraqis, who were deploying. The Marines were to slam straight through Kuwait into Iraq. Our brigade was doing the flanking movement for the 24th Division. The other two units in the division, 3/15 and

2/15 Infantry with Bradleys and M1s, were supposed to hit the big stuff while we flanked and headed up to take the airfield.

Our goal was Objective Brown, outside of the Toledo airfield. I was the vehicle Commander and had the Lieutenant on my vehicle. When the time came we rode out at oh-dark-thirty and worked our way through a marsh covered over with two or three feet of sand. It looked like solid ground, and it would have been for a car, but when a tracked armored vehicle hit it, you'd break through and start sinking. It slowed us down some.

We traveled all that day and into the next night before we reached our objective and made contact. At that point we had traveled—well, it seemed like the longest movement to contact in history, until we went back into Iraq in 2003. It was the equivalent of driving from the panhandle of Florida to Atlanta, maybe 250 miles. Something ridiculous like that.

Objective Brown wasn't the airfield, but a mass of wadis and some rolling hills outside of the airfield. It was the defensive position for one of their infantry battalions, as Toledo was an Iraqi air base. Brown was probably five or six miles from the flight line of the airfield and about a mile from the highway that looped around the outside. We had satellite reconnaissance photos of the battalion and knew they were set up there. It was actually right in the town of Ur. If you remember your Old Testament, Abram was born in the town of Ur. God changed his name to Abraham, but old Abram was born right where Saddam's battalion was stationed.

Well, at the time our NODs (night observation devices—night vision goggles) were PVS-7s. They weren't very good. The hatch was open, and I had my head and shoulders out of the hole. We were getting close to Objective Brown, and I could see some people tagging me with flashlights. I told the lieutenant, "They're flashing flashlights at me. They're signaling me." All our vehicles were

aligned, and we were a pretty good distance from whoever was signaling me, 300 meters or more—although at night, in the desert,
it's really hard to tell distance.

I wasn't exactly sure what was going on, and I was distracted by
watching a firefight way off in the distance, tracers going back and
forth. Then Simmons, my driver, told me, "Hey, my night sight quit."

I told him, "Well, put another battery in it."

"I just put a battery in it. It just quit."

And I said, "That's bullshit. You didn't put a battery in it. Stop
lying. Just put a battery in it."

These guys who were signaling us, I wanted to find out if they
were surrendering or what, and my driver kept fucking with the
night sight. Then he told me, "We got a leak somewhere."

Jesus, what now? I said, "What do you mean, we got a leak?"

He said, "Something's . . . I'm getting splashed on by water."

What? I didn't know what the hell was going on, so I stuck my
head down inside the hatch and when I did, I felt that the outside of
his periscope, for his night sight, was broken. So I said, "Simmons,
how did you break your periscope?"

He's playing innocent. "I didn't do anything."

I told him, "Bullshit. You took it out to put a battery in it and
you broke it putting it in. How did you drive all the way up here
with it broke?"

He was insistent. "I didn't do anything to it."

Then the water splashed up on me. *What the hell?* "Where the
hell's the water coming from?" It wasn't coming from the sky, it
was coming from the front of the vehicle. Oh shit, I thought, here
we go. "Did you bust the radiator?" The radiator sits up on the
front, and I thought that was it, or we'd broken a fan drive and it
was overheating and spraying me. But the water was cold.

So I turned around and took a good look, and the water can

on the front of the vehicle was leaking everywhere. I yelled at Simmons, "What the hell did you do to the water can?"

He yelled back at me, "I didn't do anything to the water can!"

About that time we started shutting the vehicle down. I was on top of the vehicle and could hear what sounded like somebody pinging a metal roof with a hammer. I lifted my CVC helmet up a little higher and said, "What the hell is that noise?"

Then Sergeant James McCormick yelled, "Contact! Contact!"

It suddenly dawned on me. For the past ten minutes I'd been up on top of my vehicle arguing with my driver about his night sight as we were getting fired upon. Those weren't flashlights, they were muzzle flashes, and between the noise of the 113's engine and the helmet, we couldn't hear the rifles. They were just pounding the shit out of us.

They were only about 300 meters away, but they didn't have night vision, so they were just shooting at the sound of our engines. The Iraqis were positioned in a pseudo-ranger triangle for security, with their machine guns set up at the corners. They also had a tank at each corner of the triangle, as well as a few assorted armored personnel carriers and other vehicles here and there.

It could have been quite a battle, but they'd already been bombed long and hard by the U.S. Air Force. We had three tanks with us, and when everybody hit them in the middle of the night with .50-cals and Mark 19 full-auto grenade launchers, the tanks launching HEAT (high explosive antitank) rounds, it was just overwhelming. Any Iraqi who could stick their hands up and wave at somebody to get their attention to surrender was doing it. We took a lot of prisoners.

The Iraqi troops hadn't been getting supplies for a long time. Not only were they short on fuel, they were all skinny because they weren't even getting enough food. An armored division, 1/64 or

2/63, went up and secured the airfield with their M1s while we were still fighting and mopping up Objective Brown.

And that was the whole ball of wax. That was it for combat. Admittedly, a lot of the units that went into Iraq for Desert Storm never even fired a shot. I seem to be a bit of a bullet magnet, always in the right place at the wrong time. That said, I left the States in August and came back the following July. I was gone for a year to fight for 100 hours. That sucked. A lot. We didn't come straight home, we went back to Saudi Arabia first and actually stayed in the Khobar Towers, which are famous for being destroyed by a truck bomb in 1996.

Before we came back, we spent some time destroying Iraqi vehicles. They were all stacked up in a line and we shot them and blew the breeches on their guns and burned them, because we didn't want to leave them for the Iraqis. We soaked rolls of toilet paper in diesel, lit them, and threw them inside next to their open fuel cells, mostly, and that worked real nice. Well, little did we know, General McCaffrey had put those vehicles aside. He was going to bring those back as show vehicles and put them on display. Nobody told us. Boy, was he pissed. You look up *conniption* in the dictionary and there was a picture of his face when he found out what we did.

But anything I'd done, on purpose or by accident, up to that point paled in comparison to what happened when I returned to Iraq in 2003.

CHAPTER 5

LOVE AND MARRIAGE, ARMY STYLE

After Desert Storm I left the 197th Infantry Brigade and went over to the 2nd ACR (Armored Cavalry Regiment). The 2nd ACR was involved in the Battle of 73 Easting, the biggest tank battle of Desert Storm, so those guys had a much bigger part in the war than I did. When I showed up in Amberg, Germany, I helped them refurbish all of their vehicles and do the turn-in process.

From there I went up to Vilseck to the Bradley Transition Team. That was a teaching assignment. The ADA (Air Defense Artillery) guys were moving from the old Vulcan cannons and 113s to Bradleys with Stinger missile pods. They needed people to transition them over to those vehicles, and I became a gunnery instructor.

They had no idea about the Bradley or anything else. We had to start from scratch—go out to the range, teach them dismount tactics, everything. I was an instructor for about a year and a half.

After that I switched over to Platoon Gunnery Training. This was a new program the Army developed that used the UCFT (Unit Conductor Fire Trainer), which was a first-generation computer trainer. The unit was designed for one vehicle to shoot in simulated battlefield scenarios. They had computers in that bastard bigger than Coke machines, and you had to have about twenty of them to run what we run now on an iPhone.

I was one of six guys selected in Germany to help General Electric with this simulator program in Daytona Beach, Florida. I was picked because of both my gunnery ability and the fact that I'd seen combat. I'd shot Distinguished, which means shooting a score of at least 900 out of 1,000, in many gunnery exercises, including multiple 1,000s. So I headed down there on TDY (temporary duty assignment) to help them work the bugs out.

We were working on a plan to have four of the platoon gunnery trainers tied together so that the guys could come in and work with their wingmen. More than one unit meant they could help each other maneuver, engage targets on the battle line, screen, or do route reconnaissance. The programs were pretty detailed, following existing maps and everything.

It was down there that I met my wife, Amy.

Actually, I'd been married once before, and I like to joke that everyone needs a practice marriage before they settle down for the real thing, but the fact of the matter is I was just too young. I got two great kids out of it though, Daniel and Janise.

When we met, Amy was with her friend Robin, and I was hanging with a guy named Dave. He was part of what I like to call the Alcoholic Infantry. They don't have their own MOS (military occupation specialties) yet, but they should, because there are enough of them.

We were at a bar in Daytona. The Atlanta Braves were playing the Toronto Blue Jays and I remember seeing Amy. She had on a white dress to about midthigh and it had a red flowery pattern on it, maybe roses. She has blond hair, but that wasn't what grabbed me—I can remember seeing her blue eyes from across the room. I knew that night that I wanted to marry her.

Amy and I traded phone numbers, but everything was casual, at least on her part. She said she was going to school and wasn't interested in dating anybody. Well, soon we bumped into each other again, and I said, "Hey, you know, could you just show us around town? I'll take you out to a nice place to eat or whatever. We're not familiar with the area." I ended up taking her to a Japanese steak house. This time Amy and I hit it off for good. This was in fall 1992.

I was stationed in Daytona for close to three months. It was only supposed to be thirty days, but it wound up being longer than that because they kept extending the project, as the test wasn't ready. Then it was back to Grafenwoehr, Germany, for me.

Not too long after I headed back to Germany, I flew Amy out there. I took her all over the place, showed her the sights—and asked her to marry me. She didn't really need any convincing. We just had that connection. I guess we felt we deserved each other.

At the time I was doing the Bradley instructing thing as a Master Gunner at Grafenwoehr. I was back transitioning ADA gunners over to the Bradley. We had a three-day weekend, and I took a so-called whether pass—as in, you take off whether you have a pass or not. I called my boss and said, "I'm going to be up in northern Germany doing blah blah blah." He didn't have a problem with it, so I left that Thursday after work.

This wasn't a surprise. I had already talked to Amy and told her to get everything organized. Well, I arranged as much surprise into the situation as I could, which wasn't much. I picked out the ring at Service Merchandise and called Amy and told her she had something to pick up there. When I came back to the States she already had her wedding dress and everything was set up. We got married at a place called Chez Paul's. Her friend Robin, who'd been there when we'd met, was the maid of honor. Amy's brother was my best man, but none of my family or friends were there. That's life in the Army for you.

That day my boss called and told me, "Hey, one of the guys is sick, you're going to have to work tonight."

I told him, "Look, I'm up in Bremerhaven, and there's no way I'm going to make it back."

He told me, "I'm going to have to write you up."

"Whatever, I don't care."

We got married that weekend and flew back to Germany. Surprise, guys, I'm married! We lived in government housing there. She started working for Northrop Grumman in Hohenfels, and we'd been there about two years when we had our son Jaycob.

Jaycob was born prematurely, and we knew something was wrong with him. We had him at the German hospital in Rosenberg. The doctors kept telling us, "Oh, there's nothing wrong with him. He's fine."

We took him to see the Army doctors at Wahlsburg and they also told us there was nothing wrong with him. We told them, "Are you sure? It's hard to put a diaper on him; his legs are tight together and he always keeps them crossed."

The doctor over there told us, "Yeah, it's no problem," but we knew something wasn't right. So when we took him home on leave, we got him checked out in the States.

As soon as the doctor saw him, he asked, "Have you guys started any therapy or anything for his cerebral palsy yet?" We were floored. We knew there was something not quite right, but *cerebral palsy*? We had no idea.

The German doctors failed to diagnose it. The Army doctors failed to diagnose it. When Jaycob was born, we didn't think that he was going make it, and that was a tough time. And then we find out that he has CP. Amy was upset and I was *really* upset, but I couldn't lose control because she didn't have any family there. I had to be the strong one, be supportive. It was a hard time.

The Army was going to send us back to the States on TDY so we could start getting Jaycob the treatment he needed. They were going to get us out of there in something like three days, handle everything, fly us back, move our things, and put our furniture in storage. However, the Major who I was working for thought it would be a good idea to do a "compassionate reassignment," instead. It turns out that compassionate reassignment takes anywhere from a year to three years to do. So, in effect, by putting us in for compassionate reassignment, he put a stop to us going back and Jaycob getting treated. A week would go by and I would call the Pentagon (again) to find out my status, or call the VA (again) and beg to be reassigned, and they'd go, "Oh, well, we're still reviewing it," or "Your case hasn't gotten here yet."

So a month went by and Jaycob wasn't getting any treatment or anything else. I actually contacted a congressman in hopes of fixing the situation. I had to get Congress involved to contact the Colonel—that's how ridiculous the situation got. And you know what? My regular rotation came up, a PCS (permanent change of station) to Fort Bragg and the 82nd Airborne Division, before I ever got the compassionate reassignment. Some things the Army does great, but as far as taking care of their people when it counts, they suck.

The 82nd Airborne didn't have any use for armor that couldn't be dropped out of a plane. While, theoretically, you can drop anything by parachute if you've got a big enough chute, planes can only carry so much weight and still take off. For most of my time with the 82nd I commanded an M551 Sheridan, which is a light tank. The Sheridan was designed to be dropped by parachute and to swim across rivers. It weighed just 15 tons, compared to the Bradley's 32 tons, in part because most of the vehicle was aluminum, except for the steel Commander's cupola. We called it the chicken box.

The main gun on the Sheridan is a big 152 mm designed to fire both conventional tank rounds and missiles. When the M1 Abrams main battle tank fires its 120 mm main gun, the whole tank rocks a little, and the Abrams weighs 60 tons. The first time I commanded a Sheridan and we fired the main gun, the whole vehicle rocked back until we were balancing on our last two road wheels. When we fell back down, I smacked my face on the turret. When I looked down, there was smoke coming out of the vehicle.

"Cease fire! Cease fire!" I yelled. I thought the breach had failed. "Everybody out. Un-ass the vehicle!" The rest of the crew poked their heads out of their positions and looked at me in confusion.

"What the hell are you all looking at me for?" I said.

"What do you mean, Sarge? We just fired the main gun."

I stared at them. "You mean it does that every time you fire it? The breach didn't fail? Holy shit."

To reduce the number of broken teeth and concussions, I learned to brace myself against the rear of the cupola. However, that didn't work out so well. One day during training I had my ass pressed against the rear of the cupola. The main gun fired, the cupola flexed, and both my ass cheeks were pinched between the steel cupola and the aluminum vehicle body. I started screaming, "Cease fire! Cease fire!"

Nobody knew what the hell was going on, but they rushed to my aid. My coveralls and my ass were stuck, and my crew had to push the cupola up for me to get free. I ended up with a huge blood blister across both cheeks, like a long purple line. It turned into a scar that lasted for years.

If you're in the Airborne, that means you jump out of planes when you go into combat—or at least you need to know how to. It takes five jumps to get "jump qualified." On my first night parachute jump I came down and landed without a problem, but I didn't know the landing area. As I was walking around, trying to get oriented, I started kicking and tripping over tank parts.

"Dammit, they should brief us that there are going to be tank parts on the ground out here, we could get injured," I said to one of the experienced 82nd guys nearby.

He looked at me, and said, "Buddy, that's *your* tank."

The chute never opened, and my Sheridan burned right in. That's why you jump separately from or after your armor.

The Sheridan was armed with a Shillelagh missile, which we fired out of the main gun. The actual range was about 5,000 yards, but they called it an infinity missile. It was an IR (infrared) missile, and it would pick up any IR signal—like a garage door opener. So we were out at the range, I launched this bad boy, and it was tracking toward the target—and then it hit a little berm. The missile bounced, and then it picked up the IR beam coming back at me.

My gunner started yelling, "Hey, the round's coming at us!"

I screamed back at him, "Dump the gun! Dump the gun!"

He was still tracking the laser, and we had a missile coming back at us. A Shillelagh missile, a 152 mm round, coming right for the vehicle, and my gunner panicked and was trying to get out of the vehicle. So I had to take the Commander's override, which doesn't really work very well, and dump the missile. The missile hit about 20 feet in front of my vehicle, bounced in the air, and landed behind us underneath the First Sergeant's Humvee. Luckily it was an inert training missile, so it only blew the wheels off the Humvee. Nobody was hurt. If it had been equipped with an actual explosive warhead, the First Sergeant would be dead, and so would I. Hell, our troop had one land in a housing area, and another fly through a drop zone with paratroops jumping. Crazy ass missile.

Part of the rotation with the 82nd Airborne was being assigned to South Korea. I tried to get out of that, due to having an "exceptional family member" (that's the military term), but that did not work out. Part of my lack of success was the fact that I wasn't part of what I call the 82nd Airborne mafia, guys who had only ever been in the 82nd and treated everybody else like shit. Inspector General (IG) complaints were filed, because I wasn't the only person that this had happened to. I was told it was just a personality conflict, when in fact some of my paperwork was deliberately mislaid. There's no such thing as a personality conflict. Some people are just assholes. My Platoon Sergeant was one of them.

When I left for South Korea, Amy was pregnant with Max, my youngest. To add insult to injury, right before I got orders for Korea we had a rat in the ceiling of our house. He chewed some wiring or something, and one day when both Amy and I were at work the house, which we owned, burned down. So the house was torched, we're living in a hotel room, and I get orders to go to Korea. Insert profanity of choice here.

All my efforts to fight the system through the IG went nowhere, so I told Amy, "The hell with this. I'm going to get us a house and move you close to your family."

We had a lot going on with the insurance company rebuilding the one house, trying to find another home in Florida, and me getting ready to head to South Korea, but somehow everything worked out all right. I was able to go home on leave to be there for the birth of my son Max, but I wasn't stateside for very long. The flight is eighteen hours each way.

Tours in Korea are supposed to be longer, but I was only there for a year. In 2000 we were on a training mission against the 3/15 Infantry. I was climbing up on the back of my Bradley, and my driver saw a guy out on the ground with a flashlight. He thought that was a signal to move forward. So he took off and hooked my right leg with the track. The track dragged my right leg down the side skirts of the Bradley. My right ankle was crushed, and my tibia and fibula were in bad shape. They had to take the track apart to get my leg out. I was air-evaced out of there and then spent three weeks down in Seoul with my leg up in traction, pins and other hardware in it.

At the time I was in 4th Squadron, 7th Cavalry, Apache Troop. A little after July of that year, I had orders to go back to Fort Bragg and flew back to the States. I'd had enough of the bullshit with that unit, though. I was in Daytona Beach on leave and I just drove to Fort Stewart in Georgia. I went and talked to the Cav Sergeant Major there and I said, "Hey look, here's the deal. I've got an exceptional family member. We're already living down here. He's going to see the doctors out of Winn Hospital, and I'd really like to be a part of this unit."

The Sergeant Major was no dummy. He said, "You're still on leave?"

"Yeah."

He said, "Just sign in off of leave here."

So I signed in off leave a week early to the 3rd Infantry Division. They sent in the paperwork, informing my previous unit that I was now with this new unit. The sergeant who had caused me all those problems at the 82nd did everything he could to get me back under his boot heel. Finally, my Squadron Commander called down to the officer in charge of the assignments and said, "Look. We're keeping this guy here. He's a good dude. We want to keep him."

The officer said, "There's no problem with him staying there, why is there an issue coming up?" When it was explained to him, he said, "I didn't know anything about it, and that assignment NCO—well, we're replacing him because he's got some issues anyway."

So I was able to stay with the 3rd ID, and that was the best damn unit I was ever in. But I wasn't at Fort Stewart very long. I was only there for about six months before I did my rotation in Bosnia.

We returned to the States—to Fort Stewart, Georgia, specifically—from Bosnia in November 2001, and we immediately started spinning back up, hitting our training hard. We went to Fort Irwin NTC (National Training Center) and Fort Polk JRTC (Joint Readiness Training Center), doing everything that needed to be done. We knew that we'd be heading over to Iraq, or rather Kuwait. We just didn't know when.

At that point we were pretty sure the war in Afghanistan had already started, but we didn't know anything more about what the Special Forces were doing than anyone else, until it hit the news. But there was almost no doubt we'd be going over to Iraq. We could see which way the wind was blowing. And we knew the Iraqis had a lot of tanks and APCs, and you don't fight armor with Special Forces—you fight armor with armor. That meant us.

My son Jaycob was about eight years old at that time, and he was dealing bravely with his cerebral palsy. Amy and I were doing whatever needed to be done to help him as much as possible. We discovered a clinic in Poland, the Euromed Rehabilitation Center. They were unique, doing things that nobody else was as far as physical therapy and other treatment for cerebral palsy. In particular, they had something called an Adeli suit to help with his treatment.

I knew I was going to get deployed soon, and so did my wife; the only question was when. So, while I was getting ready for Kuwait, my wife was preparing to go to Poland with Jaycob and Max, my youngest, who was three or four at that time. Jaycob could get this intense physical therapy much cheaper over there.

I have to say, my wife Amy was astonishingly courageous to head to a second-world foreign country all on her own with two little kids. We weren't getting any support from the Army whatsoever, as far as any of Jaycob's issues were concerned. We had to take it all upon ourselves to get this treatment for him. I was getting ready to go and possibly fight on behalf of our government, but did we get any help with Jaycob? No.

Amy actually left a week before I was deployed. It was around Christmastime. For me, it meant one more week without seeing them, and it was a pretty sad time. A trying time. I hadn't told her I was going into combat. She had enough to worry about, being in another country by herself, in the winter, with two small children, one of them handicapped.

We finally went over to Kuwait in December 2002. The fact is, however, that I could have gotten out of it. I was on PCS orders and was supposed to be leaving Fort Stewart before we deployed. I had a sweet-ass gig lined up at Camp Mabry in Austin, Texas. There I would be working with National Guard and Reserve people, completely low stress. I already had my reporting date and everything else.

My Troop Commander at the time was Jeff McCoy. He had 21 years in the Army and was undoubtedly the best Commander I ever had. He was a stocky little barrel-chested Irish fireplug of a guy from the mountains of Colorado. I got lucky because toward the end of my career I had three really great Commanders.

McCoy asked me, "Hey, I know you've got combat experience from the first war and you really know what you're doing . . ." He hemmed and hawed for a little while, then said, "Is there any way that you can stay?"

I'd already talked to the wife about the new orders. We had a house in Florida, but we were looking forward to going out to Austin. We had heard a lot about it, plus it was going to be a good career move for me. At that time I hadn't really done much on the training side of things. I'd been straight combat arms all the way through, except for the gunnery training I did in Germany.

This was a really tough decision to make. I remember talking to Jason Christner, my Platoon Sergeant, and he said, "Hey, I really want you to stay. We're going need you here." I respected his opinion—Christner was a true professional soldier and had been wounded in Somalia.

After thinking about it, I decided to stay. So I called the DA (Department of the Army rep) and he said, "No can do. You know you can't get out of your orders. You're already on orders assignment to Mabry. Besides, your squadron doesn't have orders to deploy yet, so you're not Stop Lossed where you can't go anywhere else."

I found out that the orders were coming, but they were two weeks away. So I called up the DA again and told him the orders were coming in. I said, "Hey, look. Here's the day, the date, and I want to get a three-week extension before I leave out of here."

He said, "Absolutely not. You are not going to be able to do it."

Fine. I may be aggressive and bull-headed and have a bit of a temper, but at this point I'd been in the Army for 16 years and knew how to work the system. I told them, "Well, okay. But I'm going to take thirty days' leave before my PCS." And they said, "Okay, that's good." Because they had no reason to deny it.

With that, I had 30 days before I had to go to my next duty station—but I never signed out on leave. I didn't really clear and I didn't sign out on leave, so I was still technically in the unit, just letting the days click down. I didn't pack anything up. I didn't ship anything. I was just sort of hoping that I would get the Stop Loss before I had to go. I had about four days left on my leave, four days before I would have had to report to my next duty station, when they hit us with Stop Loss.

I didn't have to go to Iraq again. I made a conscious decision to go with my Commander, my Platoon Sergeant, my First Sergeant. I wanted to go with those people. I chose to serve with them.

I wanted to go to war because the bottom line is, human nature's a bitch. You never know how you're going to react even if it's the same situation you've been in before. It wasn't going to be the way it had been during Desert Storm. We weren't going to be the backup element, we would be the men who led the charge. I knew that. I wanted to be in the charge. I just didn't realize I was going to be THE guy to lead the invasion.

CHAPTER 6

EIGHT BALL AND THE
LIPSTICK LIZARDS

There were endless things to do before we headed out to Kuwait. We packed up a million things and started shipping them out months ahead of time.

Whenever we were out on training or maneuvers, everybody would always visit my Bradley. I had a coffeepot, and creamer and sugar for the guys who liked coffee that way. They would come by and we'd spend a lot of time drinking coffee and talking during breaks in the action. As the time to leave approached, I went to Sam's Club and got all the coffee and all of our other supplies, and the plastic containers to put them in. (Just so you know, if you have something with an aroma, like soap, and you store that with your creamer and your sugar, even though they're in different containers, all your coffee's going to taste like soap. Six thousand miles away from the nearest grocery store and all the coffee we had tasted like Irish Spring. Quite a disappointment.)

Once we arrived in Kuwait we moved to an instant tent city called Udairi. It was in northwestern Kuwait and was only put in place in January 2003. Now it's this big complex, and they renamed it Camp Buehring after one of the highest-ranking U.S. officers killed in the war, Lieutenant Colonel Charles Buehring. They run the Predator drones out of there now, but back in 2003 it was just a tent city in the middle of the desert. It was us, camels, goats, sheep, and the bedouins. And sand berms.

We didn't ship our Bradleys over there. My Bradley, which I named "Carnivore," was PREPOSed—prepositioned. Sometime between the end of Desert Storm/Desert Shield and 9/11, it had been put into storage in Kuwait, waiting for the next dustup. Maintenance people would go out to where the vehicles were and start them up occasionally, make sure they were working, but when we got there and were assigned a vehicle we had to do the PMCS—primary maintenance checks and services. If something wasn't working, or wasn't the way it should be, that's when we called a mechanic.

My Bradley, the Carnivore, was officially an M2. M2 Bradleys are designed to carry infantry and have seats in the back. An M2 crew consisted of the driver, the gunner, the vehicle Commander, and a seven-man dismount team. We turned our M2 into an ad hoc M3. The M3s are cavalry/scout vehicles and carry more gear than people. The first thing we did to it was rip the seats out of the back. That enabled us to load all the ammo that would fit into the back.

The Commander and gunner are in the turret of the Bradley, and the Commander's hatch is on top of the turret. The driver is below, in the body of the vehicle, and he has his own hatch, in front of and below the turret. There is a large door at the rear of the vehicle for loading, as well as a cargo hatch on the top of the rear deck.

The Bradley Fighting Vehicle has a 25 mm main gun, and there is a coaxially mounted M240B machine gun. Wherever the main gun was pointed, so too went the coax. The M240B fires the 7.62 NATO round, and our belts were loaded with standard FMJ (full metal jacket) ball ammunition in a four-and-one mix (four rounds of ball with one tracer). The ready box for the coax holds 800 rounds.

Our Bradley also had a TOW (tracked optically, wire-guided) missile launcher. The launcher held two missiles, and the range on those is in excess of two miles. We had the standard load of 12 missiles with us. The ironic thing is, in all my time in Iraq, I only fired one TOW, and that was during my second tour.

The basic load is 1,500 rounds of 25 mm for the main gun. I loaded my Brad with 4,500 rounds of 25 mm, heavy on DU—depleted uranium—rounds. We used saboted tungsten ammo in training, but when we went to war we were issued DU. The DU round was nicknamed the "silver bullet." Depleted uranium is both heavy and hard, and the projectile itself was shaped like a fat needle. It worked even better than tungsten, and had a similar trajectory, but was too damn expensive to use during training. We thought we'd be getting into huge battles with tanks, so I wanted as much armor-piercing stuff onboard as possible. We hadn't really gone up against the BMP-3 yet (the Soviet-built armored vehicle the Iraqis favored), so we weren't sure what they were worth, but I wanted every advantage.

There are two ready boxes for the main 25 mm gun on the Bradley. One is designed to hold 70 rounds, and that is usually filled with armor-piercing ammo. One ready box holds 230 rounds, and that is usually filled with HE (high-explosive) rounds. I reversed the equation, and filled the big ready box with 230 rounds of DU. The range and velocity of these rounds are classified, but let's just say I could hit something—and kill it—beyond the range of our optics.

The 25 mm HE round isn't something to sneeze at either. It simply looks like a big rifle cartridge, with a green tip and a yellow stripe. Twenty-five millimeters equates to an inch, and a round that's only an inch in diameter doesn't sound like much, but the kill radius on the 25 mm HE is 5 meters, with a 10-meter wounding radius. And it did every bit of that, let me tell you.

The 25 mm had three rates of fire—high, low, and semi. High and low were both full auto, just different rates. Semiauto was one round downrange with every pull of the trigger. The gunner could switch between the ammo boxes with just a quick flip of a switch, but the HE rounds had a completely different trajectory than the lighter, faster DU rounds. We had two different aiming reticles for the two different rounds, and the gunner had to know which one to use. Switching between ammo types—and actually hitting what you were aiming at—meant the gunner had to be paying attention.

We rigged an additional M240B machine gun on the back deck of the Bradley. We put it on a tripod and fastened it down with some straps so Sully could use it while standing in the open cargo hatch. On my side of the vehicle, I had the coax, which I could operate with the Commander's override and swing it around to identify targets. I could see to the right out of my hatch, but I couldn't see off to the left because of the turret. Both the driver and the gunner are on the left side, but they're always inside of the vehicle, so we don't really have good vision on that side of the vehicle. With Sully having that 240 in back, he would be able to cover that side of the vehicle much better.

Having that second machine gun saved my ass more than once. The basic load is 4,800 rounds of 7.62 for the coax, and we had 6,000 rounds on board when we rolled out on the invasion.

Our load was also supposed to include two AT4s, shoulder-fired antitank rockets, and we had four with us. We also had two M4 carbines, for the driver and dismount, and two Beretta 9 mm pistols, for me and the gunner. We only had a total of 30 rounds, two magazines, for the pistols. That's not a lot, but remember, the only time you're supposed to be leaving the Bradley in combat is if it's on fire or disabled. I'll say it again: never get off the boat.

The M16 has been the issue rifle for America's troops since the 1960s. It fires a small, .22-caliber bullet, but at a very high velocity, and a magazine holds 30 of them. The M4, one of many variants of the M16, was designed in the 1990s and features a shorter 14.5-inch barrel with a cutout where an under-barrel 40 mm grenade launcher (the M203) can be mounted. Thus equipped, it is designated the M4/203. That's what we had.

The 40mm grenade fired out of the M203 is a big, slow round with a near rainbow trajectory. The great majority of the ammunition we used was HEDP (high-explosive dual-purpose) rounds. The explosive warhead is surrounded by a conventional casing that fragments and works like a typical frag hand grenade—except you can hit people hundreds of yards away with them, something not possible with a standard hand grenade.

I estimate I had a metric ton of ammunition in the back of the Carnivore. We had so much that there wasn't room in the back to do anything, except maybe lie down on the boxes. With the ammo we probably weighed about 36 tons.

Jason Sperry was my driver. He was an E4 (Specialist) and liked to rap, like a chubby Eminem. I gave him a lot of shit, but the fact of the matter was he had been in the Army for two years and knew his job. He was from New York, had a very young wife and a small child, and had joined the Army as a means of supporting his family.

Michael Soprano, who was my gunner, was an E5 (Sergeant)

from the Atlanta area. He'd only been on my crew four months at that point, but he knew what he was doing. He looked a bit like a dark-haired James Dean.

Michael Sullivan—Sully—was our loader/observer/dismount. He was from Florida, and I believe his father had a furniture store in St. Petersburg. Sully wore a dual hat, because in addition to being the designated guy to jump out and inspect something on foot when necessary, he worked as a loader. The Bradley system is loaded by traversing the turrets around at an angle. You then open the doors up on the side, one guy in the back hands the ammo up, and the gunner drags the ammo over. The gunner then either hooks the links to the rounds that are still in the ready box or he feeds it up into the main gun. Sully had arrived in the unit just before it deployed to Kuwait. He'd only been in the Army for a few months and had just turned 19. I guess you'd say he was "black Irish," because he looked Italian. He was a pretty meek, mild kid, and when I say meek and mild I mean he was a huge teenage pain in my ass—up until the shooting started.

I was the vehicle Commander. I had another driver, Private First Class Jesse Gardener, but he broke his leg a few weeks before we went into Iraq. He wound up in Headquarters Platoon driving the First Sergeant. So it was just the four of us in the Carnivore. I look back at the pictures of us, and while I look young compared to now, they look like babies. Heck, they were kids: Sully was just 19 and the other two were barely into their 20s. But they were soldiers to the core, and they damn sure got the job done when we faced the shit. I'd just had my 39th birthday and had been in the Army for 17 years. I had more time in the Army than the rest of the crew combined.

I wasn't the only one to name my vehicle—everybody christened their rides. Staff Sergeant John Williams in Third Platoon called his Bradley "Casanova." He was starting to lose his hair, just like me, and both of us shaved our heads. That worked a lot better when wearing the CVC helmet. Williams was a stocky, friendly faced guy, and a former national archery champion. When I asked him why he picked that name for his Bradley, he told me, "The same reason you named yours 'Carnivore.' It fits your personality. You're a rough guy, but me, I just love the ladies."

"You can shave your head like me all you want," I told him, "trying to look like Bruce Willis, but I'm the one who's got dimples. The ladies love the dimples."

"I've got something for your dimples . . ."

I'm short, and I've stopped waiting for that last growth spurt, but the fact of the matter is you don't want to be tall and riding around in armor—all you're going to do is bump your head—so I guess I was made for the Bradley.

Staff Sergeant Forest Geary named his vehicle "Circus Freaks," and I didn't even want to ask about that. He was a fifth-generation soldier from Odessa, Missouri, and one of the few in the unit not taller than me. Staff Sergeant Martin Crawford's Bradley was "Can't Puck Wit Dis." Lieutenant Justin McCormick's was "Criminal Minds." In case you're wondering, it's not a coincidence that all the armor names in Crazy Horse started with C. It cut down on the confusion.

Crazy Horse troop, 3/7 Cavalry, belonged to the Spartan Brigade for the 3rd ID, but we sort of fell underneath the 4th Brigade for aviation as a squadron asset. So while we were at Udairi, most of the other brigades were somewhere else, like Camp Jersey. At Udairi it was mostly us and a few Air Force types.

Once we got ourselves organized we did training exercises daily. We'd go outside the wire around Udairi, get on line, and run. We were practicing and making sure we could stay on line for the frontal attack because we knew when we attacked, we were going to have to attack on line. You'll see how well that plan worked out when it came to actual combat, but the theory is sound. Both of our scout platoons were going to attack on line with the tank platoons. It was like a big squadron movement to contact. We rehearsed that pretty regularly and got damn good at it.

Depending on the exercise, we had between 150 and 200 meters between vehicles. With 12 Bradleys lined up side by side per troop, and three troops, you're looking at about a two-and-a-half-to three-mile-wide swath of vehicles that could swoop in and roll your ass up.

We began getting sandstorms, so at night we moved our Bradleys in between the tents to protect them from the wind. We were living in these big tents—I don't think they were officially Iraqi tents, they were more like bedouin tents, but they were big.

I can't tell you how bored we were over there with nothing to do. I remember it as nine months in the desert with nothing to do, but really it was only three months—it just seemed like nine. Guys were so bored they were making a game out of spitting in each other's mouths. Soldiers would sit on the bunk naked, with their junk hanging off the edge of the cot, and they would see who could throw an AA battery the hardest at the other one's nuts. How bored do you have to be when *that* becomes your entertainment?

We were right next to the Air Cav (1st Cavalry Division), and two of our guys, Soprano and Christner's gunner, would go sit in the Porta-John together. They would sit in there with the door unlocked and wait until a pilot came by. Then, when the pilot would open the door, they would yell in falsetto, "Oh God, can't you knock?!" while they hurriedly pulled their pants up. That was our entertainment. Sorry, dear reader.

Want to hear about military stupidity? The Brigade Commander put out an order that there wouldn't be any self-gratification allowed. How would you even enforce that? It was ridiculous, of course, so guys would come up to their Troop Commander with their hat in their hand and say, "Sir, I was taking a shower, and I washed myself too hard, and I had a discharge. I just wanted to go ahead and report myself, so you can take me to the Brigade Commander." And it got to the point where every morning there'd be a long line of joes in front of the Troop Commander's tent. He finally came out and yelled at them, "Look, if you touch your shit and it goes off, I don't want to hear about it." Just about everybody in line would go, "Awwwwwww," and walk away.

While we were training a lot, we also had a lot of free time, and there was absolutely nothing to do. I mean NOTHING. We had to invent things to do. For entertainment we used to catch these little lizards that were all over. We didn't know their names, but we'd take the lizards and with alcohol markers we'd draw lipstick on 'em and put polish on their nails. Alcohol markers are like Sharpies, permanent markers. We'd keep the lizards in a .50-caliber-ammo can and give them all different names. We had one dressed up like the chaplain. Pet lizards and scorpion fights, that's how we kept ourselves occupied.

There were scorpions everywhere, little green ones, and we would catch them and let the scorpions fight each other. Then we caught this one black scorpion that was just huge. He must have been eight inches long with his tail stretched out. His body was almost two inches wide and he had pincers like a little lobster or a big crawdad.

The little scorpions, we would throw them all in a bucket and we'd make them fight. The black one would just grab a green scorpion in each pincer and bite their heads off. It was awesome. We painted a white 8 on his back with correction fluid and called him Eight Ball.

At some point we had this lizard, and while he wasn't as big as the scorpion, we figured we were going to have the ultimate bucket match to the death. Everybody was betting on Eight Ball to kill the lizard, of course.

The scorpions and the lizards, they're cold-blooded. They lie around all night and don't do anything until the sun warms them up. So when we'd pick 'em up every morning, it was like they were dead. You could play with them to get them going. Well, I kept this lizard in my cargo pocket for a long time, to get him warmed up and ready. The time came, and we threw him in the bucket with Eight Ball.

Eight Ball backed up when he saw the lizard. Little did we know, those lizards live off scorpions. That lizard looked at Eight Ball and was like, "Hey, what's up, bitch?" and jumped up and bit Eight Ball in the face.

Eight Ball grabbed him with both claws. He's got one leg in one claw and he's got the lizard's body in the other claw, mashing down on him as hard as he can, and he was jabbing his stinger into this lizard's head. Well, the lizard just kept crushing down with his mouth until he straight-out killed Eight Ball and started eating him. Son of a bitch. The biggest scorpion ever, the champion of Udairi, the Kuwaiti world champion of scorpion fighters, and this stupid lizard with lipstick on killed him.

We wouldn't let the lizard eat Eight Ball. We took the rest of the scorpion away from him and we buried Eight Ball. We gave him a military funeral with full honors. He served his country well.

I was always very good at getting people to do things they didn't think they could do. A lot of times my guys thought I was an asshole. Maybe I was one, but I got things done. However, when you have a bunch of guys out in the desert for months, with not enough to do, you're going to have friction even if everybody gets along at first.

When my crew messed up, I didn't really chew their ass and make them do push-ups or clean things. I would just give them the shovel. We had two T-handled shovels on the Bradley. It's always nice to have two shovels in case you get stuck or throw track, so you can dig out faster. Two shovels work better than one. I would always tell the guys, "Get the fucking shovel and start digging." And they'd do it. If they got me really mad, I'd tell them I wanted a fighting position for the Bradley.

The day we got our ammunition, Sully was fucking with me bad. All day. We were loading TOW missiles out of the Conex shipping container, breaking DU (depleted uranium) ammo out of the break-handled boxes and putting it in the Bradley's ready boxes, but not loading it into the guns yet, and Sully kept screwing with me. He'd draw a circle in the sand around himself and dare me to cross it. "It's my line in the sand. What are you going to do?" he'd taunt me.

So I'd get him and I'd roll him up in the circle. I'd give him a big wedgie and I'd make him eat the desert sand, and then he'd do it all over again. I put his face in the sand again and said, "No more circles, right? We're done with circles?" I'm not tall, but I'm stocky and have a lot of muscle underneath the padding. Plus, I like to fight.

"Yeah, we're done, Sergeant Jay. We're done." And I'd let that fucker up and he'd rinse his mouth out and he'd draw a square. "You didn't say nothin' about squares." So then we'd go again.

That went on for about four hours. Me rollin' him up, him drawing squares, stars, isosceles triangles, octagons . . .

When we'd packed everything up in the States to ship over to Kuwait, I bought Copenhagen, Mountain Dew, gum—small everyday things. I always kept extra stuff inside the Bradley to square other people away, because, you know, when somebody runs out of their dip they're really hurting. It's always nice to be able to pitch them a can of dip or something else that lifts their spirits. That's why I had the coffeepot in the Bradley. Guys could always count on coming over and being able to get a warm cup of coffee or play a video game. I was the senior Scout, and guys from the different platoons could come over, sit down, and relieve a little stress. We called it the Crazy Horse Café.

Coffee wasn't coffee. Coffee was normalcy. Coffee was a little bit of America in an alien place. Coffee was forgetting your troubles, if only for a few minutes. Just sitting there with your crew, your buddies, talking about nothing for as long as possible, which was never long enough. If you haven't been there, you just can't understand.

I also bought a bunch of Mountain Dew for my guys. Mountain Dew was the Red Bull of the day, and I shipped a lot of it over there. I would always tell the guys, "Don't ever drink the last soda. You can drink all the Dew you want, but don't drink the last soda." Well, we were getting ready to move into the desert before going into Iraq, and I looked in the Bradley and saw the last Mountain Dew was gone.

"Where the fuck is the last Mountain Dew?"

Jason Sperry, my driver, and Sully were up in front. I asked them, "Which one of you fucking guys took it?"

They both chimed in, "It wasn't us."

I said, "Get them shovels."

"Awwww." So they're diggin'. "How big?" they asked me.

I told them, "I want to be able to put the Bradley hull down." I was really pissed.

They said, "What?"

I said, "Hull down. I don't even want to see the turret anymore. I want you that fucking deep." In case you're wondering, a Bradley is just over nine feet tall.

So they're digging and digging and digging. About 35 minutes later, they walked down to the tent. "Sergeant Jay, we found your Mountain Dew and you owe us an apology."

"What?"

"You owe us an apology."

I said, "All right. Explain this to me."

They walked me over to the Bradley, and they had a half-liter bottle of Mountain Dew. You could tell where they crawled underneath the Bradley and stuck it underneath the ramp, at the gap of the ramp. They just set it on the ground there, and they're pointing underneath the ramp: "Look, there it is. It fell through the gap."

Well, I'm the guy who shipped over all the Mountain Dew from the States, and what I shipped over was cans. I told them, "Uh, guys? That last Mountain Dew was in a can."

"No, Sergeant Jay. It was in a bottle. You're just mistaken."

"It was a can. And don't tell me that bottle fell there, it can't even fit through that gap."

We went back and forth, and finally I just got tired of arguing. I said, "Fine. I've got a Mountain Dew. We're good to go. Just leave it at that. Put the shovels back."

In mid-March 2003, a sandstorm started to kick up. It didn't last as long as some, but it was still bad. We had to close all the hatches. The sandstorms are crazy: you can barely talk on the radio and you can't see 10 feet.

We spent the night all buttoned up inside the vehicle. The next morning was a nice sunny day. There was really nothing going on outside and we were on the very end of our desert laager, so we were as close to Iraq and the berm as we could get. Everybody else was in line with us.

Sully came in and said, "Hey, they're doing an NBC drill." (NBC stands for nuclear, biological, and chemical.) We were in the back of the Bradley playing Nintendo and lounging around. I looked out and could see everybody down the line running around in MOPP 4 gear and closing the hatches on their vehicles.

One big worry we had was Saddam shooting missiles loaded with anthrax or sarin gas or chicken pox or whatever at us, so we did all sorts of NBC drills where we got into our protective gear as fast as possible. MOPP stands for mission-oriented protective posture, and the number afterward indicates the level of protection. MOPP 4 was the highest level of protection. In addition to a gas mask we had to put on gloves, overboots, and a protective suit. If you think it gets hot in the desert, try standing around in a uniform covered by a full-body protective suit.

I said, "Hell. Sucks to be them." Since we were all the way at the end of the line, no one would notice if we didn't play along.

We finished the game and we shut the Bradley off. I was just getting ready to lie back and stretch out on the TOW missile boxes (because there was nowhere else to lie; we'd packed the Brad to the hatch with ammunition) when I heard on the radio, "All clear. All clear."

I said, "Looks like the training drill's over with."

And then I heard the Commander come across and say, "Roger, just got a call from Squadron Fox and they confirm that the missile that landed did not have chemical agents in it."

Um, wait, what?

Our Fox group responded to any biological or WMD (weapons of mass destruction) attacks. They rolled out in big six-wheeled vehicles that have all sorts of seals and protections. Officially the German-designed vehicles are called M93 CBRN (chemical, biological, radiological, nuclear) reconnaissance vehicles. Turns out Saddam had launched a SCUD missile and it went right over the top of our site and landed a mile or so to our south; that's why everybody went to MOPP 4 protective gear.

With the Bradley running and the video game going, we didn't hear anything because the missile's rockets weren't running. It was just the *whoosh* of it coming over. We didn't hear the explosion when it landed either; the desert is so wide open that sound really disperses.

At that point we dug around to find our masks and MOPP gear. Better late than never, right? I think mine was under a bunch of 25 mm ammo in the back.

That rocket going over apparently jarred command, because for the next three days they had us moving. Continual movement, so we were harder to hit, I guess. Between that movement and the sandstorms, we barely slept for three days. And I mean *barely*—10 minutes here, half an hour there.

So of course that's when command decided we should start the invasion.

CHAPTER 7

DEATHTRAP

Our first objective once we rolled through the berm and into Iraq was supposed to be a chemical manufacturing site, used in the creation of WMDs.

The 3/15th Infantry cut the holes in the berm, and while they were doing that Saddam launched another SCUD. It landed close to the Alpha Troop Commander's tank, maybe 400 meters away, and blew up in the desert. At that point we knew things were getting serious.

You can still see those berms on Google Earth. They are big ridges made of earth and sand that have been pushed up by heavy equipment. And there wasn't just one berm—there were three. The 3/15th Infantry and 34th Engineers had to cut lanes through them with dozers. The first berm was the Kuwaiti border, and the last one was Iraqi. In between the two was the United Nations berm in the UN Zone, and there were tank ditches on either side of it. There was a UN outpost in there as well.

The gap between the first and last berms was 10 kilometers. The 34th Engineers were actually the first unit inside Iraq, as they cut through the Iraqi defender berm. After they did that, the 3/15 Infantry charged in and headed straight for the nearby Iraqi outpost, but there was nobody there; it was abandoned. Once units started to punch through the berm they got organized on the far side and started spinning up. Some were heading north on Highway 1, others were heading out on Highway 8.

My unit, 3/7 Cav, consisted of three armor troops, Alpha, Bravo, and Charlie, also known as Apache, Bone Crusher, and Crazy Horse—because that just sounds cooler. Apache Troop was to head up the main highway to the town of As Samawah and Objective Pistol. They were the main element. Our mission was to take a dogleg to the west, to the chemical manufacturing site at As Salman. We had two Fox vehicles with us that were supposed to do a chemical survey of the objective. Bravo Troop was going to be behind us, and the headquarters troop, supply trains, and aviation assets would be behind Bravo.

Things always go wrong, of course. The road was dusty and it was one or two in the morning, and Sergeant Williams in Third Platoon stopped suddenly for some reason. Sergeant Soby, his wingman, rammed him in the back so hard it cracked the fuel cell on Williams's Bradley, the Casanova. Williams, of course, didn't want to give his vehicle up and miss the fight, so the guy in the back of his Bradley was ankle deep in fuel, sucking diesel fumes, for days.

We hadn't been rolling through Iraq for very long when we spotted what looked like some big long missiles and SCUD tents, so we went charging up the valley toward them. It turned out to be bedouins. Their tents, when folded up and from a distance, looked like SCUD emplacements.

Apache Troop had the first engagement—they identified it as a ZSU-23 (an antiaircraft gun), but it was actually an old tank hull. I ID'd another tank but didn't engage it because I could tell it was destroyed, and there was no heat signature. There were vehicles scattered everywhere from the 1991 Gulf War.

We hooked up with everyone else at our first refueling site. All the fuel trucks were with us, in the supply train behind Bravo Troop. The site was maybe 125 or 150 miles inside Iraq. Bradleys can go a lot farther before needing to be refueled, but we had M1s with us, and they are total hogs; they suck the diesel down twice as fast. We pulled aside and let the M1s refuel first.

There are two different ways you can handle refueling, a tail-gate or a service station. A tailgate is where you stay in your fighting position and the trucks pull up behind you and top you off individually. It takes longer, but it's the safest way to do it in a combat area. We hadn't been in contact yet, so we did a service station—that's where the fuel trucks stop and everybody cycles through and tops off their tanks.

After the fuel stop we drove through the rest of the day. I remember it was hot. That sun beat down on us all day. We passed a few towns, though I don't know if *town* is the correct word. They were dusty desert villages, just some mud huts and tents and bed-ouins. At this point we were ducks in a row rolling up the road, because that's bad desert there. You can't get into line formations or anything else because there are so many wadis, which are basically big desert ditches. When it rains the wadis fill up and flood, a lot like they do in California or in the deserts we have in the south-western United States. Trying to drive across them was a no-go, so we stayed on the highways, which are paved and slightly elevated.

In case you're wondering, we did have a CD player in the Bradley and had it hooked up through the radio. The setup was such that anytime we got a radio call, the music would cut out, so we wouldn't miss anything. I preferred AC/DC.

We drove through the day and into the night, then had another refueling stop, which was named Exxon. At that point we were all pretty smoked. We'd been up for the better part of three days before they'd cut through the berms, and we'd been on the move for another two. Plus, I'd been standing up pretty much the entire time.

Why was I standing up? The Bradley has ballistic periscopes and mirror reflectors, but you just can't see that well through them, not nearly as well as when you stick your head out of the hatch, which was what I did. It's a lot more dangerous, because you can always catch a bullet in the face, but when you're not in direct contact it's usually better to get your head out there. The only problem was standing for two days on my platform (with more to come) caused my knees to swell up unbelievably. I think that was due to the lack of movement affecting the blood flow, not to mention gravity pulling everything down. If I remember correctly, there was a well-known TV reporter embedded with some unit who had the same problem, which caused blood clots in his legs, because he was stuck in a Humvee for days without really being able to move.

At that point I made a mistake that almost cost me my Bradley. I was using my night vision goggles to look for a spot to set up the next refueling site. With no depth perception in the NVGs, I saw a place I thought was flat.

"Sperry. You see that spot up ahead? Go turn around there."

We rolled up, and much to my surprise the spot wasn't flat, and we slid down a steep embankment and almost turned over.

"Goddammit! Hold on, hold on. Everybody still here? Shit. Sperry, can you get us back upright?"

"Yeah, Sarge, I think so."

Sperry was able to get the Brad back on the road, but it was close. We managed to find a good spot for Exxon without flipping the Bradley.

When we pulled aside to let the M1s refuel first, I told Sully, "Hey, I'm going to get some sleep, you stay awake for as long as you can and then wake me up." All of the other crews were doing the same thing.

Next thing I know, the entire scout platoon was asleep, laid out on top of their vehicles like lizards. The muffled sounds coming across the radio were sort of like a dream, or maybe they'd made their way into my dream. Either way, I woke up and said, "What the hell?"

Sully was out, just laid out on top of the vehicle. Everybody in the Bradley was asleep. All around us were the crews of other Brads, asleep on their vehicles as well. "Hey, wake up, the fuelers are waiting on us."

As we were just waking up we could see cruise missiles coming in and flying over us. It was still a starry night, and cold, and it was very cool watching them. You could hear them coming in, and then they'd *whoosh* by overhead. They were flying nap of the earth and coming right over the top of us. I don't know where they were headed. Baghdad? When you care enough to send the very best . . .

When we started moving, one Fox vehicle rammed another and cut a tire on it. Maybe they were watching the cruise missiles fly over, I don't know. At that point, our exhaustion was a big safety factor. Plus, night vision does not give you good depth perception, as I'd just learned. Their vehicle Commander called First Sergeant Roy D. Grigges and told him they were going to have to change a tire—oh, and there was a specific procedure to change the tire on one of those vehicles, which meant it would take four hours.

"You've got twenty minutes," Grigges told them, "and we're

fucking rolling. We're in enemy territory, it's nighttime, we're on the move, and now you've got nineteen minutes." Grigges was from Ocala, Florida, and was the best First Sergeant I ever worked with.

The Fox guys said, "But it's not recommended to drive on a flat tire!"

Grigges was reasonable. He told them, "Okay, I'll drop a case of MREs [meals, ready-to-eat] off with you, and the next unit coming up will pick you up. We'll just leave you there by yourself."

Needless to say they drove on the flat.

Somehow before we got to Exxon we had found ourselves the lead element for the squadron. Alpha Troop was supposed to be in the lead, but they had fallen behind us—I think they ran into mine-fields. Everything at this point was just a big push to get forward, get forward. Our objective was the small town of As Salman, and we were supposed to make sure there weren't any chemical weapons factories there. We were to send our Fox NBC vehicles into town first. After that small town, the road bent north and went straight into As Samawah. We had some objectives in As Samawah, but they were secondary to the WMD check at As Salman.

Past Exxon, back on the march, we came to another checkpoint in our route. At that point the Troop Commander, Captain Jeff McCoy, contacted me on the radio. "Hey, you are now the lead element for the squadron, and we need you to push north."

"Roger that, sir."

He wanted us to turn off the main road using Route Mule, cut across the desert, and rejoin the main road just before As Samawah. He was giving me coordinates and numbers for our maps, which we called graphics (for topographic maps). This would have been very helpful had I brought those graphics along.

Our graphics were very detailed—very, very detailed. On top of that, we'd covered hundreds of miles. We literally didn't have room for all of the maps that we could have brought with us, and we still brought a shitload. It was like a vehicle tarp, there were so many maps, and they were covered front and back. It was just impossible for us to have all the maps that we were going to need to get from point A to point B, and I figured there was no chance in hell that we'd need *those* graphics. Turned out I was wrong.

We'd been traveling east all day and needed to turn north. I had Sully in the back of the vehicle going through all the maps, trying to find a zone designator. I did my best to pick up the trail by memory, but that wasn't working so well. And our GPS? We were so deep in the desert, there weren't any satellites, and my instrument wasn't working.

"You have to go north," Sully told me, sitting on ammo and buried in maps.

"I know I fucking have to go north!" I yelled at him. Finally, I had Sperry just turn off the road and start heading north. In the dark. We found a couple of trails made by guys driving pickup trucks and riding camels. They would go in the right direction for a while, but then they would veer off. They can't go over big hills. They can't go over wadis. They can't go over depressions. So, the trails twisted and turned and I was doing the best I could running north. Whenever the trail we were on started spinning off, either hard right or hard left, we really didn't have a lot of choice but to not follow it. Because if we followed it, we didn't know where the hell we would wind up.

Everybody following me was having a hard time, because the stars had disappeared and it was pitch black and I was sending up a dust cloud behind me like Pigpen in *Peanuts*. I put Sully in the back of the vehicle, and he was breaking chem lights and tossing them off the back. That might have worked better if the vehicles following us didn't keep running them over.

A few times, we went down some steep embankments that we shouldn't have, let alone the wheeled vehicles we were leading, but they did, and they made it. Everybody behind me was calling me on the radio: "Could you just go straight?"

I told them, "There is no straight!"

Wingman 3-2 for Third Platoon, way back behind me, got on the radio and said, "All you have to do is follow this trail . . ." and he's describing it for me.

"That trail doesn't exist," I told him.

"I'm driving on it!" he said.

"No, you're driving on the trail I'm making." The Bradley was crushing stones, and by the time Third Platoon got to where I'd been, there'd already been a scout platoon, a tank platoon, a head-quarters platoon, and another tank platoon driving behind me. Hell, there *was* a road by the time Wingman 3-2 got there.

It probably would have been easier if I'd had a working compass on the vehicle.

You read that right. The lensatic compass on the Bradley wasn't working. I don't know if there was too much metal (ammo?) inside of the vehicle for it to work, but it was useless. I did all the navigating using my $40 Timex watch from Walmart, which had a built-in compass. Seventy-five miles across the desert in pitch black, using my watch compass, dropping chem lights behind me like bread crumbs, and I managed to pop us out on the highway three miles from As Samawah, almost exactly where we were supposed to be. Sometimes it's better to be lucky than good.

After hours of driving in the dark, weaving back and forth, up and down hills, along camel trails and long-forgotten 4x4 tracks, we popped out onto Highway 8. Finally, a paved road.

"Who the hell are these guys?" my driver, Jason Sperry, said. I couldn't see him, but we all had our CVC helmets hooked into the radio so we could talk.

Laid out in front of us was an American armored battalion. The vehicles were in a laager position, and the troops were just lying on top of their tanks and scout vehicles with their shirts off. They were on the hoods and back decks in sleeping bags or walking around sleepily in T-shirts.

"I'm guessing they got to take the direct route up," Soprano said. He was up in the turret with me and eyed the joes wandering around in their T-shirts. "I'm also guessing they haven't seen any combat yet."

We hadn't seen any combat either, and as it turned out no one had, except maybe for a few Special Forces teams. "We don't have time to chitchat or sightsee," I said over the radio. "Let's get on the road and get organized. Where the hell is my wingman?"

I hooked up with Sergeant First Class Anthony Broadhead and his M1 Abrams tank, the Camel Toe. He was the Sergeant for Second Platoon, a 21-year veteran of the Army who, like most of the unit, had never experienced combat. He was a big guy from Virginia Beach, Virginia, laid back and easy to work with. His call sign was White 4, and mine was Red 2.

General George Armstrong Custer, whose unit we belonged to, was defeated at the Little Bighorn at the hands of a Sioux Indian chief named Crazy Horse, so that's why we took the name. The insignia of Crazy Horse Troop is an Indian skull named Nowatay. We had it spray-painted on our tracks and on our shirts, and we spray-painted that bad boy all over Iraq—our version of "Kilroy Was Here."

Each troop had six platoons—a headquarters platoon, a mortar platoon, two scout platoons with Bradleys, and two tank platoons with M1 Abrams main battle tanks. First (Red) and Third (Blue) Platoons were scout platoons; Second (White) and Fourth (Green) were tank platoons. (Being Red 2 put me in First Platoon.) The plan was to have the First and Second Platoons working in hunter-killer teams, and Third and Fourth Platoons working together as well. Being a "hunter-killer" meant we'd be in the front, tasked with finding the enemy so they could be destroyed. All told, there were about 150 guys in Crazy Horse.

My vehicle was still in the lead, and I got a little confused, having been up for the better part of 100 hours. There was a northern objective and a southern objective, and I wasn't sure which way we were supposed to go. I did know we were somewhere south of As Samawah, Iraq. It didn't help that it had begun raining, reducing our visibility—not that there are many landmarks in the desert.

"Sully!" I called to my loader in the back of the Bradley. "You've got the maps. Do you know which way we're supposed to turn?"

"That's not on the maps," he told me. "That was in the op order we were given."

"Well, do you remember whether we were supposed to go for the northern or southern objective? Anyone?"

"No, Sergeant Jay, sorry."

"No, Sarge, not a clue."

I called Tony Broadhead on the radio. "White 4, Red 2, do we head north or south from here?"

"Red 2, White 4. Ummm, wait one."

The Troop Commander, Captain McCoy, got on the radio. "We're burning daylight, people, we need to move and stop dragging ass."

Shit. Well, just because I didn't know quite which way to go was no reason to be late. "North," I told Sperry, so we turned north and Broadhead and I led the way, with First and Second Platoons following. In total we had two M1 tanks and three Bradleys in our group.

Sergeant Williams got on the radio. "Heading to the southern objective now with Third and Fourth Platoons," he announced. I guess that settled that. After thinking back on the orders the troop had been given, I was pretty sure that meant that Williams would be heading to the chemical factory to check for evidence of WMDs. So that would make my objective a bridge.

Even though it burns more fuel, an M1 can outrun a Bradley without even trying, so I was setting the pace. Broadhead stayed on the asphalt road and I was on his right flank, driving through fields. The M1 is great for some things, but when it comes to maneuvering off-road it's a pig. It's just too big and heavy. Which, if you ask me, is completely ass backward. The main battle tank of the United States Army can't go off-road? Whiskey Tango Foxtrot.

We got up to 30 miles an hour in the light rain, and I had to keep wiping the mud and dust off my goggles. Then we hit the outskirts of town. We passed a junkyard, then some sort of big refinery, and big piles of trash. Before long we started driving by houses.

We began seeing people, and we waved at them, but they stared at us like we were aliens. I don't think it really clicked with them that we were Americans; they just wondered what their military was doing there, exactly as we would if we saw tanks rolling down the street. Americans would just think it was our Army and wonder what they were doing. If you don't know anything about armor, one tank looks like another, and we weren't flying big American flags. It was early enough that I think some of them wandered outside just to see what the noise was.

They could probably hear us coming a mile away. Hell, they

could probably feel us in the soles of their feet. A 60-ton M1 at speed sounds like a screaming bulldozer on steroids. Broadhead's tank made the ground vibrate like the *T. rex* in *Jurassic Park,* and its tracks were trashing the asphalt road.

"Whoa, shit!" I heard Sperry say, as he slewed the Carnivore around a low wall, then had to swerve to avoid some people. Our tracks sprayed mud sideways. "Armor coming through here people, fucking *move!*"

"White 4, Red 2, you wanna slow it down some? We're swimming through soup and dodging chickens over here."

"Red 2, roger that."

We closed in on Objective Pistol, which was a railroad bridge in the town of As Samawah. Our mission was simply to hold it so the tank battalion coming up behind us could cross it. Most of Saddam's armor was further north, and everyone assumed the real war would start when the armor went head-to-head. As Samawah was just a small town, of no specific strategic importance, and we weren't expecting much of anything to happen there. Everyone knew Baghdad was where the real fight was going to happen. Still . . .

"Guys, heads up," I told my crew. This was the first town of any size we'd encountered in our run north. Apart from a few mud huts and bedouins in tents, we had hardly seen any Iraqis, much less the Iraqi army. "I know you're tired, I'm tired too, but now's not the time to get your ass shot off 'cause you're not paying attention." How much sleep had I gotten over the last three days? I tried figuring it out in my head. Less than an hour a day. No wonder I was so tired.

"Dismounts, three hundred meters!" Broadhead called out. I saw them.

Broadhead and I rolled to a stop, vehicles idling. We were within 300 meters of a bridge over a canal in As Samawah. Just past the canal bridge was Objective Pistol. Broadhead was in the middle of the road, and I was still off the road to his right.

There were about 30 guys on the near side of the canal bridge, in and around a small concrete building or bunker reinforced with sandbags. They had several vehicles as well and were not in uniforms. We could see they had AKs, and maybe an RPG-7 (rocket-propelled grenade launcher). You'd have to be a damn good shot to hit either of our vehicles with an RPG at that distance, and their AKs wouldn't do anything unless Broadhead or I caught a round in the face.

The AK-47 is probably the most-produced military rifle in world history, and it has a reputation for reliability. While they aren't necessarily as accurate as our M4s, someone who knows how to shoot could definitely hit a man's head at 300 meters with a few shots. My helmet theoretically would stop an AK bullet, but I didn't really want to test that theory. Soprano traversed our turret and pointed our 25 mm main gun toward the group.

"Don't fire," I told him. "Just hold on."

The M1 Abrams is America's main battle tank (MBT) and has been since the early 1980s. It is both longer and wider than the Bradley, and just about double the weight of a Bradley. Instead of a 25 mm full-auto main gun it had a 120 mm cannon on the front, with a .50-caliber M2 machine gun for backup, as well as an M240 7.62 machine gun coaxially mounted to the main gun. Ammunition for the M1s main gun comes in two types—an armor-piercing DU round, and a HEAT (high-explosive antitank) round. The HEAT round doesn't cause a general explosion like a bomb; rather, it is more focused, like a shaped charge, and designed to defeat armor. M1s have a crew of four—commander, gunner, loader, and driver.

The M1 was designed to be superior to the top-of-the-line Soviet MBT, the T-72, of which the Iraqis had plenty. No one had any doubt that the U.S. Army would win any tank battle with the Iraqis. The M1 would also withstand a direct hit from an RPG-7 warhead. My Bradley, on the other hand—let's not find out.

While a few had seen some action during the 1991 Gulf War, for all intents and purposes the Bradley Fighting Vehicle was untested in combat. The design itself was the result of a decades-long internal Army struggle so divisive it was the basis for a movie starring Kelsey Grammer, *The Pentagon Wars*. The movie concluded that the design of the BFV had been compromised by politics so badly that the vehicle literally was a deathtrap. It was too big, too heavy, too slow; the armor wasn't thick enough and the main gun was far too small to be effective. Personally, I loved the damn things, but I hadn't seen any serious combat in one. I had a feeling this war was going to settle the argument, one way or the other.

We reached the bridge at approximately 7 A.M. on March 23, 2003. I don't believe either side had fired a shot in the war up to that point. We were the first major American force (apart from Special Forces teams) to reach that far north.

We stared at the group on the bridge, and they stared back. After a few seconds, Broadhead, who was standing up in his turret, waved at them. That may sound dumb, but it wasn't.

Our rules of engagement at the time were very limited. We had all been told that the Iraqis were just waiting for the Americans to arrive. As soon as we showed up, they would start hugging us and throwing flowers and asking us to kiss their babies and date their girlfriends. If we saw anyone with weapons, we weren't to fire at them, because as soon as they saw we were Americans they were going to join us in fighting Saddam.

I don't know if you watched the news, but it didn't quite happen that way.

CHAPTER 8

FIRST CONTACT

Objective Pistol was a bridge that went over railroad tracks. We could see it maybe a couple of hundred meters beyond the canal bridge in front of us.

Broadhead waved at the crowd of armed Iraqis manning the crossing, and, as soon as they realized we were Americans, the guys manning the bridge opened up on Broadhead with AKs and RPGs.

"Shit, are they shooting at us?" Soprano asked me.

"At Broadhead," I told him. "It'll be our turn soon enough. Heads up!" I told my crew over the radio. "This just turned into a shooting war."

Broadhead ducked down and got on the radio with command. "Contact! Contact! I have troops engaging me with small arms." He provided our location and, just to make sure, asked, "Am I cleared to return fire?" I am almost positive this was the first engagement of the war involving regular army troops, just after 7 A.M. local time, March 23, 2003.

Captain McCoy responded immediately. "Roger, White 4, return fire."

Broadhead opened up with his .50-cal on the fortified position, and the sound of the big gun was huge, echoing off every wall and building along the road. As powerful as the .50 is, it didn't do shit against the concrete and sandbags. The Iraqis kept firing back, now at us, too. Some ducked down, but the rest just stood in the middle of the road. At that distance, mostly firing on full auto, they were doing good to just hit the road near us. Well, nobody said every fight had to be fair.

"Gunner!" I called out to Soprano. "Targets, three hundred meters, HE, fire!"

Whatever doubt I might have had about the fighting effectiveness of the Bradley and its 25 mm main gun was quelled right then and there. Our main gun barked a short burst, and the Carnivore shivered from the recoil. The 25 mm high-explosive rounds landed in the middle of the men shooting at us and bodies flew everywhere. Their bunker was hit, one of their vehicles was struck—the HE was like an explosive tornado right in the middle of them.

"Shit, that worked," Soprano said.

I grabbed the Commander's override, which gave me control of the main gun, and turned the 25 mm on their bunker. With just a few rounds I destroyed it. Broadhead and I kept firing, taking out another 10 or so guys in the open.

Four Iraqis jumped into a truck and hauled ass in the other direction, and Broadhead and I lit it up. The truck flipped over and went off the road.

"Red 2, let me call this in," Broadhead radioed me.

"Copy."

Broadhead called in a contact report to command, and I relinquished control of the main gun to Soprano again.

A few seconds later, Broadhead was back on the radio. "Red 2, White 4, proceeding toward the objective."

"Roger that, on your ass." We still hadn't reached our objective, the railroad bridge, which we could see in the distance. "Sperry," I told my driver, "stay with him."

Broadhead took the lead, running straight down the middle of the road, and we pulled up onto the road behind him. We rolled slow and careful, checking either side for threats or an ambush, but there was nothing. All the civilians who'd wandered out to rubberneck as we'd rolled up had vanished. As we approached the bridge, I found myself staring at all the dead men, even though I'd seen plenty of bodies before.

"Keep your head on a swivel," I told my guys.

Right after we'd crossed the canal bridge, an Iraqi army truck appeared in the distance, heading straight for us. It stopped and spun around, and we could see it was full of Iraqi soldiers. There was a civilian pickup truck between us and the army truck, so we couldn't fire. At this point the adrenaline got the better of Broadhead, and he started chasing the army truck in Camel Toe. The huge diesel engine roared. I was his wingman, so I told Sperry, "Stay on his ass!" We immediately took off after him.

We drove right over the railroad bridge and kept going, past our objective, leaving the rest of the troop on the other side of the bridge. At that point the M1s were almost out of fuel, and the rest of them were waiting for the fueler to catch up. Sergeant Christner's Bradley had some sort of comm issue and lost radio, and everybody else was way back there wondering what all the shooting was about.

As we went roaring down the road chasing Broadhead in his M1, Sully saw three dismounts firing at us from the left, trying to set up a machine-gun position. He turned the M240B on them and killed them all with a long burst, and I looked back to see what had happened. Nineteen years old—that was the first time he'd ever pointed a gun at another human being, much less pulled the trigger, but he didn't hesitate. I was tough on them, treated them like the kids they were sometimes, but my crew wasn't stupid: we were at war, and they knew it. War means killing the other guy before he kills you. We soldiers don't make policy or decide whether to start a war, but we damn well are going to do the job we've been trained for if we're sent into battle.

The Iraqi army truck we were chasing turned into some sort of walled compound on the left side of the road. I watched as Broadhead's M1 pulled into the gate and just stopped, blocking it. Even over the roar of the Bradley I could hear the shooting.

"Knock down the wall next to him!" I yelled at Sperry.

It's hard to argue with mass, and 34 tons (plus ammo) beats concrete every day of the week. As the dust settled I popped out of the hatch and beheld absolute mayhem.

The compound wasn't big, maybe 20 by 40 yards, and there were vehicles and Iraqis in uniform running everywhere. Everyone I could see had AKs or RPGs, and they were firing at us with all they had. The truck we had chased was right in front of us, the back of it still filled with Iraqis.

"Shoot!" I yelled at Soprano.

"What?" he yelled back. The noise was incredible. We were only feet apart and could barely hear each other.

"Shoot!" I yelled back. "Shoot the fucking guys!"

"Where?"

"Where?" I yelled at him in disbelief. "They're everywhere! Pick a direction and fucking start SHOOTING!"

At that point one of the 15 or so guys standing in the back of the truck launched an RPG at me. The backblast from the rocket engulfed the man behind him in smoke and steam, and blew him out of the back of the truck. As I watched the RPG flying toward me, it was as if time had stopped. The round came at me like someone throwing a softball. The RPG went right by my face and smashed into the antenna mount next to me. Unbelievably, it did not explode but went spiraling smoke up into the air, landed somewhere behind my Brad, and then exploded.

RPGs were everywhere in Iraq. The launcher is a simple tube the user rests on his shoulder, and the rockets are inserted into the front of the launcher. Press the trigger, and the rocket-propelled-grenade's motor is ignited and it shoots out, deploying stabilizing fins as it goes. For what they are, they're reasonably accurate, but how effective they are ultimately depends upon the skill of the user. Generally, the Iraqis couldn't shoot worth a shit.

Soprano was still looking at me like he was confused, so I grabbed the Commander's override and launched six 25 mm HE rounds into the back of the truck. Bodies went flipping everywhere, and the truck broke in half. Apparently that truck was so close Soprano couldn't see the guys in the back of it in his sight, which was still set on low magnification. My grabbing the override was all that Soprano needed to figure out what was going on, and he got back on the gun. The truck went up in flames.

I pulled my Beretta pistol out and fired seven shots into two Iraqis who had come out of their bunkers right next to my vehicle. When I shot at them, they were less than two feet away from me and climbing up. The first Iraqi fell after the third shot and I had to fire four more times at the second Iraqi before he fell. Then the pistol jammed.

Iraqi soldiers were all around us, mere feet from the Bradley, getting closer, and they kept trying to climb up the sides. One came out of a building, firing at me. Most of the rounds hit the turret and bounced off, but at least one of the rounds hit my vest. I fell down into the vehicle, thinking I was dead. Surprisingly, I wasn't, even though I didn't have a plate in my vest—only the command group had armor plates. Turns out it was a pistol round, a 9 mm or .380, and only went through the first layer of my vest. I had a purple bruise on my chest for three months from that bullet. I grabbed Soprano's M4/203, popped back out of the hatch, and started taking enemy out. I was shooting people charging me, hiding behind vehicles, climbing up the sides of my Bradley. It was insane. We were taking a huge volume of fire, from every direction.

There was a small guardhouse right next to Broadhead's tank. A guy kept popping out of it and firing his AK up at him. Broadhead turned the M1's main gun on it and from point-blank range let go with a 120 mm HEAT round. The little building disintegrated, and concrete blocks went flying everywhere. My Bradley got hit with concrete chunks as well as body parts. Broadhead continued to light up the dismounts with his .50 and fired main gun rounds into the buildings.

There was another small pickup truck full of about six guys in uniform trying to get away, and Soprano hit it with the Bradley's main gun. His first round hit a soldier in the chest and he literally disappeared. The next three rounds destroyed the truck and everything in it. I wouldn't have believed the 25 mm was able to do that much damage if I hadn't seen it myself.

Sully was in the back, firing the 240 into a group of Iraqis charging us. Soprano was chewing everything up with the 25 mm, and I was nailing guys with the M4 as fast as I could pull the trigger, reloading, and shooting some more. I saw movement to the right and yelled, "Pivot right!" Soprano slewed the turret.

There was a group of five or six Iraqis holding their hands up or on their knees, hoping we wouldn't kill them. Iraqis were bleeding out everywhere, vehicles were on fire, screams filled the air, and I could see about 60 Iraqis on the ground in the immediate vicinity, dead, dying, or wounded.

Everyone in the compound was wearing what we called "salad suits," which was the Iraqi military camouflage. We found out later we had rolled into a Ba'ath Party police station, and that was their uniform of choice. Police or not, they were all trying to kill us, but we didn't even know the compound was there until we drove into it.

"Sully, on my six!" I jumped down from the Bradley with the M4 and Sully joined me, while Soprano and Sperry provided overwatch. Sully had his M4 in his hands and was trying to look everywhere at once.

"Hey, I see movement around back, I'm going to check that out," Broadhead yelled to me.

"Roger, I'm going to clean this area up." I was looking for prisoners more than anything. I told Sully, "Cover those guys, and see if anybody else wants to surrender—but watch your ass!"

There was a brand-new New Holland tractor just sitting inside this compound, and it seemed out of place to me. I shot it a couple of times with the M4. Soprano was in the turret, hand on the Commander's override of the coax in case something happened. The area was a kaleidoscope of smoke and flames and blood and moans.

Three guys showed themselves in a nearby building, and I shot them with the M4. Somehow we'd parked the Bradley on top of a bunker, and I saw movement inside it. I stuck the muzzle of the M4 in there and emptied it. In all I fired fourteen 30-round magazines through that M4 on three-round burst, but I finally was out of ammo. After tossing the M4 on top of the Bradley, I picked up an AK-47. Sully was rounding up casualties in the open, and I started checking buildings. There were a few guys moving around inside one of the rooms and I emptied the AK through a window at them, then reloaded and went in and cleared it. Finding fresh magazines for that gun was never a problem; there were rifles lying everywhere.

I found one guy hiding in a little building, and as soon as I walked into the building he came at me. I buttstroked him with the rifle and knocked his two front teeth out. He half fell into me, and I grabbed him by the front of his shirt, took him outside, and threw him on the ground. He was an officer, obviously—he had the best uniform on, and it was all clean and pressed.

Between Sully and me we rounded up close to 15 EPWs (enemy prisoners of war). Broadhead was still running around in the field beyond the compound we were in, dealing with machine-gun and mortar teams and dozens of dismounts with AKs (although we didn't know that at the time, we could hear the shooting). As we were standing there, about eight vehicles drove up on the road and stopped next to the compound. Most of them were pickup trucks, and all of them were painted white with orange fenders and/or bumpers front and back. We'd never seen those before but naturally assumed they were Fedayeen vehicles, because that's who got out.

The Fedayeen Saddam was a loyalist paramilitary group established in Iraq in 1995. Saddam used them to do all sorts of nasty stuff. Wearing black track suits and carrying AK-47s and RPGs, they looked like Iraqi ninjas. From the eight vehicles about 60 men dismounted, not much more than 30 meters away from us. The funny thing was, they never even looked in our direction—they were gesturing and pointing at the bridge, the direction we'd come from. We didn't fire on them immediately because we weren't quite sure whose side they were on; we'd been told the Iraqis would greet us with chocolate and American flags and puppies. I wondered if perhaps they were there to help us.

Most of them ran to the first truck, a Toyota with a heavy machine gun in the back of it. There was a guy there giving directions, pointing back at the canal bridge, which was being held by an M1 and a Bradley. Sully and I looked at each other, him with an M4 in his hands and me with an AK.

"What the fuck?" I said. Did these guys really not see us? Standing broadside to us, only 30 yards away, were 60 guys and 8 vehicles, and they don't even know we're there?

I signaled Soprano in the turret to get ready to fire, and Sullivan and I took aim. He took the guy on the machine gun and I aimed at the guy who I thought was in charge.

"Wait until I fire," I told my crew, as I was still waiting to see whose side the Fedayeen were on. When they took out an RPG launcher and aimed it at the bridge, I knew. I had the AK on full auto and fired three rounds, hitting their Commander in the chest; he turned and fell to the ground. Sully took out the machine gunner and Soprano let about 35 rounds of 25 mm fly into the men and the vehicles on full auto. They were so close Soprano could hardly get the barrel of the gun down low enough to engage them, and we had the same problem with the coax, but where that main gun did hit it was the nastiest thing I had ever seen. We were out of HE in the ready box, and so Soprano engaged them with DU (depleted uranium) rounds. The 25 mm ripped and dismembered the men all to hell, turned them inside out, and the trucks broke apart like toys; meanwhile both Sully and I were shooting everybody we could see with our rifles.

The weird thing was, they didn't seem to know where the fire was coming from; I think they thought our guys at the bridge were shooting them. One of the Fedayeen ran and hid behind a wall, but the wall was between him and the bridge, not between him and us. We could see him fine. He was about 50 feet away from me, on the far side of the road, and I was shooting at him and shooting at him and the damn AK was not zeroed. It wasn't a hard shot, he wasn't really moving, just squatting behind that low wall with his rifle, but I couldn't hit shit. The rounds were flying over his head or hitting the dirt at his feet, and he had no idea where the bullets were coming from. I wasn't the only guy shooting at that time, and wherever Broadhead was it sounded like he was in the middle of a small war.

Finally I shot at the wall, just to see where my AK was hitting, then adjusted my aim and with the last shot in the magazine hit the man in the head. He fell over sideways and didn't move. By that time pretty much everybody else in and around the trucks was dead. Two of the trucks had tried to get away, but didn't make it.

"Stay with them!" I yelled at Sully, pointing to the EPWs still cowering on the ground. I grabbed another magazine for the AK and headed for the road on foot.

Everybody was down, but not out, and there were a number of Fedayeen crawling around in the ditch beside the road with their AKs. I shot half a dozen guys, then ran back to Sully and the Iraqis, and everybody was right where I left them.

"All right!" I started looking for the guy with the good uniform and found him in the group.

"Call the Commander," I yelled up to Soprano. "Tell him we're going to be bringing him prisoners."

Mr. Iraqi Officer with the nice uniform just looked at me as I pulled him up and started walking him to the back of the Bradley. Only one or two of the EPWs could fit in my overstuffed Bradley, and officers are usually the only guys who know anything. He was between me and the other prisoners as I pulled him toward the back of the vehicle. Just then a mortar round landed right in the middle of the group of prisoners on the ground. I was blown backward onto my ass and tasted blood, but I seemed to have all my parts. There was shrapnel in my hands, but luckily I still had my CVC helmet on, with its Kevlar cover. It protected my hearing and my skull. If the ground hadn't been sand, or those prisoners hadn't been there to absorb the blast, or the EPW I'd been bringing to the Brad hadn't been between me and the mortar explosion, it probably would have killed me.

The Iraqi I was leading got hit by a big piece of scrap metal and most of his nose was gone. Blood gushed down his face and was coming out of both of his ears. Some of the prisoners I'd grouped together on the ground were screaming and spurting blood, and the rest weren't moving at all.

"Mortar!" I yelled to my guys. "Get ready to move! Get ready to move!"

The hell with taking any prisoners. "Run!" I told the Iraqi I'd dragged over to the Bradley. He probably couldn't hear me with the blood coming out of his ears, but when I kicked him in the ass he got the message and took off running. There was no need for him to die, and I had a feeling things were going to get messy. The other EPWs still able to move understood my hand signals and made for the buildings as well.

You never know what's going to happen in a war, but that guy, that officer, he made it back to our troop's position later so he could be treated for his wounds. Not only did half his nose get shot off, he took a bullet in the stomach. He was the one who told us that the compound we rolled into was a police station, even though they were wearing military uniforms. Headquarters ended up medevacing him out of there. I wonder where he ended up.

CHAPTER 9

CARNIVORE, CAMEL TOE, AND CIRCUS FREAKS

I climbed into the back of the Bradley and had just gotten into the turret when another mortar round hit the top of a palm tree over us and exploded, like an air burst.

The blast knocked me back down into the turret and threw Sully down into the cargo compartment. My right eardrum burst, and the entire Brad got nailed by shrapnel—pieces of twisted steel were sticking out of the hull like broken glass on top of a wall. Sully got hit by shrapnel in his hands, and I had shrapnel in my legs, arms, and shoulders. My hands were even burned a little; that's how close we were to the round when it went off. The mortar shrapnel shredded everything on top of the Bradley—our duffel bags, the M240 we'd mounted on the back, our water cans, the GPS unit, and my binoculars. It also trashed the M4 that I'd thrown on top of the Bradley; only the SureFire flashlight on it worked after that.

Sperry panicked when the mortar round went off above us, and he floored the Carnivore. He ran over the New Holland tractor, then over a car—not easily, by the way, but he kept gunning it until we were over the top—while I was trying to get back in the hatch. He ran over a chain-link fence and some concertina wire, then smashed into a big diesel fuel container, leaving me with about 30 gallons of diesel sloshing around my feet, and he still was hauling ass, the engine wide open. Through it all there was an Iraqi hanging on the outside of the Bradley for dear life. I grabbed my Beretta and shot him three times, then that fucking pistol jammed again, so I had to hit him with the pistol in the face before he fell off. Finally I was able to climb out of my hatch and kick the driver's hatch to try to get Sperry's attention.

"Sperry! Sperry! Jason! Asshole!"

The hatch wasn't closed and I reached down inside through a gap and grabbed Sperry. I had to shake him to get him to stop, he was so panicked. "Plug in your fucking CVC so you can hear me on the comm," I told him, then got his hatch closed and got myself back in the vehicle.

We found ourselves in a field outside the compound. Sully was down, and I didn't know how badly he was wounded. While I checked over Sully, Soprano slewed the gun around and engaged soldiers in the field who were shooting at us with AKs. There were guys everywhere, and at that time Broadhead showed up again in Camel Toe.

Sully was still alive, just stunned, and when I got back in my spot I saw that Broadhead had run right up on us. Just as I looked at his tank he opened up with his .50-cal, the rounds passing right in front of me.

"What the fuck are you doing?" I yelled at him, then turned around and saw he'd engaged an RPG team setting up to engage the Bradley. Beyond his tank I saw a Fedayeen truck skid up, guys behind it with RPGs, and used the Commander's override to hit them with a burst of DU rounds that whipped right past Broadhead's face. It was like playing chicken, with guns. Big guns.

The field was full of guys firing at us with their AKs, and the incoming rounds were pinging off the hull and trashing Sully's disabled M240 even more. We were just about out of ammo for the M4s and Berettas, and we were down to the coax and only DU for the main gun. Rounds were flying everywhere and I was slewing the turret back and forth, engaging guys with DU. The problem, though, was the cargo hatch in back was open, so I couldn't slew the turret all the way around to fire or the concussion would turn Sully's brain to jelly.

I kept trying to contact command on the radio but couldn't. In the fog of war I either didn't realize or couldn't remember that our radio antenna had been first hit by an RPG and then completely destroyed by the mortar hit. Target-rich environments aren't so great when most of your weapons are either disabled or out of ammo and you don't have a working radio to call for help.

I learned later that when Sergeant Christner's radio went out, he was doing everything else he could to get information about what was happening on our side of the bridge. The rest of the unit wasn't even quite sure where we were. Christner desperately wanted to find out how he could assist me and Broadhead, but with the confusion and my radio being out, he was unable to do so.

Iraqi mortar rounds started landing all over, and we could see a mortar team out in the field, between 300 and 400 meters away. Broadhead turned his main gun on them and blew them up, then called me on the radio—I could talk to him, maybe because he was so close, but that was it.

"We need to get the fuck out of here. My gunner needs time to reload the ready box."

"Roger that. You lead out and I'll follow you so you don't get an RPG in the grille." The weakest part of an M1 is its ass, where the grille and exhaust are.

Broadhead charged out of there and headed for the road. I fired the 25 mm right past him at a truck filled with dismounts in the back. Broadhead just rammed the truck and knocked it out of the way, then floored his tank.

The Camel Toe popped out on the road with us right behind it, and in front of us was a large, blunt-nosed flatbed truck. There were half a dozen Iraqis in the back of it, one with an RPG. The guy with the RPG fired, but the warhead hit the road and rolled off into the ditch before blowing up. The backblast blew out the rear window of the truck, which veered off to the side and hit a wall. All of the men who were in the back of the truck flipped out and landed in the road, holding their heads and faces, which had been burned by the backblast. I grabbed the control for the main gun and put a long burst into them, and then Soprano hit them with the coax for good measure.

A huge barrage of what I first thought were mortar rounds started falling all around us, so many that it looked like the world was raining dirt. We discovered later it was Iraqi artillery, D5s, pounding us. They hit the road; they hit cars; they struck buildings, Iraqi civilians, everything. The D5s were big 152 mm artillery pieces.

What with the M1 being faster than a Bradley, and our brief pause to finish off the truck, Broadhead got close to a 400-meter lead on us. As his M1 hit the bridge, artillery rounds were falling right behind him, blowing huge holes in the road.

We were close to the bridge and rolling as fast as possible when more rounds hit in front of and all around us. One of them was so close it damaged the Carnivore's track, and we started jinking wildly.

"Fuck, Sarge, that hit fucked up our track!" Sperry announced. "I can't go straight anymore, or right. It'll only go left."

"Do what you can," I told him.

Sperry did a great job keeping control of the Bradley and turned off the road just before the bridge. He got us into a protected spot between a berm and the raised railroad tracks.

It only took me a few seconds to realize that we were the only American unit still on our side of the river. We were probably a mile from the American forces posted at the bridge, with Iraqis all around us, in a Bradley with a busted track and no radio. I discovered our coax had been damaged in the firefight as well, so neither of our M240s worked. Shit.

We could see both the compound we'd thrashed and another, larger one beyond it. We didn't know it at the time, but that larger compound was a Fedayeen training barracks, and the area was swarming with Iraqis. We'd had no idea that either the police station or the military compound were there. Let me edit that statement: I wouldn't be surprised if somebody in the U.S. command structure knew that the two compounds were spitting distance from our objective, they just neglected to tell us.

The Fedayeen facility was four times as large as the police station compound, and I could see hundreds of Iraqis organizing and looking for someone to kill. They'd heard me and seen Broadhead driving around, but at that moment they weren't quite sure where we were. Or, possibly, they knew where we were and were working up the courage to come after us again. Meanwhile, the mortar and artillery teams were still dropping rounds everywhere.

"Sperry! Get in the back and start loading HE into the ready boxes!" The HE came in 25-round links, and filling up the 270-

round box took 10 minutes. "Soprano, see if you can spot those fucking mortars." Meanwhile, I checked out Sully.

Both his hands were cut up from shrapnel, but his CamelBak, a soft-skinned canteen that covered his back, had helped save his life. He was stunned, though, and a little bit out of it. I was bleeding from everywhere and couldn't hear out of my right ear, but I was alive.

While back there, I grabbed our spare antenna and started trying to attach it, but it was really hard for me to grip anything. I was losing dexterity in my hands because of the shrapnel, plus I was fuzzy-headed from the mortar round going off right above us. I'm pretty sure I sustained a concussion. I always carry a Leatherman multitool, but I wasn't able to get it open because of my injuries.

"Soprano! Don't you have a multitool?"

"Yeah, Sarge, here."

He had a Gerber Multi-Plier, which was designed to be opened with one hand. I was able to get it open, twist the wires together on the radio mount, and tighten them while holding another part. Just then, somebody must have spotted us, because we began taking fire from something heavy, maybe a 12.7 mm (their equivalent of a .50-cal machine gun). It was kicking up dirt all around us, trying to pound through the berm.

"I got it!" Soprano was listening to the net as I worked on the antenna mount, and he yelled out when he heard Sergeant First Class Talmadge Lee Bennett's voice over the radio net. MacGyver can kiss my ass.

I can't tell you how happy I'd been to hear that Bennett was our mortar platoon leader. He was from Jacksonville, Florida, and had been in the Ranger Battalion for a number of years. He was the man you wanted on the other end of the radio when you need indirect fire and you needed it to bracket the target quick. I got on the comm as fast as I could.

"This is Red 2, Red 2, does anybody copy, over."

"Roger, Red 2, Jesus. Where the hell have you been? Uh, over."

Let me tell you, they were as happy to hear from me as I was from them. They'd been doing everything they could to raise me on the net. I reported our situation to Bennett, told him we needed some mortars and quick, and gave him the grid coordinates. Soprano had spotted the mortar team along a tree line, and we were getting tired of them hanging 120 mm projectiles in our general direction. I could see them with my binoculars—which were badly damaged, so at that point it was a monocular, but that one side still worked. The tree line was actually a date grove, and I could see a whole bunch of bad guys in there, waiting to do some serious damage to the Americans.

Our mortar track was an M113 with a 120 mm mortar mounted in the back of it and had a range close to four miles. Bennett fired one ranging round and then waited for our call, as he couldn't see what he was aiming at. That first round hit, and it was close enough.

"Fire for effect!"

Our mortar track opened up, blew apart the Iraqi mortar team, and killed everybody in the area. They fired 20 rounds, and after that there were no more Iraqi mortars making the sky rain mud. We were still taking fire from the heavy machine gun, however, wherever the hell it was, and now we were taking small arms incoming as well. My radio kept going in and out, so I was only getting part of the troop's conversation.

At that point I saw a missile fly out of the town. I wasn't sure if it was a SAM (surface-to-air missile) or SSM (surface-to-surface missile), but I think it was a SAM. It got everybody on the net all hot and bothered—missiles tend to do that. Meanwhile I was pulling parts off Sully's M240 in the back, trying to get the coax

M240 in my turret working again. I got it running without too much trouble.

During the fight our TOW launcher had been damaged. I don't know if it took an RPG or what, but the hydraulic arm that raised and lowered it had been blasted away. The way the launcher was hanging, it was actually interfering with the turret traversing. We had to climb out of the Bradley with the tanker's bar, which is nothing more than a giant 60-pound crowbar, and crank on it. We pried the launcher up and then ratchet-strapped it down to keep it out of the way.

Even though our mortars had pounded the Iraqis, they were still all over the place, and we kept taking fire. The Troop Commander, Captain Jeff McCoy, called me up on the radio.

"Red 2, did you plan on coming back to this side of the river any time soon?"

"Roger that, sir, we're still working on the track." That D5 round put a bunch of gashes in the hull and the wheels, and hit the Adler arm for the sprocket gear, which provides the tension. We could see the track shoe was messed up, but it looked like the only part we were missing was a pin. We put a pin in, but we didn't have any tension on the track, which meant we couldn't really turn or drive faster than a slow jog, but at least we'd be able to move.

I radioed in the details of my situation and requested air support.

"Red 2, I'm going to send the platoon to you, and to seize the objective. If you're in a protected position just wait there."

Broadhead and I had crossed the bridge around 7 A.M., and by now it was barely an hour later, yet it seemed like days had passed. He'd run the Camel Toe to fumes and was still getting refueled when the rest of the troop headed toward the bridge. Staff Sergeants Carter and Geary were heading to the bridge in their Bradleys, accompanied by Staff Sergeant Fred Housey in his M1.

Geary was in the lead and had made it almost to our side of the bridge when all hell broke loose. The wood line in front of me opened up with small arms fire, RPGs, and mortars, and the D5s started coming down again. Something big landed right next to Geary's Bradley—Circus Freaks—and blew the ground out from underneath his track. Circus Freaks slid down the bank on the edge of the road, hanging by one track at such an angle that he couldn't engage anything with his main gun or coax. Carter and Housey pulled back under orders from Captain McCoy, because a direct hit by a D5 could take them out. So much for our rescue.

All of the Iraqis scared out of the area or shut down by our mortars saw Geary's track just hanging there and came running back. They were everywhere, and beyond his track on the low ground (which I couldn't see) were even more Iraqis. They had all come from the military compound and were sticking to the low ground and wadis to make their approach. I couldn't see them, but I could hear a hell of a lot of shooting.

I got on the radio to Bennett again and called in more mortars on the positions I could see, and his crew filled the air, but there were too many Iraqis, moving too fast, and a lot of them I couldn't see because of the low ground.

My crew and I could only watch Geary's Bradley taking fire, and after fifteen minutes it was getting bad. I could see him popping up from his hatch, firing his M4 in every direction just to make the Iraqis keep their distance. My radio was going in and out, and most of the time I could only reach Bennett. I never could reach Geary. Carter and Housey had displaced across the bridge and I kept looking for someone to come help Geary, but no one did. I learned later that Captain McCoy had been working on a plan to get Geary and coordinate counterbattery fire, while the rest of the vehicles were fueling. He also didn't know just how bad Geary's situation was, but at the time it seemed to us like Geary was on his own, as if the squadron had abandoned him. I thought it had to be us or no one.

"Guys, he's screwed, we've got to go help him. What do you want to do?"

In Kuwait, when we had nothing to do, we were each other's worst enemy, but when the bullets started flying, my crew did what had to be done. They could see the shit storm of lead raining down on Geary, knew that we'd be heading into a world of hurt, but still they looked at me and said, "It's your call, Sarge."

"Fuck it, let's go."

CHAPTER 10

STEEL BEAST

Wounded, the Carnivore could only do five miles an hour, and we might throw track if we tried any serious turns, so we couldn't exactly race to Geary's side. We got the Carnivore rolling toward the bridge and almost immediately spotted 20 Iraqis off to our right who had worked their way into a ditch directly across from our position. They had been expecting to ambush us, and instead we surprised them. I slewed the turret around and engaged them with the coax M240, and we continued our slow crawl toward the bridge.

Another Iraqi mortar barrage came in, but it fell short of Geary's Bradley. The Iraqis didn't seem to have any concept of friendly fire, because they were dropping rounds on their own guys.

As soon as we pulled out from behind the berm the amount of incoming rattling off our Bradley grew immensely. Soprano let a long burst of 25 mm go into the wood line, and I opened up with the coax on the dismounts getting close to Geary. There were a few in front of his vehicle on the road, and the ones we didn't kill took off running.

Sperry pulled the Carnivore onto the road near Geary's Bradley, and we dropped the ramp. We hadn't been able to reach him on the radio, but he'd seen us coming and knew what he and his crew needed to do.

"Let's go, let's go!" I yelled. I headed out on foot with the AK-47 I'd picked up at the police compound and covered his crew as they headed toward my Bradley. I don't know why I left the Bradley. I could have covered Geary and his crew from my hatch, but for some reason I climbed down. There was a huge amount of fire coming at his vehicle from the far side, down low in the field where I couldn't see, and I hooked around the back of Circus Freaks. There I found a cutout leading into a ditch running alongside the road, jumped down there—and found myself looking at 20 Iraqis, firing wildly up at Geary's track. Oh, shit.

They were close enough to hit me with rocks, and I opened up with the AK on full auto. With all the shooting, my AK was just more noise, and a lot of them fell down before they even knew I was there. When that AK was empty I picked up another one, off one of the many Iraqis I had already killed, as more Iraqis ran into the ditch and headed my way. I don't even know if they knew I was there, they might have just been looking for a way up the bank to kill Geary and his crew. When the second AK was empty I picked up a drum-fed PKM machine gun. When that was empty I picked up another AK. The Iraqis would run toward Geary's track, hit the ditch, and turn my way. It was like shooting down a hallway. There were no tactics on my part, no strategy; all I was thinking was, Which rifle do I pick up when this one's empty? They were so close I hardly had to aim.

I don't know how many guys I shot down in that ditch while Geary and his crew were transferring to my Bradley—50? More? More. A lot more. It was surreal. They weren't expecting to see me,

I wasn't expecting to see them, but yet again I just happened to be in the right place, at the wrong time—for them.

As soon as I didn't have bad guys running at me, I retreated up the bank and got back into the Carnivore, which was now over-stuffed with people. Geary, his gunner Dakel—I counted faces. We had his whole crew.

"What the fuck, Forest, did you think that was a good place to park?" I said to Geary.

"Jesus Christ" was all he could say, eyes wide. His guys were as freaked out as we were.

Cramped didn't even come close to describing it—I guess it was a good thing we'd used up almost all of our ammo, because otherwise Geary and his boys would never have fit. We all wanted to head back across the bridge to rejoin our troop, but the D5s started falling again between us and the bridge, sending up huge clouds of dirt. That berm had been a safe haven for us, so we headed back to it as fast as the Carnivore could roll—which wasn't nearly quickly enough for our tastes.

We found out later that the Iraqi D5 artillery team could see us on the road but couldn't find us when we parked by the berm. That area was blocked from their view by trees and buildings, so their observer did not have a line of sight to us. We were in the perfect spot. They would launch rounds randomly into our general area. They would fire one, then fire another at a different spot, but you could tell they didn't know how to hit us, because they weren't adjusting. It was just random. They were looking for a fire pillar or smoke plume to know they hit us, and they never got it. As we were heading back to our protected spot, however, we took another RPG. It exploded next to the track, and we limped the last few meters.

Geary's people were in pretty good shape, and I was able to

contact Bennett on the radio to call in some more mortars. Good news and more good news. We replaced some track on the Carnivore, but it wanted to pop off if we even looked at it funny, so we wouldn't be able to go anywhere faster than a crawl.

By that time the rest of the squadron was refueled, and not only were they hoping to come save our asses before we got killed, they wanted in on the fight as well. Captain McCoy put the call in for some air support, and pretty soon some Kiowa Warriors and A-10 Warthogs were doing gun runs on our side of the river, killing anything and everything that wasn't us. The A-10 is an awesome piece of equipment, a slow-flying, tank-killing angel of death.

Finally the rest of the squadron drove across and set up a bridgehead to protect us as we limped back across the two bridges. It had only been four or five hours, but it seemed like a lifetime since Broadhead and I had chased that truck into the compound. The Kiowas and Warthogs kept doing gun runs as we crossloaded ammo off Sergeant Wallace's Bradley, then topped off our fuel. I was finally able to get our radios working consistently.

When everybody was gassed up and organized, we went back across the river in force. Geary's crew was still in the back of my Brad. As soon as we crossed the railroad bridge the mortars started up again. We spotted the mortar teams back in the tree line again and called for indirect fire. Our mortars answered theirs, only ours were a lot more accurate. Across the net, I could hear Sergeant Christner, one of the guys who talked me into staying in the unit instead of heading out to Texas, in his Bradley adjusting fire.

We set up our vehicles in a blocking position around Geary's Bradley. Geary and I checked out Circus Freaks and knew it would be hard to recover, but we had to try.

"How do you want to do this?" I asked Geary, hunkered down behind the Carnivore, out of the line of fire.

"If we try the wrong thing it's going to roll, and then we're fucked," he said, looking at Circus Freaks. "What do you think?"

I had Housey put his tank on the road to pull Geary's Bradley, while we would push with the other two Bradleys. We tried pulling and pushing, but that damn Bradley wouldn't move, and we started taking more fire. The gunner on Housey's tank was firing at the Iraqis with the .50 and keeping them at bay while we worked on getting Geary's vehicle unstuck, but one machine gunner on overwatch soon wasn't enough. Iraqi soldiers showed up in everything—cars, trucks, even an ambulance. Yes, an ambulance with a Red Crescent on the side pulled up in front of the Fedayeen compound, and about ten soldiers got out and ran into the building. They immediately began shooting at us, so we engaged the structures with 25 mm HE. A van full of armed Fedayeen pulled up next, and we killed all of them as well. The fire got to be so heavy we had to abandon our rescue attempts. Our vehicles moved away from the stuck Bradley and set up in an overwatch position.

A good overwatch position is one that allows you to cover your guys and bring the hurt down on anyone who shows up wanting to cause trouble. You're usually exposed, but danger comes with the job. A defilade position, on the other hand, is one where you're protected from incoming fire.

The Carnivore set up in a defilade position in the ditch next to the road. Geary's guys helped us refill our ready boxes. While things weren't as crazy as they had been, our troop had random engagements all day. Bad guys were grabbing civilians and walking behind them with AKs, moving from building to building. This was the first time we had to deal with Iraqis in civilian clothes, mixing with civilians, shooting at us. Command eventually rewrote the rules of engagement with regard to how to deal with civilians in the area, but as the guy with his hand on the trigger, it was a tough call to make. Do I risk getting killed by a bad guy using a civilian as a hostage, or do I engage and maybe kill someone whose only crime was being in the wrong place at the wrong time?

Command called in air support, and Apache attack helicopters (AH-64Ds) came and hovered in the area, engaging all threats. The only problem was that they liked to hover behind our position, and the Iraqis kept shooting rockets at the aircraft.

"You need to change position or relocate" was the radio call that went out to the pilots from our troop.

"Negative, negative, we're in a good spot here," came the reply.

"You need to leave," we told them. "They can't see us, but they can see you, and the rockets they're shooting at you are impacting on us!"

Our Kiowa Warrior scout helicopters (OH-58Ds) showed up then, and helped ID enemy positions so the mortars could put more fire on them. Shortly thereafter the Commander got on the radio.

"Red 2, you need to displace and pull back to our side of the river. There is an air strike inbound." I learned later the Kiowas had spotted a missile site and several other high-value targets beyond where we'd been positioned.

We began moving back across the river. As we did, the Iraqi mortars started falling on us once more, but again their mortars fell short. McCoy and Broadhead took over watching Geary's Bradley from a distance while we waited for the air strike. And waited. And waited. After six hours, we were finally told the air strike wasn't going to happen (command was worried about collateral damage), and the troop moved back across the bridge. We crossed with Second Platoon, so we had a total of four tanks and six Bradleys. Geary and his crew went back over to his vehicle to do what they could, in hopes of recovering Circus Freaks. When it started getting dark we backed away from the road a bit, farther out in the center of the field, and tried to get some sleep in shifts.

At that point we'd all been up for many days without any real sleep, and we were honestly delirious. We were on 50 percent security, with half the guys up and half of them sleeping. I was so exhausted and drained that I was seeing in black-and-white instead of color, but I took first watch. Lead from the front.

There was a call across the radio that we were taking sniper fire and that one of the Bradley dismounts was engaging it. When you're on watch you're in the gunner's position, using the thermal sight to scan for threats. I looked around using the thermal sight but couldn't see anything. I got on the radio. "Engaging what?"

"Sergeant Wallace's dismount, Murphy, is engaging enemy sniper fire he can see through his NODs."

Roger that, I could hear Murphy's rounds zinging over the top of my vehicle, but I still couldn't see the sniper he was shooting at. I climbed out on top of the Bradley and looked in the direction he was shooting with my night vision, but I still couldn't see anything. I called Wallace on the radio.

"Tell Murphy to stop firing, he's getting real close to my vehicle. I'm on the NOD, let me take a look."

"Roger that. Murphy says the guy is firing every five or six seconds."

Murphy finally stopped putting rounds right over the top of my Bradley and I scanned the direction in which he was shooting, seeing nothing. Nothing. Finally I noticed that I kept getting a light splash on top of my vehicle. I looked up and saw our firefly.

At night, one way we identified each other was by putting infrared (IR) lights on top of our antennas. We called them fireflies, because they blinked every few seconds. I watched the firefly on top of my vehicle and counted the time between flashes, then got on the radio.

"Wallace, get Murphy on the radio and have him call out when the guy shoots."

Murphy got on the radio, and in just a few seconds he yelled out, "All right, he's firing!"

I yelled into the radio, "He's not firing, you moron, you've been shooting at my Bradley for half an hour!"

That firefly was only a foot over my head. The next morning the whole back of my turret was paint splashes because Murphy had shot it close to thirty times. That's how tired we all were.

When it was my time to sleep, I took my turn on the turret floor of the Bradley. My legs were horribly swollen from standing up for the better part of five days, and even as tired as I was it was hard to get comfortable. Being pincushioned by shrapnel and having a burst eardrum wasn't making it any easier. We took mortar and small-arms fire all night as the Iraqis probed us, which was pretty inconsiderate of them.

Geary worked all night getting his Bradley back up. He was able to recover Circus Freaks, finally. The next morning he spotted a dismounted team that had made it within 200 meters of my Bradley. His gunner took them out with the coax, and we all moved back up onto the road. We continued to watch troops move into that Fedayeen compound all day, and we let our Commander know about it, but our orders were just to sit.

The police station and Fedayeen compound were approximately 800 meters from the railroad bridge, and we were about 500 meters from them. We could see *a lot* of activity inside that compound. We had sporadic contact in the area, nothing major, but I started getting a bad feeling.

I got Broadhead on the radio. "White 4, Red 2, you need to call the Commander, tell him to let us go in there and clean the place out before those bastards start dropping mortars on us again."

"Roger that. Wait one."

A few minutes later Broadhead called me on the radio. "It's a go."

Broadhead took the lead, and I followed right on his tail, everybody else rolling behind us. His tank hit the gate, and a few seconds later I punched a hole in the wall next to where Broadhead went in. The wall I knocked over landed on guys who were getting ready to shoot an RPG into the side of Broadhead's tank.

The Fedayeen training compound was maybe 100 meters square, with buildings all around. It was like being in a football stadium, with buildings instead of bleachers, and everyone in them trying to kill you. We took fire from a nearby guardhouse, and I told Sperry, "Run over that fucking thing." Guardhouse 0, Carnivore 1.

Dozens—hundreds—of guys ran out of the buildings firing AKs, PKMs, and RPGs at us. If I'd thought the police compound firefight was bad, it was nothing compared to this, as Iraqis came from every direction, every building, and started trying to kill us with all they had. It was like being inside an anthill. The sound of guns firing was a constant roar. They were wearing the same salad suit camouflage that the Iraqis in the police compound had on the day before, a British-type pattern that didn't do them any good inside the walls.

"Holy shit!" Soprano yelled. He couldn't shoot people fast enough.

"How many guys are out there?" Sully shouted.

Hunkered down inside the Bradley, literally surrounded by people trying to kill us, I traversed the turret in a 360-degree arc with my finger on the trigger of the coax. Do you know how many enemy have to be swarming your position before spinning the belt-fed machine gun in a complete circle seems like a useful option? Surrounded by bad guys firing from the buildings around us, Soprano seemed to dump 25 mm HE into almost every door and window. Broadhead's .50 was going continuously, and he was slamming the buildings with 120 mm HEAT rounds, the explosions rocking everything.

Groups of soldiers would run from one building to another, firing at us. We kept driving and shooting, driving and shooting. We took out communication towers. Somebody would fire an RPG at us from a small building, and we would blow it apart. Groups of soldiers would rush us, and we would mow them down or drive them back with our machine guns. Soprano was working the main gun and the coax, switching back and forth. I was firing the M4 as fast as I could empty and reload the carbine.

I spotted an Iraqi pointing an RPG at us, and before I could do anything I saw it coming at us in slow motion again. I knew we were fucked. There was nothing we could do; I could only watch it coming in to kill us.

All of a sudden there was an explosion that knocked me back down inside the hatch. When I stood up I had splinters all over me, the air was filled with this white cloud, and I could taste it on my lips . . .

"Goddammit!" I looked down.

I'd bolted a wooden ammo box on the Commander's side of the track. In it I had my little Coleman stove, my coffee, my sugar, my creamer, and a couple of coffee cups, even a piece of Corian countertop we could use as a little tabletop while we sat around and BS'ed. That was the Crazy Horse Café, which I'd written on the side of the box. The box that was now gone.

The RPG hit the Crazy Horse Café and blew up. It blew the box off the side of the Bradley, and the box acted like reactive armor—it gave its life to save the Carnivore. However, all I could do was taste my sugar and creamer swirling through the air in a white cloud, like a cocaine bust gone wrong, which made me even angrier. The Iraqi who'd killed the Crazy Horse Café was standing there looking at the swirling cloud of coffee and creamer, and I put a burst into him. Fucker.

My radio wasn't working for shit, and I could only communicate with Broadhead. I found out later that the rest of the platoon was behind the compound where they'd discovered a number of mortar positions. They were as busy as we were.

In military parlance, "black on ammo" means you are out. By the time we stopped taking incoming, we were black on 7.62 for the coax and black on HE for the 25 mm main gun. We were black on ammo for the M4s and Berettas. We literally had nothing left but DU rounds for the main gun, and my commandeered AK.

Broadhead dismounted his tank and was inspecting one of the Iraqi arms rooms when an enemy soldier walked in on him. Just like the Old West, it was a quick draw—Broadhead with his pistol and the Iraqi with his AK-47. Broadhead emptied his M9 pistol into him. The Iraqi officer only got one round off, and it hit the floor.

There was a flagpole in the compound and I had Sperry run over it, which made me feel all sorts of warm and fuzzy. We took their flag, which now hangs in the 3rd Infantry Division Museum at Fort Stewart.

How long were we in there? I could only guess. Time seems to lose meaning in those situations, but we were told later it was less than half an hour. It seemed a lot longer. There were bodies everywhere. We were still taking a lot of sporadic fire from the buildings and could see movement behind a lot of the rubble. The last thing we were going to do was clear the buildings on foot: we'd need a company of infantry, so Broadhead and I pulled back.

We joined Christner and the rest of First and Second Platoons to the north of the compound where they'd been providing overwatch. We had six Bradleys and four M1s on line, and we just pounded the shit out of the compound with whatever ammunition we had left. We also called Sergeant Bennett with the mortar platoon and had him drop rounds into the compound. Fuck moderation. We shot through the walls, through the buildings, into the fuel tanks behind the compound, everything. Burning fuel splashed everywhere, helping us level the place. I later heard that we'd killed an entire battalion of infantry inside those walls. There was a small number of wounded and prisoners that we dealt with as best we could, then we got relieved by Apache Troop. When we headed back across the bridge, the area behind us was nothing but a huge fireball.

Life is strange, to say the least. God really has a dysfunctional sense of humor. Two years later, during my second tour with Crazy Horse, I was talking to George, my interpreter in Baghdad. He was a great interpreter—I think his English was better than mine. George had a bunch of scars—bullet wounds—but a lot of the Iraqis we worked with did. You learned not to ask about them, because there was no way to know if they had earned them fighting Iran, the Kurds, or us. George was telling us the day he gained respect for the Bradley. It was back in 2003 at the beginning of the war, and he was in an infantry battalion at a base in a town called As Samawah.

That got my attention. "Um . . . oh, really?" I said. Sully was with me on the second tour as well, and he sat up, his eyes darting between me and George.

"Yes. This steel beast pushed the wall down to my post and started killing everyone."

"At As Samawah?" I said, just to be sure.

"Uh . . ." Sully started to say, but I shushed him.

"Yes," George told me. "It shot us in the buildings, killed us when we attacked, killed us without mercy. But I was not scared, I was brave. I jumped up and fired an RPG at the beast. My aim was true. But I could not believe what happened. There was a huge ball of fire, and black-and-white smoke . . . but the smoke cleared, and I saw it did nothing to the vehicle, the Bradley. Nothing. Then the soldier on top of the vehicle turned and shot me with a machine gun four times."

By that point Sully was biting his lip so hard to keep from laughing that it was bleeding, and there were tears running down his face. George looked over at him, saw the tears, and said, "Yes, it is very sad."

George told us there had been 1,500 soldiers inside that compound. He was one of only 10 who survived. He would go on to tell me how he was pulled from the pile of bodies by his soon-to-be wife. What are the chances? The guy who destroyed the Crazy Horse Café two years later became my interpreter. I never did tell him that I was the one who'd killed all his friends.

Finally, we were officially relieved and off the line. Still, the first thing we did was track down the HEMTT fuel and ammo carriers and top off. HEMTT stands for heavy expanded mobile tactical truck—we called them Hemmitts. They are eight-wheel-drive off-road-capable supply vehicles and carried all of our fuel and ammo. The fuelers have big tanks in back, but the ammo carriers are just giant flatbed trucks.

Sully and I were finally able to go see the medic, Sergeant Todd Cardone. He would patch me up many more times. Amazingly, none of our injuries were life-threatening, even though—at some point—I'd been shot in the leg. Maybe while protecting Geary's Bradley? I honestly couldn't say for sure when.

It was a small bullet or fragment, and it's still in my leg to this day. It went in the side of my left leg about four inches above the ankle and damaged some nerves. Part of my leg and the top of my foot are still numb, and the doctors are afraid that removing the bullet might cause more nerve damage. The medics bandaged that up, and my hands as well, but that was really all they could do for me in the field. My eardrum was definitely burst, but they couldn't do anything for that either. The shrapnel wounds to my arms were officially Purple Heart number one for me, the medal nobody wants to get, and the bullet in the leg was number two. The medics were pretty sure I had a concussion, too, but seeing as they couldn't do much of anything to treat it, they just let me go back into the line. That was the first, but not nearly the last, serious pounding my head took over there.

Captain McCoy came over to see how we were doing. We were just glad to be alive. Thirty-six hours of taking incoming, of being swarmed by the enemy, of not knowing if the next RPG would take us out . . . Soprano had a flag from Hooters, and we opened it in front of the Carnivore and took a picture. That picture ended up in *Soldier of Fortune* magazine, ultimately. To be honest, at that point I'd never been inside a Hooters in my life, but it was a piece of America, a symbol of what we were fighting for. Not only that, the fact that Hooters employed pretty girls in short shorts probably was hugely offensive to the guys who'd been trying to kill us for the better part of two days, so it was a win-win.

My crew and I were just happy to be alive. Heading to Kuwait, we knew we'd probably see some combat, but those two days in As Samawah—it was insane, incredible. We drove up not expecting much of anything and got hit by more than 2,000 men. Between the fighting and the lack of sleep, everything seemed surreal to me. I had to fight myself just to think clearly.

While we were monkeying around with the Hooters flag, a Toyota Hilux pickup approached the troop's position, and after the last two days every eye and gun swung in the pickup's direction damn fast. The truck skidded to a stop, and the men inside nearly busted their wrists deploying VS-17 visual signaling panels. In this case, they meant "Don't shoot us." The guys in the truck were a Special Forces team and needed to get on our radio net, fast.

They had located Chemical Ali, Ali Hassan al-Majid, the King of Spades in the Iraqi Most Wanted playing cards deck, the fifth-most-wanted man in Iraq. The bearded spec-ops guys had pinged his cell phone and knew right where he was, not too damn far from where we were sitting. They needed an air strike and needed it fast.

The request went up the chain but was denied because Ali was located right next to a school, and command didn't want to cause that kind of collateral damage. Those Green Berets were pissed, but they knew the score. They threw their shades on, piled back into their pickup to head out for their next job, then paused.

"Dudes, can we get some gas?" they asked Broadhead and me. "We're bone dry."

"I'm a Bradley, he's an Abrams," I told them. "Diesel."

Broadhead decided to help out. "Give them the gas you have for your generator," he told me.

Thanks a lot, Tony. "It's all I've got," I told him.

"It's only ten gallons. You'll find someplace to fill it back up." With some grumbling I gave them the 10 gallons, and with a grateful wave they sped off in their pickup. You hate to give anything up in a war zone, because you never know when you'll be able to get more. Scavenging can become an art form.

U.S. forces almost nailed Chemical Ali with an air strike the next month, but it wasn't until August of that year that he was finally captured. It was the Iraqi Kurds who had given him his nickname, after he used chemical weapons in attacks against them. He was charged with a number of crimes including genocide, tried, and ultimately hanged on January 25, 2010.

I then went over to the mortar team to thank them for their help. That is when I found out that not only did the Iraqis pound my side of the bridge, they'd pounded everyone, everywhere. My first sergeant, Roy D. Grigges, and the Second Platoon leader, 2nd Lieutenant Charles Tucker, a 23-year-old West Point grad from Haleyville, Alabama, had both been wounded by the mortars. Grigges had been with the Commander near the objective when the mortars started landing. One mortar round landed so close it almost turned his armored personnel carrier over.

While Sully and I were getting worked on by the medics, our squadron CO, Lieutenant Colonel Terry Farrell, walked up. He's a handsome guy with dark hair and looked young for an LC, which is probably why they chose him to speak to the media. He's a Brigadier General now, in charge of the National Training Center. We provided him with an informal after-action report of our adventures in As Samawah during the previous 36 hours. Not long after that he gave a television interview to Fox News. Your battle roster ID is your troop, the first initial of your last name, and the last 4 of your Social Security Number, so my battle roster was "Crazy J 1248." That is why the Colonel, when he was talking to Fox News about the battle of As Samawah, kept referring to me as "Crazy J." The name stuck. As nicknames go, it's a pretty good one, and a pretty good way to get one.

CHAPTER 11

AMBUSH ALLEY

Colonel Farrell let Crazy Horse go 100 percent down for the afternoon. We'd led the way and been the first unit to fight, and he thought we'd earned a little rest. Like we were going to argue?

We parked on the reverse slope of a ridge and the troop took artillery all afternoon and into the evening. At least, that's what they told us. We were so dead tired we slept right through the barrage. Luckily, the incoming headed in our direction missed and hit behind our position.

The U.S. military got quite a bad reputation during the Vietnam War for inflating enemy casualty figures. The body count exaggerations got so bad that eventually nobody believed them. During the Iraq War, casual observers may not even have noticed that we rarely released numbers of confirmed kills to the press or public, except in rare instances. That doesn't mean we weren't counting.

Part of a soldier's job in combat is BDA—battle damage assessment. During the entire engagement at As Samawah—when my radio was working—I called in the BDA for my vehicle, which included enemy KIA as well as number and types of vehicles destroyed. We weren't involved in a jungle war, and the enemy generally didn't carry off their dead, so our body count resulted from counting actual bodies. When the whole troop came over in force and we were trying to unstick Geary's Bradley, we did a body count around that vehicle. I don't know how many people Geary shot with his M4, how many Soprano hit with the coax while we were en route to or parked beside Geary's Brad, or how many I shot in the ditch while protecting Geary's crew during their transition to my vehicle, but we counted a total of 221 bodies around that location.* I've read that the official BDA just for my vehicle on March 23, 2003, the day we crossed the bridge and entered the Ba'ath Police compound, was 488. I've heard the unofficial body count was over 1,000. I was too busy, that day and the next, to keep an accurate total, but Crazy Horse Troop did their best to kill everyone who was trying to kill us. We were just better at it.

I was awarded the Silver Star for my actions rescuing Geary and his crew, and there was some talk about putting me in for the Medal of Honor, but politics apparently reared their ugly head on that. They quite often do, when you're talking about any award at or above the Silver Star level. As far as I'm concerned I didn't do anything that anybody else wouldn't have done, I just happened to be the guy there at the time. Most of the time medals should be called the "Hey, Dumbass" award, and this case was no different. Actually, in this case it was a team effort. When it was time to do the right thing, we all stepped up. Broadhead received the Silver Star for his actions at As Samawah. Sperry, Soprano,

---

* *On Point: The United States Army in Operation Iraqi Freedom,* by Col. Gregory Fontenot, U.S. Army, Retired; LTC E. J. Degen, U.S. Army; and LTC David Tohn, U.S. Army. Office of the Chief of Staff, U.S. Army (2004), p. 130.

and Sully were all awarded Bronze Stars for their actions as well, and Sully and I received Purple Hearts.

While we were asleep, the other Cav troops went back across the bridge and secured it. The next day, an infantry unit came up and did a blocking position on the town, locking it up a bit tighter. As soon as they were in position, however, the Iraqis opened up with D5 artillery again. One of the infantry's Bradleys, parked behind the berm just across the bridge where I'd hidden out for most of the day before, took a direct hit that killed everybody in the vehicle. It was pretty vicious. I don't know if the Iraqi spotter moved, or they just got lucky, but things like that make you think. What if that had been us? Why did they get hit, and we didn't? I got a medal, and they got killed. There was no reason to it, and trying to make any sense out of it could drive you crazy.

That day the Iraqis were throwing D5 rounds everywhere, and our whole troop was displacing all day, moving around to keep from getting hit by the artillery. First Sergeant Grigges told the Hemmitt fuelers and the ammo truck to stick with him no matter what, but I don't think he quite thought that order through. As we were getting hit by artillery, he was trying to haul ass and maneuver away from it in his M113, and he had that huge 5,000-gallon Hemmitt fueler right on his ass, not letting him get away. The fueler, following orders, wanted to stay with him, and Grigges was trying to get away from the fueler, because, well, it's a big bomb. That was funny as hell to watch, like the Road Runner and Wile E. Coyote.

That evening I picked up two combat engineers on my vehicle, because once we'd been blooded, command assigned engineers to the squadron. One of the engineers' vehicles, an M113 APC, broke down. We abandoned it, took everything off it, and spread the crew among our vehicles. The Carnivore got two of them, including a great Korean kid named Sun, so then we were six. We also managed to fix Sully's M240B, so all of our weapons—minus the M4 shredded by the mortar round—were back in business.

Our original objective was to hold the bridges so the armor units—a tank battalion—could pass through us. We would follow them through to the other side of town and hold the bridge over there, then do a feint and make the Iraqis think we were attacking that way. After dodging artillery for the better part of a day, Captain McCoy decided that a change of plans was in order. Instead of going through the town, we'd go around it. As Samawah was just costing us too much time, and we weren't going to be able to get where we needed to be if we kept banging our collective heads against this town, where we hadn't even thought we'd see much resistance.

The Squadron Commander decided that since Crazy Horse Troop had done so much in the battle of As Samawah, he would give us a break. That night, at dusk, Apache Troop moved out. Bravo Troop followed them. Our job was to follow Apache and Bravo, protecting the field trains. We had the fuelers, the ammo trucks, the headquarters platoon, all the soft-skinned and supply vehicles with us. We were heading to a town called Nafen, en route to An Najaf. All three troops would be following the same route, but because we were bypassing As Samawah, command told us enemy contact wasn't likely, and it would be an easy move. Riiiiight.

We were supposed to take a lateral route, almost a scenic tour, that had us going through farm fields on back roads and then along some canal roads, but the canal bridges weren't big enough to support us. We started along that route, but soon realized we had to turn around, and actually took a mortar round at that first bridge. I could cross the bridge, but Broadhead couldn't, and that seemed to be the story line all the way through Iraq—the Bradleys could make it, the tanks couldn't. The problem for armor in Iraq was the deep canals everywhere. The canals are 10 feet deep and 15 feet wide, with concrete banks and fast-moving water, so there's no way you can ford them. So we had to cross using the bridges, which were designed for trucks and tractors. The Bradleys could make it across most of the bridges, pushing our luck, but at 60 tons the M1s just couldn't. We actually had two tanks fall through bridges, so command said to stay on the main road. We stayed on the main road.

The official designation of the road we took was Route Appaloosa, and it paralleled the Euphrates River. Appaloosa headed in a general northwest direction and stretched between As Samawah and An Najaf, the two largest cities in the area.

There were three roads that went north from As Samawah. Command knew there was a lot of enemy in the area north of As Samawah, including armor, but the trick was to get them to show themselves. Our plan was to get into a fight and bait them into engaging us in force. We wanted to get into a decisive engagement with them and make them commit, thinking we were the main effort. Because we were Cav, we had our own artillery, our own reconnaissance, our own aircraft, and our own armor—we could throw a lot of weight around for our size. Once they committed, we would then bring the armor brigades in and crush them. It didn't quite work out that way.

It was dark when Crazy Horse Troop started rolling. The Carnivore was in the lead, with Broadhead and the Camel Toe right behind us. We weren't moving fast, and we weren't trying to—we were leading over 100 wheeled vehicles of all types. Apache and Bravo, two troops filled with aggressive guys just itching for a fight, were out front, and we knew they'd take care of the heavy lifting.

The road we were driving on was elevated, with fields and occasional houses off to either side in the distance. We'd been on the road an hour and had covered about 10 miles, when Specialist Bobby Hull in Broadhead's M1 spotted a cow off in the field. For whatever reason, Hull decided to shoot at the cow using the tank's .50-cal—and that touched off the longest ambush in military history. For the record, that is only the first of two cow-initiated ambushes I experienced in Iraq.

When Hull shot at the cow, guys hiding behind the cow ran in every direction, and beyond the cow was an Iraqi BMP. The BMP is a tracked infantry fighting vehicle, and as soon as those guys started scrambling away from the cow the BMP opened fire on us. That was apparently the signal for the ambush, because the world around us exploded.

"Contact dismounts east!" Broadhead yelled over the radio, which was not good, considering the BMP was to our west. We started taking mortars from the distant houses. Soprano spotted a pickup truck on a side road with a 14.5 mm heavy machine gun mounted in the back and took that out with the 25 mm. We were ducks in a row on that road, and moving slow. The Iraqis had a target-rich environment.

When responding to an ambush, there are two ways to react: you can fight, by assaulting the ambushers, or you can run. Acting as an escort to 100 slow-moving vehicles, we couldn't really do either. Our job was to protect those vehicles. We could slow some vehicles down and let other vehicles pass us, but we had to keep them inside our formation so we could provide protection. Our major defense was speed. When the mortars and bullets started flying everybody sped up, but with that amount of traffic, nobody was going as fast as they could, much less as fast as they wanted to. Our plan was to get out of the ambush zone, as fast as possible. The only problem was, it never seemed to end.

Staff Sergeants John Williams and Heath Thayer in Third Platoon were doing all they could in their Bradleys. They would stop and fire at the enemy and let the fuel trucks pass through them, then race up ahead of them and do it again.

Mortars were hitting the road when the medical platoon passed through it. One of the medic trucks was hit, on fire, and taking small arms fire. The medic platoon's First Lieutenant, Sammy Gram, stopped his truck in the middle of the firefight and engaged the enemy until his soldiers were in another vehicle and rolling.

BMPs were positioned in alleys between buildings and would take keyhole shots, shooting through a narrow slot across the road. They could hear us coming and were just launching rounds across the road hoping that somebody would run into them. Their 30 mm tracers would zip right across the road. I just slowed down as I was coming up, and when I could see the corner of their vehicle I would just start shooting into (through) the buildings to get at them. I'd watch for the explosion, then we'd roll up to where the next one was firing. We were hitting the BMPs with DU rounds, and a few not hiding behind buildings we hit from 1,000 meters while driving down the road.

As we kept moving forward, getting closer to town, there were a lot of trees on the side of the road and houses built right up next to it. A lot of the houses had little concrete-block walls, and Iraqis were hiding behind the houses, behind the trees, behind the walls, and had dug foxholes right on the side of the road.

"Run over them," I told Sperry, pointing at the foxholes on the right side of the road. He did, and the weight of the Bradley crushed the guys in them, while Sully shot the Iraqis to the left. There was no finesse to it, but there rarely is in war. Half the time Sully was shooting his M240B with the buttstock sticking straight up into the air, shooting right down into the ditches, that's how close the Iraqis were.

Soprano engaged the Iraqis who were farther out and firing RPGs at us. Looking back behind me, all I could see were white lines from the firefights. The barrel of Broadhead's .50 was white hot. I fired the AK-47 I'd picked up to replace my gunner's shredded M4, reloading from the pile of loose mags we'd collected at As Samawah. When Sully's ready box was empty, if he didn't have time to fill it between incoming, he fired his M4/203 into the enemy. They were everywhere.

Up ahead I saw the back of a Bradley. We'd caught up with the forward unit and had to stop. All the ready boxes in my Bradley were out of ammo, and my crew was scrambling to upload. Sully was getting the ammo ready when I saw eight mortar tubes and more than 100 dismounts in the wood line to my left.

"Contact left, one hundred meters, multiple dismounts and mortar tubes!"

All I could do was watch as the mortars fired at me and the dismounts charged the road. The first mortar round knocked me down into the turret. Mortar rounds hit almost on top of the Bradley. A direct hit would kill us all. I heard our vehicles in front and behind me start hammering the wood line. Broadhead called over the radio.

"Red 2, stay down inside the turret, you've got guys almost on top of you. I'm going to take care of it."

I kept inside the turret, opened the turret shield door, grabbed Sully by the leg, and pulled him down into the safety of our Bradley. Heavy machine-gun fire hit the side of my vehicle and raked back and forth.

"We're getting hit!" Sully yelled.

"No shit!"

Then Broadhead's calm voice came over the net: "Red 2, you're clear." Broadhead had hosed down my Bradley with 7.62 mm machine-gun fire, killing three Iraqi soldiers trying to climb aboard. Dismounts were swarming everywhere.

If you're wondering what the hell had happened to Alpha and Bravo Troop, when they went rolling down the road they weren't getting much fire. The Iraqis could see that both troops consisted of armored vehicles, so they were waiting for a more inviting target— which was us. When Alpha and Bravo did receive fire, they usually did the smart thing and hit the gas pedal. They just didn't know we were getting hammered as hard as we were.

The Squadron Commander, Lieutenant Colonel Terry Farrell, was riding with Alpha Troop. He had no idea what we were going through until the squadron Executive Officer (XO), First Lieutenant Keith Miller, called him up. Miller was riding in our train. He was normally a happy-go-lucky guy, a third-generation soldier who had joined our troop just before we headed to Kuwait, but when he was finally able to get through to the Colonel on the radio, he in no uncertain terms expressed his wish that Alpha and Bravo start killing the bastards shooting up the supply train. That's why we ran up on the back of a Bradley—Alpha was stalled in a big firefight and had stopped to slug it out with the Iraqis instead of speeding out of the kill zone like they'd been doing.

I had never seen anything like what was happening in front of me at that moment. My entire troop was all firing at the same time, in every direction. It was massive—120 mm, 25 mm, .50-cal, and 7.62 mm, tracers and explosions, incoming AK and RPG fire, Iraqis running and screaming, BMPs blindly firing straight across the road. We might have technically been in their kill zone, but in fact they were in ours. Our training and weapons and armor were the best in the world. We were just too well equipped.

The cross talk over the radio was constant and, considering what we were facing, surprisingly calm and professional. I heard everyone from Staff Sergeant Harris, our maintenance Platoon Sergeant, to First Sergeant Grigges. Everyone was working the net, laying fire into the Iraqis, calling out targets. Sergeant Christner had his Bradley firing on an Iraqi mortar position to our left front. Enemy mortar rounds landed all the way around him, but his crew was very lucky and didn't take a hit. Every round he fired hit true, and the mortar team died in place. Staff Sergeant May, Christner's M1 wingman, fired 120 mm HEAT rounds into another mortar position.

Geary's Bradley was running a lot better and he got some payback—his 25 mm was barking like a mad dog in a cat farm. He only stopped firing long enough to reload his coax machine gun.

I heard Harris talking to Sergeant Willey, and with their .50s they were killing Iraqi troops who had moved to within feet of the road. They couldn't use the sights on their vehicles because the Iraqis were too low and close, so they were holding their NVGs (night vision goggles) with one hand while they fired their .50s with the other, walking the tracers into the dismounts. Third and Fourth Platoons were firing up 200 dismounts in a nearby wood line. Sergeant First Class Lessane and Staff Sergeant Hamilton, from Fourth Platoon, were engaging dismounts who had been trying to work their way up to the support vehicles in the dark. They didn't even get close.

Remember how Williams's fuel cell had been cracked right after entering Iraq? Well, at this time, he had commandeered Sowby's Bradley and was towing the Casanova behind it. He ended up renaming his new ride Casanova 2. His 25 mm was to the front, though, and he was able to slew his turret and engage targets as fast as he could identify them. We emptied and reloaded our ready boxes at least twice. The wood lines on both sides of the road were on fire before we finished our very slow roll-through.

The crazy thing was, while we got stuck in that one spot for a while, we kept moving, and the fighting never stopped. There wasn't a collection of guys, then a pause, then another; it was a continuation. It never stopped, not for 23 miles. We kept expecting to drive out of it and never did. Well, it felt like never. That night we got hit by everything but tanks; we never identified any tanks.

As we rolled around another corner, we identified and engaged a group of Iraqis with mortar tubes and DSHKs (heavy machine guns we called "dishkas") on the side of the road. Through the thermal sight we could actually see them hanging mortar rounds. We hit them with the 25 mm, which again performed exceptionally.

All of a sudden, a voice with a southern accent thick as grits came across the radio net—"Somebody stop 'em, they're shooting at womens and sheeps, and them sheeps ain't doing nothing but eating grass!"

It was as if time had stopped. Everybody stopped shooting.

I looked at Soprano, and he looked at me, and at the same time we both said, "Did he say 'sheeps'?"

The squadron wasn't sneaking quietly through the woods. We were getting engaged by 1000s of Iraqis across a well-planned ambush route, and somebody sitting in a lounge chair on the moon could have heard the racket. We were shooting anything we saw in our thermals that showed hot and wasn't running in the other direction. Did somebody accidentally shoot sheep or civilians standing around watching the fireworks? I do know that the sergeant in Third Platoon who was so worried about them "womens and sheeps" filed a complaint against another member of the unit. We did find some dead sheep (sheeps?) near an Iraqi mortar position, and some of the fighters were wearing traditional clothing, which made them resemble women from a distance, but I never heard about any women being killed. Nobody got convicted of any war crimes.

Dawn started to break, finally, on March 26, 2003, and I was able to see that it was Alpha (Apache) Troop to my front. They were taking such heavy fire that they stopped again and called in an air strike. While we were engaging the tree line full of dismounts, we heard on the radio net that A-10 Warthogs were coming in to drop 500-pounders.

Just then, Soprano jumped from his gunner's seat. "It's jammed," he said. "Your gun."

Soprano could shoot that main gun, but when it came to working it he lacked a few skills, and it had jammed on him. I crawled down and started working on it, and in short order I saw that the DU ammo that was in the ready box and loaded into the gun was caked in mud. Clay mud, mud that was so hard it was like concrete. Son of a . . .

The last time we had loaded ammo, Geary and his crew had been in the back of the Brad, and they'd walked all over the loose ammo in muddy boots. It wasn't my job to load the ammo into the ready boxes, it had been Sully's responsibility. How had he not noticed it was caked in mud? Motherf—

While I was yanking and cursing at the gun and mudded-up ammo, the whole troop was upstairs watching and cheering as the A-10s did their passes and dropped 500-pounders on the Iraqi positions. The bombs hit so close our guys at first thought one of our M1s had been hit, but the pilots were better than that. They did two more runs, strafing anybody else still moving with their 30 mm cannons. Everybody was still cheering, and I missed it all.

I popped up, a 25 mm DU round caked with mud in my hand and murder in my eye. It was the round that had been in the gun and jammed it up. I spotted Sully in the back of the Brad.

"Come here!" I yelled at him and tried to grab him. I was going to stab him with that round, I was so mad.

His eyes went wide and he scrambled back from me, where I couldn't reach him. "No. Sarge, calm down!" He wouldn't come close enough for me to brain him or stab him with the round, and that's probably a good thing. Eventually I calmed down.

We weren't taking any more incoming at that time, because we had beaten them. When you've got an entire cavalry squadron on line, just pounding the shit out of everything, any opposing forces fade away or get chewed up pretty quickly. Any hot spot out there we shot, and then we brought in A-10s. After having been on the receiving end of an uncomfortable amount of incoming, the Commander's concern about collateral damage had been greatly diminished, otherwise he'd never have authorized the A-10s to drop their 500-pounders.

We had vastly outgunned and outperformed the Iraqis, but you can't engage that many enemy forces without damage. The squadron lost one M577 APC, two Hummers, one five-ton truck, and one ambulance. My vehicle had been rocked by mortars (again) but had come through it intact. Amazingly enough, we suffered no killed or wounded, even after nine hours of fighting. Nine fucking hours. The hell with "Route Appaloosa"; that stretch of road will forever be known to those of us who were there as Ambush Alley.

Broadhead came the closest to being injured. He'd gotten hit in the wrist with shrapnel from a mortar round as he was closing the hatch on his Abrams—but his watch gave up its life for his wrist. The shell fragment was stopped by the stainless-steel case of the watch. Sometimes it's better to be lucky than good, and that time we were both.

The cover of *Life* magazine had a picture of Alpha Troop's medic carrying a small child who had been wounded during that engagement. While we didn't lose anybody during the battle, that medic was never able to forget the war and sadly took his own life years later.

We'd been told that there would hardly be enemy activity on the road north to Objective Floyd and had been put in the rear with the supply train to stay out of the fight. The ambush zone no one could have foreseen had stretched for over 22 miles, and we had no idea what to expect next, if anything.

CHAPTER 12

JUNKYARD DOGS

The troop stayed in place, and the Hemmitt fuelers rolled up and down the line, topping everybody off in a tailgate maneuver. Just sitting there not being shot at was a relief, but it was short-lived. We had rolled through Alpha Troop during the fighting and now pushed through Bravo toward our objective.

Objective Floyd was another damn bridge, this one across the Euphrates. The 1st BCT (Brigade Combat Team) had moved in from the north of An Najaf and locked up another bridge over the Euphrates designated Objective Jenkins, in the small town of Al Kifl. The Division designated every class-70 bridge (any bridge that could take a 70-ton load) in the area as an objective. With 3/7 Cav to the south and 1st BCT to the north, the goal was to isolate An Najaf from any reinforcements. There were an estimated 2,000 or more troops already in An Najaf, and command didn't want any more.

The road split, and Alpha and Bravo Troops took a left and

headed north on Highway 9 to secure that area. We went straight, through a small town, crossed the bridge over the Euphrates, and rolled another 900 meters to a one-lane canal bridge.

The Carnivore was in the lead, with Broadhead right behind us, and as soon as we rolled over the little bridge the Iraqis hit us with an antiarmor ambush. At least 50 dismounts appeared, and a volley of RPGs flew at me and Broadhead. Jesus Christ, I thought. Again?

RPGs came over the top of my vehicle. They came so close to me standing in the Commander's hatch that I honestly had to do the *Matrix* maneuver—bend backward in super-slo-mo to dodge the warhead. A smoke trail came across and got in my eyes, and I felt the swoosh, *that's* how close they came. But we were just high enough, sitting on the bridge, that the angle at which they fired sent the RPGs over the top of us.

Broadhead yelled "Contact!" and opened up with his .50.

No shit, *Contact*. I couldn't yell "contact" because I was ducking and diving. The whole squadron was on my ass in 10-foot intervals, so I couldn't back up. About that time an Iraqi technical (pickup truck with a heavy machine gun mounted in back) opened up. The heavy slugs started slamming my hull and whipping past my head. There was a house nearby that resembled a big glass box, and a bunch of people in it started shooting at me as well.

"Somebody shoot that motherfucker!" I yelled as the 12.7 mm tracers buzzed around my head and glass was flying everywhere.

The rest of the troop was lined up along a bit of a dogleg in the road, which was both good and bad. They could see me under fire, so everybody started launching rounds at that house and shooting the shit out of the technical. Rounds from Broadhead were flying in front of me and the rest of the troops' rounds were coming behind me. I watched tracer rounds walk up the fucking road toward me; meanwhile we couldn't get our own main gun low enough to shoot at the guys below trying to kill us. Three more RPGs flew over Broadhead's tank.

"Back up! Back up! Back up!" I yelled at Sperry, not that he needed to be told the obvious. The Carnivore started crawling backward.

"You're coming into my gunsight!" Broadhead yelled at me. The two Bradleys behind Broadhead's tank were trying to turn around, but there was nowhere for him to go.

"You need to move the fuck out of the way, my ass is in peril up here," I shouted back. There were Iraqis on both sides of the road shooting at us, and RPG rounds were hitting the guardrails and exploding.

Behind us Sergeant Wallace had an angle and was firing like a madman—25 mm, then coax, then 25 mm again. He must have killed 25 guys in less than 30 seconds. While that was going on, Lieutenant McAdams was hanging out of his hatch firing his 9 mm pistol into five Iraqis who were moving in a ditch to his left. It was then that Staff Sergeant Wasson from Third Platoon took an RPG in the back that had bounced off his turret. Luckily the Iraqi who launched the RPG had forgotten to take the pin out, so instead of dead, Wasson was just in severe pain—imagine being hit in the back with a baseball bat by someone very strong and very angry. The RPG made him black out for a minute, but he still stayed in the fight.

We managed to get back across the canal bridge. Both the road and the bridge were narrow there, only big enough for a Bradley to turn around, not an M1. As soon as we got back across and could get an angle, I started pounding that fucking building. I shot into that field at the dismounts and the technical, Sully worked the M240 in back, and Soprano the coax, and we kept at it until we were black on ammo.

I got on the radio and called the supply crew. "I need ammo up here!"

We were still taking rounds when the Hemmitt rolled up the shoulder, backed up to us, dropped the tailgate, and Sergeant Bell in back kicked off a huge amount of ammo. "Thanks, Sergeant Bell, you rock!" we called out to him.

He gave us a thumbs-up and a smile. "Kill 'em all!" he yelled back. I love those Hemmitt guys—no damn armor on their vehicles to speak of, and they'll roll into anything. They're *my* heroes.

The Hemmitt tore off, and I started going through what was there and found I had 120 mm HEAT rounds and .50-cal ammo—exactly what I needed if I was an M1.

Broadhead called me on the radio. "Hey, I've got three hundred rounds of 25mm here . . ."

I said, "I've got HEAT rounds and .50-cal, want to trade?"

That was funny, but I can't give enough credit to those guys in the headquarters support platoon. The PFC driving that fueler or the E5 driving the ammo truck: they won that war, because those dudes kept us in ammo. They would roll right up in their thin-skinned vehicles, ignoring the incoming like it wasn't even there, and top off our tanks or kick out some ammo. And I was always able to get more, no matter how much incoming I was receiving, except for fuel later on in the push, when we were rolling so far ahead of our supply trains we had to siphon gas out of Iraqi tractors. Filling up the Bradley's 150-gallon tank five gallons at a time was no fun at all, but it was better than running dry.

Once we were squared away, command called us up and told us that we were going to hold the canal bridge. The ground was low on both sides of the road, there were guardrails, and there were only a few buildings off to the left, so it was as good a place as any to set up. We positioned the Carnivore just short of the bridge, where the road was wider.

We had no sooner settled into position than a huge sandstorm rolled in. If you've seen the movie *The Mummy,* that's exactly what it looked like. A horseshoe-shaped brown cloud, 10 miles high. Visibility went from 900 meters, to 50, to 10, and it got almost as dark as night. The sand got into everything, but at least I had goggles. I still couldn't see very far, but I didn't get sand in my eyes.

Broadhead and I were at the front of the column of support troops, along with Sergeant Wallace in his Bradley, Sergeant Housey in his M1, and Lieutenant Garrett McAdams in his Bradley. McAdams was a young professional soldier from South Carolina. He had graduated from the Citadel and was so tall and skinny we joked about having to tie him to a rock during the sandstorm to keep him from blowing away.

Third and Fourth Platoons were at the rear of the column, with Staff Sergeant John Williams acting as tail gunner in the Casanova. He started taking small arms fire from the town on the other side of the Euphrates, but not too many people were dumb enough to try to cross that bridge. If they did, they didn't last very long.

Williams was a good man, with a good crew. Sergeant Thomas Hudgins was his gunner, a good ol' boy from Georgia who was always cracking jokes. Specialist John Pecore was the driver. He was a tall kid from Texas, and Williams liked him a lot. Williams's dismount/loader/observer was Specialist Clint Leon, who hailed from Arizona. With them watching the troop's back I didn't have any worries.

The sandstorm got so bad we lost communications with the rest of the squadron. So there we sat, in the middle. We had Iraqi soldiers on at least three sides of us, with no visibility. We tried the thermals, but they didn't work through the sand, day or night. The Commander told us to stop any vehicles from coming into our perimeter. With our Bradley not really set up for traffic control, I did this by standing up on top of my turret, waving my arms for everyone to see my signals to turn around.

It started off with a car.

It came rolling into view through the sand, and for all of my waving I might as well have been invisible. The car swerved around the Carnivore and drove into the front of the Lieutenant's Bradley. The driver jumped out with an AK-47 and Broadhead shot him three times with his pistol. The Iraqi dropped his AK and ran into a ditch. He later crawled out of the ditch, bleeding from three very visible gunshot wounds, and walked off into the woods.

"Let him go, he's done fighting," Broadhead called out over the radio, so we did. We pushed the vehicle off the road and shot it with 25 mm HE until it caught fire. It didn't take long for me to realize that I would get killed if I stayed up on top of my turret.

The new plan would be to fire coax (which had a four-in-one tracer mix) in front of the oncoming vehicles so they would see the tracers and turn away. Broadhead moved off the road to my right rear where he could get a different angle on the vehicles, just in case either of us had to shoot. This worked much better, and a lot of civilians did hasty U-turns after seeing us loom up through the sand or seeing tracers whip past their bumpers. However, we kept seeing one truck roll up close enough to see us through the sand, pause, and then move away. He did it over and over. We thought he was a bad guy, but didn't want to fire until we knew for sure.

Finally, the driver grew some balls or made his peace with Allah and came roaring down the road at about 80 miles per hour. We fired in front of him, and I was waving and waving, but he kept coming. He had to slow down to make it around me, but when he saw the Lieutenant's Bradley on the road right behind me, blocking his way, he locked up his brakes. There had to be 15 guys in the back, and he launched a half dozen of them over the cab of the truck. The rear of the truck was still packed with Iraqi soldiers, however, all with weapons, and they were right next to my Bradley.

"Sully, kill those motherfuckers!" I yelled. He was in the back with the M240 and let loose with one 200-round burst and killed them all, raking the gun back and forth, not taking any chances. I got on the main gun and started throwing HE rounds into the truck, and it caught on fire.

We had barely finished firing into the truck when two more vehicles, cars this time, came roaring down the road at us. The sandstorm was still going strong, but it wasn't consistent—at times we could see 400 meters, others only 40 feet. Lieutenant McAdams and I fired coax in front of the cars, then into the cars when they didn't stop. One of them rammed the Lieutenant's Bradley, but no one made it out of the car. McAdams pushed the car back up the road to slow any more traffic. We pushed the burning truck off the shoulder of the road.

The area was getting to look like a junkyard, with half the vehicles on fire. Between all the burning vehicles and the shooting, everyone had to know the Americans were in town. If I'd been living in that area I would have stayed the hell away from us, but I also realized we were on a main road, so we couldn't automatically assume everyone driving toward us had evil intentions. The sandstorm complicated things as well. Just as the Lieutenant got back in his position, Soprano called out.

"Got a bus coming down the road toward us. It's hauling ass."

I put a wall of tracers in front of it, but it did not stop. This was a big, city-type bus, and we assumed it was full of civilians and only driving fast to make it a harder target for anyone in the area with itchy trigger fingers—I'd seen the same thing in Bosnia. I got on top of the turret and was waving like a madman, trying to get that bus to stop. At the last second I could see he was going to ram us.

Soprano had good eyes and spotted the driver. He yelled out, "Hey, that guy's getting out of his seat."

I knew that wasn't good and said, "Shoot that guy!" We didn't know if he was going to bail out of the vehicle or what was going on. With one hell of a fine piece of shooting, Soprano shot the driver as he was running backward in the bus. One round of 25 mm HE and he was dead, but the bus still rammed the Lieutenant's Bradley at about 30 miles per hour. McAdams's whole Bradley rocked, and he was knocked back down inside the turret.

McAdams got on the radio. "That hurt." Several of his crew were almost knocked unconscious. We pushed the bus back sideways to block the road, getting pretty damn tired of being rammed.

To disable the bus Broadhead shot it a few times with his .50, and suddenly there was a huge explosion—the bus had been packed with explosives and had been on a suicide run. The driver had been running to detonate the bomb when Soprano killed him.

The official campaign history of the U.S. Army's Operation Iraqi Freedom, *On Point,* credited Bravo Troop with the destruction of that bus.* I don't know if someone in Bravo took credit for it or credit was mistakenly given to them, but Michael Soprano, my gunner, took out that bus driver and probably saved the life of Lieutenant McAdams, if not of his whole crew. That's not to say we were the only troop taking fire—far from it. Alpha and Bravo troops had to fight hard just to get to their positions, as the area was filled with Saddam's paramilitary forces, with more on the way.

---

* *On Point: The United States Army in Operation Iraqi Freedom,* by Col. Gregory Fontenot, U.S. Army, Retired; LTC E. J. Degen, U.S. Army; and LTC David Tohn, U.S. Army. Office of the Chief of Staff, U.S. Army (2004), p. 205.

Night showed up, but it didn't make much difference with the sandstorm, at least in the amount of light we had. A sandstorm is filled with static electricity, and there was an orange glow everywhere that had nothing to do with the burning vehicles. It was very otherworldly, like being on Mars.

The vehicles running down the road weren't the only activity in the area, and we were taking small arms fire from every direction. Between the dark and sandstorm they couldn't really see us, only hear our engines, and were just shooting at the noise and in the general direction of the burning vehicles. If dismounts got close enough to see us, we could see them as well and took them out pretty quickly.

Sergeant Wallace came over the radio. "Heads up. We've got a fuel tanker headed our way." He was the only one who had the angle to see around the burning bus, and in his thermal sight he had spotted a full-sized fuel truck driving down the road toward us. It got closer, and closer, and while we were pretty sure the driver's intentions weren't good, shooting at what in effect was a big bomb was not something we wanted to do.

The tanker couldn't get around the burning bus and instead rammed it and started pushing it toward us. A fuel truck pushing a flaming bus straight at you is not a good combination. Broadhead opened up with his .50 and took out the driver, and the forward momentum of the vehicles stopped.

The troop watched the two vehicles for a while, especially the fuel tanker. "What are we going to do about that fuel truck?" Broadhead said to me.

"If we shoot it we won't be able to see anything in the thermals," I told him.

"We've got to take it out," he argued. "If we leave it there, they might try ramming it closer to us and blowing it later tonight."

"If we blow it, we won't be able to see shit," I told him again. We could hardly see anything around the bus anyway, but some visibility was better than none.

The next thing I know Broadhead made a command decision and launched a 120 mm HEAT round into the fuel truck. That truck burned for what seemed like forever but was really three days. A lot of fuel went into the canal, and the canal was on fire too. We had flames across half our horizon. Son of a . . .

When I finally got past the urge to kill Broadhead and could use words suitable for the radio net, I called up McCoy and told him that I couldn't see anything because of the thermal package in front of me.

"Sir, I want to push forward onto the bridge and take control of it, put more standoff between me and the supply train."

"Roger that." He had the soft-skinned vehicles pull tighter together to give us more room to fall back, if needed. Williams, at the rear, was dealing with some dismounts hitting him with small arms, but he hadn't had any vehicles try to ram him—yet.

The bridge was big enough for one Bradley. We set up in the middle of it, and that was where we were going to make our stand.

In one way we actually had it easier than Alpha and Bravo Troops, because of the bridge—the enemy could only come at us from the east and had to come across the bridge if they were going to get to the support vehicles. Alpha and Bravo, to the north of us, were set up with fields all around. They had no way to predict from which direction the enemy would be coming.

CHAPTER 13

LINE IN THE SAND

The sandstorm lessened for several hours during the day, and we took the opportunity to sleep in shifts. The bridge was a good spot to sit. When the sandstorm thinned out, we could see that the road in front of us went more or less straight and flat for about 2,000 meters, then turned a dogleg and went out of sight.

That morning the Troop Commander, Captain McCoy, came forward to survey my position.

"How you holdin' up, Jay?" he asked me.

"Tired and cranky," I told him. "But we'll hold this bridge. How about you, sir?"

"The .50-cal on the tank is tits up, otherwise we're doing fine," he told me.

"Yeah? Hold on a second." I gave him the AK-47 I'd picked up in As Samawah and the AK magazines we had been collecting all night. Some of the AKs lying around from the guys we'd killed were in sorry shape, but mine worked, and I wanted my Commander to have one he could depend on. There were plenty of others around for me to grab, and I could test fire them off the bridge if I needed to. One thing I learned about combat—you'll always have an opportunity to get a resupply. You may have to kill someone to get it, but it's out there.

Most of the time, during the day at least, I could spot the trucks coming around the curve 2,000 meters out. The Iraqi troop trucks were pretty easy to identify, and we had good resolution in our optics, but I would always wait to engage them until I was positive.

Usually I would have the opportunity to contact the Commander on the radio. "Sir, I've got a truck coming, looks like a troop truck, I'm going to go ahead and engage."

"Roger, Red 2, go ahead and engage."

We would wait until the trucks were about 800 meters away. Soprano was as good with the main gun as I was, and we'd usually only have to fire one shot. *BOOM* with the 25 mm and the truck would roll off the road into the ditch. I'd call the Commander back up. "Yeah, it's on fire, dismounts on the ground, engaging," and I'd hit them with the coax. Between the distance and the sand there were always a few soldiers who were able to scramble away.

With Broadhead on overwatch, my crew and I went out and did BDA during a break in the storm and collected weapons off the dead. We tossed them onto the back of the Bradley when we were out there but didn't really have a place to store them. When we got back to the bridge we threw them into the canal. The Iraqis came at us in everything that had four wheels: two buses, four cars, four Toyota trucks, one fuel tanker, and three Iraqi army trucks. I checked all of the vehicles. Every one had soldiers in them with a shitload of weapons. There were a lot of dead men, more than I could count in the short time I had for my recon.

The rest of the day was quiet, but I knew night would bring more activity.

The sandstorm grounded most of our air assets, and the ones that could fly couldn't get anywhere close to us. We were too far away from our artillery, much less mortar support, to call in any indirect fire, so defending that objective was solely on the shoulders of those of us on the ground, there at the bridge.

The first truck that came down the road after dark had about 30 Iraqi soldiers in the back. Soprano took it with a 25 mm round into the cab at 1,100 meters. The truck rolled another 300 meters before it stopped gently on the right side of the road in a small pond. Iraqi soldiers jumped out of the truck and were running around like ants. Lieutenant McAdams had the angle to engage them, so he opened up with coax from his Bradley, then moved up to 25 mm HE. The high-explosive rounds killed most of the soldiers and blew large holes in the ground. As the first truck was burning, another troop truck tore around it, headed straight for the bridge.

"These guys don't learn." Soprano fired a 10-round burst of 25 mm HE into the truck. The truck broke apart and caught fire like it was made of kindling. After that truck, there was another one, and another one. They kept coming down the road, and we kept shooting them. The troop trucks were the size of our deuce-and-a-halfs, and most of them were filled with soldiers. The horizon became littered with burning and blackened vehicles and with all the hot spots a lot of the soldiers who escaped the vehicles were able to get to for cover.

The sandstorm was bad, but you could still see the burning trucks from more than 1,000 meters. This wasn't random; the Iraqis knew we were there and they were trying to get at us no matter what it took. Thank God they could only approach us from one direction. We again called for air support, but were told it was a no-go.

At one point Sun, one of the two engineers we had on board, called out to me while he was looking through his NVGs. "Sergeant Jay, there two guys out there walking in the field toward us." His Korean accent was strong, but I had no problem understanding him.

"Take 'em out then."

"Okay." He opened up with his M4. He fired, paused, fired some more, then looked through the goggles again. "Oh, I think they still moving," he said and fired again.

This honestly went on for close to half an hour, until I'd finally had enough. "Sun, quit the fucking shooting, you're going to use up all of your ammo."

"It's okay, Sergeant Jay, I shooting Sully's ammo," he told me cheerfully.

"Stop shooting at them!" I told him. "If they're not dead by now they deserve to get away."

When morning rolled around I sent Sully out into the field to see what Sun had been shooting at. He called me on the radio. "Sarge, there's nothing out here but a cow that's been shot about a hundred times."

"They must have been hiding behind the cow," Sun told me. "There was two guys."

"Two guys."

"Yes, two guys walking in the field, holding a backpack between them."

"Two guys," I said slowly, "walking in the field?"

"Yes."

"Holding a backpack between them?"

"Yes."

"Right where that cow is."

"Yes."

"*Right* where that cow is?"

Sun looked at me for a few seconds, then his eyes went wide. "I no shoot cow, Sergeant Jay. I no shoot cow!" He seemed offended that I could even suggest such a thing.

The troop trucks showed up all night, at irregular intervals, and through the next day as well. We shot them, they ran off the road, we shot them and the troops scrambling around them some more, until the trucks were burning and everyone around them was dead. Then it was time to wait for the next one. The sandstorm abated for several hours during the day again, and we got what rest we could. While we were able to kill most of the soldiers in or around the vehicles, many were getting to cover. Those soldiers weren't giving up, however; they were working their way closer to us on foot, and the amount of small arms fire we were taking was growing. Because we were the point of the spear, all the ammo flowed up to us. The Hemmitt drivers and the crews of the other Bradleys ran ammo up to us whenever we were running low.

A lot of civilians have heard of AWACS planes and have a picture in their head of a jumbo-jet-sized aircraft with a white dish mounted on the top. We had something even better looking over us in Iraq, the JSTARS. The Joint Surveillance Target Attack Radar System uses an Air Force's E-8C (basically a Boeing 707), and instead of all the high-tech sensors filling a giant dish on the top, they are in what looks like a long fuel pod under the forward fuselage. JSTARS can simultaneously track 600 targets on the ground at more than 250 km (152 miles).

As night fell, we got the word from command—JSTARS had spotted 44 T-72 tanks, an entire tank brigade, on the move toward Sergeant Williams's position. Oh, shit.

McCoy got on the radio. "White 4, I am going to need you to reposition." He told Broadhead to move to the rear of the column to help support Third and Fourth Platoons.

Not 10 minutes after Broadhead left, Captain McCoy called me. "Um, Red 2, JSTARS reports that they have approximately one thousand troop trucks moving on your position."

"Sir, can you repeat that, did you say one thousand troops?"

"Negative, Red 2, that is one thousand troop *trucks*." If each truck carried up to 20 soldiers, I would be facing nearly 20,000 soldiers coming to take my bridge.

"Uhhhhh, Roger that. Sir, is there a chance I can get any indirect fire to support my position?" *Pretty, pretty please?*

"Negative, Red 2," McCoy told me. "You are still out of range."

"Roger that, sir. How about air support?"

"We're working on it."

Ten minutes later, the CO called, and I was hoping it was good news about the air support, even though I could see the sandstorm was still nasty. Nope. "Red 2," he told me, sounding tired, "JSTARS now reports that they have twenty BMPs moving toward your position from the southeast." First the troop trucks, now armored personnel carriers? The hits just keep on coming . . .

McCoy started doing whatever he could to make things as tough as possible for the Iraqis, but he hardly had any space to work with, much less pieces to move around the board. Broadhead was already in the rear, doing what he could to support Third and Fourth Platoons, to suppress the incoming small arms from the town until the tanks showed up. Then the real fun would begin. Headquarters Platoon had already tightened their positions all they could, but thin-skinned vehicles weren't going to be enough—the XO, First Lieutenant Keith Miller, had our troops start digging fighting positions and placing claymore antipersonnel mines on either side of the road.

Vehicles couldn't make it across the canal, but dismounted soldiers could. Contact was sporadic through the night, but no one was immune—the unit was fully engaged, including command. Captain McCoy was working on getting air support for us when Iraqi soldiers came running out of the darkness at his tank, positioned in the center of the column. McCoy grabbed the AK-47 I had given him earlier, aimed it at the Iraqis charging his side of the tank, and pulled the trigger. He stitched all three of them, emptied an entire 30-round magazine, fighting the rifle to keep it from climbing off target on full auto.

My Bradley was in the best position I could get, blocking the bridge. With Broadhead gone I moved Sergeant Wallace (Wild Wally) up on my right side and had McAdams watch our rear. There was nothing for me to do but wait: they would have to get through me to make it to the rest of the troop. Not knowing if I could stop everything coming down on me, I planted some C4 on the canal bridge. As I was hanging off the bridge, I dropped my demo bag into the canal—that was the last I saw of the Gerber multitool I'd commandeered off Soprano to fix the radio at As Samawah. Son of a . . .

While it may seem like we were just one unit, fighting to defend an insignificant bridge, that was the pivotal point of the conflict—if Saddam crushed us it could have been the turning point of the whole war. It would have been an entire cavalry squadron getting slaughtered. Because once they went through us, the armor, it would have been our fuel trains, our aviation assets, aviation fuel, aviation mechanics, cooks, supply guys, ammunition, headquarters maintenance element for the squadron, *everything*. Our entire package was sitting right there between me and Sergeant Williams.

Everybody was invested equally on this one. Our headquarters platoon, the people who normally are behind the lines, had dug foxholes and set up claymores, that's how bad it was. Captain McCoy called me on the radio.

"Red 2, I just wanted to let you know I have been moving heaven and earth to get you some air support, but as yet I have had no luck. The sandstorm is shutting everything down." He'd been trying to get helicopters, get fixed wing, get something flying our way to give us some air support, but the sandstorm was just too tall. The attack air was all grounded. They brought in F-15s and F-18s, but they couldn't see anything. The ceiling on that fucking sandstorm was 15 miles. They couldn't drop on radar, not from that high, because they didn't want it to land on us. Even with all their smart bombs, they couldn't see through it, at least not accurately enough to keep from killing us. I knew McCoy knew the situation when he told me, "It's been an honor working with you, Crazy J. You're a super scout, thanks for leading us. I'm proud to have served with you."

"Roger that, sir, the feeling is mutual." We had a lull in the action, and for once my radio was working. I had a good, calm, five-minute conversation with my Troop Commander, a man I both respected and admired.

"When you boys are out of ammo, or out of the fight, you need to get the hell away from your Brad, get away from the road, because I'm going to have the entire troop firing at your Bradley on the bridge."

"Yes sir."

The First Sergeant, Roy Grigges, called us up on the radio as well. He knew the score. "It's been an honor and a pleasure working with you guys." I told him the same. I'd been in the unit a long time, knew these men, knew their families, and they knew mine. Hell, Crazy Horse was a family.

When he signed off I called Sergeant John Williams, at the

other end of the column in the Casanova. He and I had a great talk. We basically made our minds up, the two of us, that it stopped there. They weren't going to come any damn further, they weren't going to attack our wingmen, they weren't going to attack our unit. Regardless of what happened, he and I were going to stay in our turrets. When the driver was gone, and the rest of the crew was gone, we were going to stay there, and we were going to fight the good fight until it was over for us. And we were calm. We weren't scared, we were relaxed.

"I'm going to fight until I'm out of ammo, and then I'm going to go hand to hand," I told him.

Sergeant Williams moved the Casanova up onto the bridge into the path of the expected T-72 tanks. He was not going to let them get by him. Williams said to me, "They ain't coming through me, brother. I'm going to fight until they get up on me, and when they take me out, they're going to take me out sideways and on fire, because they ain't crossing the fucking bridge."

"Roger that." The Carnivore at one bridge and the Casanova at the other. Somehow that seemed right.

I knew John Williams and his whole crew. I knew they would hold the bridge, and protect our rear or die trying.

When I got off the radio I looked at Sully. He'd been listening to the net, and my end of the conversation, and from the look on his pale face, he knew exactly what was going on.

"So we're drawing the line in the sand here?" he asked me.

"Yeah."

He just nodded. Nineteen years old, and a pain in my ass, but he'd proved himself to be a true soldier when the time came. He'd started the war a meek kid, and in five days he'd killed dozens of Iraqis, saved the lives of the crew over and over again, and never quit, not even in the face of overwhelming odds.

I got the attention of everybody in the Bradley and let them know the situation. "I don't know if we are going to make it out of this. If you see a fireball in the turret don't worry about us, we're done. Just get off and run to the closest farmhouse and stay there till daylight."

CHAPTER 14

EVERY TRUCK IN THE COUNTRY

I knew there were all sorts of dismounts working their way toward us, because during the breaks in the weather—the sandstorm would be heavy, and then it would be light—we could see them and hear them shooting. We'd destroyed so many vehicles that 2,000 meters out, where the dogleg was, the road was actually blocked by burning trucks. The trucks kept coming, though, so they'd stop and the soldiers would get out and start walking, moving up in the ditches. Guys would stop from time to time and shoot for a while in our general direction. They knew we were there, but couldn't see us. Hell, we couldn't see them any better than they could see us, because the thermals didn't work for shit in the sandstorm. They didn't know where we were until they were right up on us.

The lack of sleep was getting to me. I had to concentrate very hard on even the smallest task, and I felt like I was moving in slow motion. As I stood there somewhere between awake and asleep, I heard the radio come alive: First Lieutenant McCormick, our fire support officer, came over the net and told everyone that we had air support, that we had aircraft stacked over us. Yeah, great—like we hadn't heard that before. The sandstorm was as bad as ever, or worse. Nothing could fly in it, and it was still too high.

Ten minutes later Sergeant Williams came across the radio net. "Contact tanks! Lot of tanks!"

He couldn't see them, but he could hear them. The tanks were maneuvering through the streets of the town on the other side of the bridge toward him.

Finally, McCoy called on the radio and gave us the first bit of good news we'd had in a while. "Be advised, we have two bombers on-station overhead," he announced.

Instead of F-15s or F-18s, they gave us two B-1B bombers, and McCoy had control of them. This was the first time any Army officer had ever had direct control of his own B-1B bomber—let alone two. The B-1Bs could not see through the sand either, but they could drop their precision-guided munitions where JSTARS told them the enemy was. JSTARS had no problem seeing through the sand, and B-1Bs regularly drop ordnance from amazingly high altitudes.

Williams barely had a chance to breathe a sigh of relief when Captain McCoy got back on the radio to him. "As of right now, JAG will not let us engage those tanks, as they are inside a town." Unbelievable. They wanted to avoid unnecessary collateral damage— never mind the fact that Third Platoon had been receiving incoming from the town for two days. McCoy was told he could only drop bombs on the tanks if they were firing on us. So we waited, the sound of tanks growing louder and louder in Williams's ears.

Sergeant Hudgins, Williams's gunner, saw a T-72 between two houses across the river and fired a 25 mm round at it, but missed.

The tank moved behind a house. Williams spotted another tank moving behind another building—the two of them were trying to get him into a crossfire. The sandstorm was so bad, most of the time visibility wasn't much more than 50 feet, which might have been the only thing that kept them from killing Williams.

Williams got McCoy on the radio. "Sir, I've got eyes on two tanks. They are maneuvering around behind buildings, trying to get me into a crossfire, and I can't get a shot at them." The tension filled his words.

McCoy was on the radio immediately. "Roger that. Wait one."

I don't know what McCoy said to whoever was on the other end of the line at JSTARS, but when he came back on the radio he told Williams, "Payload is now inbound, and you are danger close. You need to get as far away as possible." McCoy was in the center of our train and working with an Air Force JTAC (joint terminal attack controller), Staff Sergeant Shopshire. He was a great kid and knew his job—bringing the steel rain.

Williams didn't need to be told twice. When the bombs from the B-1Bs hit, I was 2,500 meters away and could feel them through the floor of my running Bradley. Williams was only 300 meters away from those bombs, and I could only imagine the fireworks show rocking his world.

Twenty minutes after the last bomb hit, Williams moved back to his last position to call in the BDA. The sandstorm was as strong as ever, but he could see the fires of the burning tanks in the town. The bombers blew their wad on Williams's tanks and didn't have anything left for me, so my hope of air support was a pipe dream. How long it would take to get more bombers overhead with fresh ordnance was anybody's guess.

It's unknown how many of the tanks the airstrike took out, but no more showed up to fight. Meanwhile, Third Platoon was still getting hit by small arms fire and Iraqi soldiers on foot charging their position. Williams stayed busy.

The rest of Crazy Horse didn't exactly have a night off. They had sporadic contact all night, and then I heard Sergeant Christner over the radio net talking to McCoy. "Sir, be advised I have two Iraqi soldiers armed with AK-47s approaching my position . . . riding a donkey."

"Did he say 'donkey'?" Soprano asked me.

Christner fired tracers in front of the donkey to see what it—and the soldiers—would do. When they turned the donkey his way and picked up the pace he knew. Christner waited until the very last second, then opened up with his M240 machine gun, hitting both men in the chest but sparing the animal. The donkey was still alive and wandering around the next day.

Just down the road, Sergeant Geary was in a firefight with 10 dismounts who had spent the night working their way close to his position along the wood line. Once they were close enough to see his Bradley, however, Geary had no problem seeing them in his thermal sight. Geary was still pissed from being stuck in a disabled Bradley at As Samawah and being used for target practice for hours. Firing the main gun on semiauto to conserve ammo, he took the first soldier with one round of HE to the chest. The man died instantly and on fire.

Sergeant May was sitting next to Geary. After a lot of cross talk, they worked the other nine dismounts into their crossfire. After a brief burst of full auto fire from both tracks, the nine Iraqis lay dead.

The sandstorm came roaring back bigger and badder than ever. At least Broadhead and one other Bradley were coming back our way—with the tanks taken out in the town across from Williams, I needed him backing me up again. The storm was so bad that Broadhead could not find his way to me. The last thing I wanted to do was draw attention to my position, knowing how many Iraqis were out there on foot (because they kept shooting at my Brad from time to time, the rounds pinging off the hull when they got lucky), but I had to help Broadhead and Sergeant May, his wingman, find us. When I turned on the Carnivore's headlights it looked just like swirling hell, and standing right there next to us were two Iraqi soldiers. The storm was so bad they walked right by me and none of us knew it.

"Fuck!" I grabbed the AK I had close at hand and emptied the magazine at them. The only reason I didn't die was quicker reflexes—that was too damn close.

Broadhead came over the radio. "Red 2, I see your lights. Rolling up now."

"Roger that," I told him, panting and shaking from the close call. (Just the latest in a long list.) "I've got a spot I want you to set up in for a good firing position."

Using the radio I talked him into place as best I could, but the sandstorm was so bad that when he moved to set up in the fighting position, he overshot it and got high-centered on a wall or something—in that orange hell it was hard to even recognize the shape of his tank. Broadhead dismounted his tank to check out what he was hung up on when he tripped and fell facefirst in the dirt, hitting his knee on a big rock.

When he got back up he could barely stand and limped back up to the M1, where he got on the radio and laid into me with a profanity-laced tirade that would have made a porn star blush. His knee swelled up so badly that he could barely walk for the next two weeks. After Tony calmed down and had said everything he wanted to about my mother, I was able to talk his tank into the right position, just in time for the sandstorm to stop and open the night up to us.

Our visibility was now 1,000 meters or more. Mother Nature's timing was great for us, but sucked for the platoon of Iraqis who had been working their way on foot to Geary and Crawford's position just down the road. The pause in the sandstorm caught them out in the open, and they couldn't outrun the 25 mm HE.

We had about 25 troop trucks on fire in front of us, and a lot more assorted vehicles in various states of projectile-assisted disassembly. I got on the radio to Broadhead.

"White 4, we are going to head across the bridge to do BDA while we have a break in the weather. You need to move up with me and set up in overwatch while I recon."

"Red 2, roger that. Moving now."

We moved across the bridge, Broadhead rolling shotgun. As we headed into the field of disabled vehicles, we flushed Iraqis like quail. They'd been hiding in ditches, behind vehicles, anywhere there was cover.

Soprano opened up on them with the coax while Broadhead's gunner, Sergeant Bobby Hull, did the same.

We fired and maneuvered, fired and maneuvered up the road, with none of the returning AK fire even coming close. Just as Hull killed the last of the dismounts, Soprano called up to me.

"Sarge, I think I've got a BMP up ahead."

Shit. Was this the first of the 20 BMPs headed our way? I dropped down inside the turret and looked in the sight. The vehicle didn't have tracks, but it was armored and had rolled into view from the wood line to our southeast.

"White 4, can you ID the armored vehicle out there?"

He was back on the radio. "Negative, Red 2. Can't see it, you're in my line of sight."

Well, I guess it really didn't matter. It wasn't one of ours. I said to Soprano, "AP, three rounds, fire!" My eyes stayed glued to the sight.

The round in the chamber was HE, and it hit short because Soprano was using the AP (armor-piercing) reticle, but the next two rounds were armor-piercing depleted uranium and hit the front of the vehicle. I could see impact, but there was no other reaction from the vehicle.

"You're on target. Smoke it." He let out another burst of AP, and this time there was a small fire, then one big explosion.

"Okay, Sperry, I want to know what we just killed. Move us a little closer."

"Hold on."

We rolled forward enough for me to see that we'd just destroyed a BRDM. The BRDM is a Soviet-manufactured armored amphibious combat patrol vehicle with a 14.5 mm main gun and a supporting coax. Instead of having tracks like the BMP, they rolled on four tires.

"Chalk up one BRDM," I announced. I was feeling pretty good about that when out from behind the burning BRDM rolled another damn truck. It was like playing Whac-A-Mole—kill one and another one pops right up.

Before Soprano could get on target, Broadhead nailed the truck with the M1's main gun, and it exploded.

"All right, enough sightseeing, get us back to the bridge," I told Sperry. "Heading back into position," I radioed Broadhead.

While we were still rolling, Broadhead set up in his old firing position and started engaging one truck after another as they rolled down the road into view. The Carnivore assumed its position on the bridge, and I stared at the wood line. The 20 BMPs were coming from that direction. How long did we have?

While we went back to killing trucks, Williams and the rest of Third Platoon were up to their ass in dismounts. Sergeant Wasson was still in pain from being hit in the back by the RPG earlier. His gunner, Sergeant Raab, engaged 20 dismounts swarming their vehicle while Wasson fought through the pain.

By that point we had so many vehicles on fire in front of us that the thermal sight was once again useless.

"Okay, I think we've killed every truck in the fucking country, are we done yet?" Soprano grumbled. "Sarge, I can't see shit with everything on fire."

"Switch to day sight. Everything's all lit up anyway."

He did. "That's not much better."

It had been two hours since the bombers had taken out the tanks threatening Williams and the bridge to our rear. The amount of AK fire we were taking from all sides was increasing and pretty much constant, but most of the rounds hit nowhere near us. And the sandstorm was getting thicker, which meant they'd be able to sneak up close again.

McCoy answered my radio call. "Go ahead, Red 2."

"Sir, do we have any air support yet? It's getting pretty busy up here."

We were constantly scanning, looking for new threats, trying to see past the fires, and suddenly there they were—BMPs, a lot of them, at least 20, working their way through the trees to the southeast, headed right at us.

CHAPTER 15

REPO MEN

I can't see for shit!" Soprano yelled as he began engaging the BMPs with DU rounds. There were too many fires to use the thermals, but the day sight wasn't much use either. This was going to get real ugly, real quick. The armored tracks moved out of the woods and began advancing down a road toward my position.

My radio crackled. "Red 2, roger that, we have aircraft back on station above you, just call out some targets when you have them."

God bless McCoy, talk about nick of fucking time! If he'd been in the Brad with me I would have kissed him.

"Sir, I have twenty BMPs in the woods approaching my position, and have grid coordinates for you RIGHT NOW." I gave him the coordinates, and we waited. We didn't have long to wait.

A B-1B dropped four 2,000-pound bombs in a line right down the row of BMPs. The bomber's aim was perfect. The explosions were huge skyrockets of dirt in a swirling maelstrom. When it cleared, there were a lot of things on fire where the column of

BMPs had been, and nothing was moving. We couldn't tell how many BMPs had actually been destroyed, but any crews left alive were either combat ineffective or pretending they were dead.

The BMPs handled for the moment, we turned our attention back to the road in front of us. Truck after truck kept rolling down the road, and while I'd been on the radio with Captain McCoy, Broadhead had been burning through 120 mm HEAT rounds like they were on sale, but the Iraqis kept coming. The trucks at first would drive around the burning hulks to get closer to us, but that just resulted in yet another truck on fire. That seemed to be a lesson each new wave of trucks had to relearn. They finally wised up, stopping at the far edge of visibility to let their troops out. The Iraqi soldiers began moving toward us in the ditches en masse. The amount of incoming fire was insane—forget "target-rich environment," we had more guys in front of us than we had ammo left in the Bradley. I got back on the radio and requested another air strike on the trucks, on the soldiers, on every square inch of dirt in front of the bridge.

McCoy was back on the radio seconds later. "Roger that. Aircraft are inbound, and you are danger close. Get your ass out of there."

I didn't need to be told twice. "JDAMs are inbound," I told Sperry and the whole crew. "Let's get the fuck back from this bridge." JDAM stands for "joint direct attack munition," which you might know as a smart bomb.

"Shit yeah." Scared as hell, he cranked the steering so we would straighten out and then hit the accelerator, thinking we were in reverse. We were still in drive, however, so we jerked forward off the steep bank at the end of the bridge and began to roll over. Somehow, we didn't, and the Carnivore teetered there, ready to roll at any second.

"Nobody fucking move!" I yelled. "Don't do anything," I told Sperry, "don't even try to back up or we'll roll." Very carefully I climbed out of the turret to look at the Bradley. We were so close to going over I was amazed we hadn't rolled.

"White 4, I need you at my location immediately with a tow cable," I called Broadhead.

"Red 2, we've got incoming!"

"I know we've got fucking incoming! Pull us the fuck out of here!" I stayed hunkered down behind the rear of the Bradley, protected from the incoming AK rounds.

"Sarge, I've got a lot of dismounts a hundred meters out," Soprano called to me, scared out of his mind. I don't know if he was more worried about the soldiers or the B-1Bs and their 2,000-pound bombs en route. "I think I can get them if I traverse the turret—"

"Don't touch anything!" I yelled at him. I was worried any shift in weight would cause the Bradley to roll over. Just then Broadhead roared up right on our ass in his M1 and climbed out as fast as his wounded knee allowed.

"Are you fucking kidding me?" he roared. "You're endangering the lives of my crew because your driver can't fucking drive."

"Fuck you and bring me that goddamn tow cable, you limping prick!" I screamed at him.

We were both terrified and angry and kept yelling and screaming at each other as we got out the tow cable. We couldn't see a damn thing, as it was still the middle of the night and we were between the two vehicles. The only light came from burning vehicles several hundred yards away. Broadhead got the cable and then we had to step out from our sheltered position to hook the cable up.

Even though it was dark, as soon as we stepped out in the open, the volume of fire we were receiving picked up tenfold. The rounds bouncing off the Bradley and the M1 sounded like rain hitting a tin roof, *clinkclinkclinkclinkclinkclinkclinkclink,* and rounds were snapping through the air all around us. Broadhead could barely walk and had to hold on to something to help him stand up—his knee was so swollen it barely fit inside his BDU pants.

"Come on, goddammit, come on!"

We looked like a couple of guys repossessing a car, crawling around half underneath my Bradley. It was so dark we had to work by feel, but finally we got the cable hooked up.

Broadhead rolled out of the way and hobbled back toward his tank. He yelled at his driver, "Okay, it's hooked up, back up!" We watched as the M1 rolled slowly backward. The cable grew taut, the Carnivore shifted, then it came fully down onto its tracks and back onto the road. I unhooked the tow cable and scrambled into the Bradley.

"Go, let's get the fuck out of here!" I told Sperry.

"Okay, *now* shoot them," I told Soprano. "Kill everything you see. Make them keep their heads down, keep them right there until the bombs hit!"

Back up on the bridge, then back on the safe side of it, roaring in reverse toward the rest of Crazy Horse, the main gun and coax both roaring—and the world exploded. The Carnivore rocked and almost rolled again and the electronics in the turret went out. It felt like an elephant sat on my chest, and all I could see were white spots. Holy—what the—I wondered for a second if I'd died, then realized the B-1Bs had arrived.

They dropped eight 2,000-pound bombs in a crescent around our position. My turret power flickered, then came back on, and I stuck my head outside the hatch. Sperry still had us rolling in reverse, but we were at an angle now and about to head off the road again, this time ass first.

"Stop! Stop the fucking Brad!" Luckily the turret power was back on, otherwise he wouldn't have heard me over the radio. The Carnivore stopped just in time, knocking off part of a guardrail. I had to shake my head.

"Everybody still alive?"

The first bomb had impacted 400 meters from my position. While that may not seem close, the minimum safe distance from the kind of ordnance they dropped all around us is 2,000 meters, 2,500 during training. After making sure nobody was seeing double, we slowly rolled back up to the canal bridge.

After that crescendo, the rest of the night was relatively quiet. We watched a few Iraqis—and by a few I mean only 15 or 20— who had somehow survived the bombing stumble out of the area. As they had no weapons, we let them go. No more trucks rolling up on us, no more BMPs.

I discovered I had two bullet holes in my pant legs right next to my thighs from when Broadhead and I were standing in the open screaming at each other. Broadhead found a bullet hole on the underside of his sleeve. How neither of us managed to get hit I can't explain.

Finally, the dawn arrived. The bridge was still there, but beyond it—it was like looking at the moon. The bomb craters were the size of houses. Big houses.

"Jeezus Christ." Sully had his head out of the hatch, looking around.

The Carnivore was in sad shape. We'd lost our radio antenna again, and two of my road wheels had holes in them from RPG hits. Sperry's periscope was destroyed and two of the armor plates for the track shoes had been blown off at some point during the last—how long had it been? Two and a half days. It seemed a lifetime.

And, once again, we were out of ammo. We had none left, as in, if the bombers hadn't shown up when they did, we were minutes away from having to throw insults at the encroaching Iraqis, maybe some rocks.

Sergeant Williams and the Casanova had survived the night, but he'd been beat up as well. He had one radio out and his night sight was going in and out. For some reason he could only run it for three hours and then he would have to turn it off for half an hour before it would work again. Maybe it was overheating. That day townspeople came up to Williams's Bradley, carrying pieces of the tanks that had been destroyed in their streets—I don't know if they wanted to give him souvenirs or what. Maybe the Casanova looked so bad they thought he needed spare parts.

The Hemmitts rolled up again and gave us a full upload of ammo. They topped off our fuel, too, but it was the ammo I was thankful for. We wiped down our weapons with a light coat of 15W40 motor oil, then checked to make sure there was nothing else that needed doing. Nope. We were squared away, at least for the moment, and there was nobody coming down the road.

I sat down to eat an MRE, then jerked when the radio came to life.

"Red 2, you have hostiles moving in and around a house to your front," Broadhead told me.

"Roger that. Watch my move and we'll go take care of them." A quick glance around the Brad showed me everybody was out cold. Wait, when did . . . ? I checked my watch and saw that I had sat down to eat the MRE and fallen asleep for four hours. I didn't even remember closing my eyes, and nobody else even twitched when Broadhead called.

"Sperry." He didn't move, and I nudged him with my foot. "Wake up. We've got some work to do."

Sperry rubbed the sleep out of his eyes and moved us up the

road. We stopped in the midst of the destroyed trucks, most of which were still smoking. I didn't wake anybody else up, because I knew how badly my crew needed to rest. When we stopped I spotted two Iraqi soldiers running down a bank to a ditch and took them out with the coax.

The sound of the gun woke Soprano up. "Hey, let me have the gun, I'll do it," he told me sleepily.

We were on a plain filled with smoking husks of trucks stretching over half a mile in every direction. It was postapocalyptic, and I wouldn't have been surprised to see zombies shambling around. There wasn't much movement to see, other than the flames and swirling sand, but here and there another Iraqi soldier appeared and tried to work his way close to us on foot.

Over the next hour we killed 10 soldiers, driving around burning trucks like tourists at Armageddon, and while we were out there we did BDA for the Commander.

In the time the Carnivore was on that bridge we had engaged close to 100 troop transports, not to mention pickup trucks and cars filled with Iraqi soldiers, and the BRDM and BMPs. Each troop truck had between 10 and 20 troops on board when they rolled up to do battle. We stopped counting at 2,000 bodies. There were soldiers still sitting in the back of many of the trucks, or stacked like logs on the floor, killed before they'd ever had a chance to dismount. Their bodies burned with the trucks. It looked like hell, and it smelled like hell, too.

We did five full ammo uploads on that bridge. Over 3,000 rounds of 25 mm, and we went through it all, as well as 7,000 or 8,000 thousand rounds of 7.62 mm for the coax. The coax shot so much, I found, when we finally got to Baghdad and I was able to clean it, completely break it down, and take it out, that it was almost welded to the trunnion.

We collected 600 rifles, stacking them on the back of the Carnivore until the teetering pile made the Brad look humpbacked. Finally, we started moving back to the bridge at a crawl.

"Dismounts left!" I yelled out. Three soldiers ran into the house closest to the bridge. Soprano slewed the turret around and put 10 rounds of 25 mm HE into it. The front of the brick house blew apart, but there was no way to know if we'd gotten the soldiers.

"Shit, we gotta go in and check," I said. The house was too close to the bridge to just hope we'd gotten them. "Sully, Soprano, let's go." We left Sperry and the two engineers in the Brad, providing overwatch to make sure nobody came at us from the rear.

As we approached the house on foot, Sully in the lead, an Iraqi ran out of the ragged hole the HE had blasted in the front wall of the house. Soprano shot him in the face with my pistol. Very carefully we entered the front of the house and found the bodies of the other two Iraqis.

"All right, check the back of the house," I told my guys. "I'm going to check these bastards for documents."

The first Iraqi had an M1911 .45 pistol on him. God only knows where he got it, and the path it took from the United States to end up in his hands had probably been long and interesting. I laid down my AK and picked up the .45 to see if it was loaded—it was. As I was checking it out to see if there were any U.S. Army markings on it, another Iraqi with an AK stepped out from behind a pile of wood just feet from me.

"Shit!" I pointed the pistol at his chest, pulled the trigger, the hammer fell—and nothing happened. Just a click. We looked at each other for a fraction of a second, then I lunged at him and with a roar hit him in the face with the pistol. He dropped his AK as I dropped the 1911. I went for the Buck hunting knife I'd carried while turkey and deer hunting in Kentucky and all through Desert

Storm. As he grappled with me I stabbed him under the arm and tried to stab him again—but I couldn't get the knife out.

I don't know if his chest muscles clamped down on the blade of the knife or what, but I couldn't pull it out of him, and he kept fighting and fighting. He took forever to die, or maybe it just seemed like forever.

In the movies, people who get stabbed just fall over and die. In the real world, it takes a long time to bleed out. He didn't go quickly or quietly. As I watched him die, I thought how stupid he was, how stupid I was. He could have surrendered, but instead he'd died. For what? Saddam and his torture chambers? And my lack of sleep had me making mistakes that probably should have killed me. Four hours of accidental nap time didn't begin to address the sleep deficit we had. Getting myself killed was one thing, but what I didn't want to do was get my crew killed. We needed a break.

Back at the bridge, we dumped the rifles into the canal while Broadhead covered us. We threw so many rifles down there that the canal was choked; you wouldn't have been able to get a canoe through it. A short time later, the Commander came over the radio net and told Crazy Horse we were going to be relieved, that another unit was going to replace us. Thank God. We'd all had enough of that damn road between the two bridges, although the sandstorm had finally died down.

The unit replacing us rolled up a while later, and they still had gun covers on their .50-cals. I looked over at Broadhead, who just smiled tiredly at me. What could you say? Their covers would come off as soon as it got dark again, of that I was sure.

What's interesting is that at As Samawah, Broadhead and I had gone tearing across the bridge after that Iraqi truck, and we'd gotten stuck on the wrong side. Geary had come across the bridge in his Bradley as part of an attempt to rescue our dumb asses. I received the Silver Star for helping to rescue his crew, but whether we rescued his crew or not, what we did was of no strategic or tactical importance to the war effort. We were just saving fellow soldiers.

At Objective Floyd outside An Najaf, however, Crazy Horse took on a tank battalion at one end of our column and an infantry brigade at the other, preventing what could have been a slaughter and a turning point in the war, in the process killing thousands of enemy troops. And nobody got a single medal. We weren't there for medals, but that just shows how arbitrary they can be. I don't think anybody even got a Purple Heart—not that you want those, of course.

Would things have been completely different for us if there hadn't been a sandstorm? Well, if there hadn't been a sandstorm, I would have been able to call in air, and we would have had a lot of other assets available to us. However, the Iraqis would have been able to see exactly where we were. I can only have so much ammo on board my vehicle and can only reload so fast. I'm still amazed that we survived, given everything we went through to secure that little worthless canal bridge.

We lived, they died. That's good enough for me.

When we were relieved, we were to proceed to Objective Rams. Finally, an objective that wasn't a bridge.

Rams was a flat field in the middle of nowhere, southwest of An Najaf. It was a short move to get there, only an hour, and it was a safe location. Once we arrived we set up in a laager position. We would have a chance to rest and repair our gear while the 2nd BCT (Brigade Combat Team) would be pulling overwatch.

I had gone so long without sleep that I don't have coherent memories of my time at Rams. It was just snapshots in my mind, shades of color. There was an MKT (mobile kitchen trailer) set up, but they were done serving, because we'd arrived so late. I grabbed a bunch of T-rats and warmed them up on the engine of the Carnivore on the way back, then set up a hot meal for the entire troop so they didn't have to eat MREs again.

Just sitting on the ground, eating and talking with my crew and the guys who walked by, seemed an almost alien experience after living inside the Brad for days. The lack of sleep, lack of food, and being under almost constant attack for a week had aged Soprano 20 years. He went from looking like a baby-faced teenager to a tired 35-year-old. Jason Sperry, my driver, wasn't much better. I didn't want to even know what I looked like. My knees were so swollen from standing up for days that it was hard to walk. For the first time since the start of the war I got to change my socks.

The meal was lukewarm eggs and sausages. It was a good meal, and it was good to see the faces of my friends and fellow soldiers. We had traveled far and been through hell, but amazingly enough we hadn't lost anybody. We were all still there.

Specialist Ryan Hellman from S-3 (Headquarters Platoon) pulled up in his Humvee with Staff Sergeant Todd Young. They knew what we had been through and wanted to check on us.

"Jesus, how you guys doing?" Hellman asked us. He eyeballed the Carnivore, which wasn't nearly as pretty as the last time he'd laid eyes on it.

I was having a hard time doing much more than blinking, and polite conversation seemed almost impossible. I looked past him at his ride. "I'm stealing your antenna," I told him.

"What?"

I took the matching unit—what we called the radio antennas because they were interchangeable—off his Humvee to fix the radio on the Carnivore. "You need anything else?" Hellman asked me.

"What do you have?" I asked him.

Young gave us some more batteries before they moved on. Captain Stephen Balog, the unit chaplain, came by to see us as well. Seeing his friendly face meant a lot and made me feel a little more human.

After eating I walked over to catch up on small talk with the First Sergeant—just being able to do that was a luxury. Turns out the .50-cal on his M113 APC hadn't functioned at all, not since we'd crossed into Iraq. The troop hadn't gotten a chance to test fire any of our weapons before they'd cut through the berm, and Grigges had been riding around for a week with a nonfiring machine gun. We put our heads together, and with a little tinkering and one big hammer, we got his .50 working again. Meanwhile, some of the guys were trying to ride one of the camels that were there. The camels belonged to the bedouins in the area. The riding attempts did not go well, except as entertainment for everyone watching.

Just being able to work on the Bradley without having to worry about being shot at was better than I can explain. I replaced some of our shot-up track shoes. I worked on our TOW launcher, which had been damaged at As Samawah, but it was a lost cause. Then, sleep.

I had a good sleep. It was a peaceful sleep. I wasn't anxious, I wasn't nervous, I wasn't worrying about the upcoming fight that everyone had been worrying about for months. I wasn't worrying about Bradleys and tanks. I wasn't worrying about anything.

CHAPTER 16

THE GREAT BAGHDAD TANK
BATTLE . . . SORT OF

The break couldn't last forever, and after three days at Objective Rams we saddled up again and headed for Karbala. Karbala was a good-sized town about halfway between An Najaf and Baghdad. It was northwest of An Najaf, and we rolled mostly through desert to get there. We didn't encounter any resistance to speak of, and once at Karbala we set up in an overwatch position.

Sitting back in the sand wasn't what most of us wanted to be doing, although we hadn't exactly been starved for action. Our job was to make sure the Iraqi army could not get into the rear of the division. Boring was a welcome change, at least for a few hours, but honestly I wasn't disappointed when we got the word that JSTARS had picked up a huge element heading in our direction. A brigade-sized element. Time to go back to work.

Finally, the terrain worked in our favor, and we lined up all three troops abreast and charged toward the oncoming enemy, just like in training—only to discover that they were camels. Lots and lots of camels. Camels moving quickly across the desert apparently look a lot like dismounted infantry on ground radar. Oh well.

We spent a lot of time around camels while we were over there. I can't say I really enjoyed it. Camels are mean. They bite you, blow spit on you, and shove you with their head if they don't like you. If you feed them crackers and run out while they're still hungry, again they'll shove you with their head. They're like mean, spoiled kids, but because most of the ones we came across belonged to bedouins, shooting the ones that pissed us off would not have been a good way to endear ourselves to the local population. They probably taste horrible anyway. I would wager that most of the people in this country in favor of animal rights have never spent any time with camels.

After we'd scared the crap out of the giant herd (or whatever it's called) of camels, command had us move north along Highway 9, the main route between Karbala and Baghdad, and set up north of town in a blocking position. There was a tank brigade still out there, somewhere, and we needed to find it. The only thing we found was an unmanned antiaircraft gun site with five 57 mm guns. Destroying them was easy—Broadhead ran over them with his tank. We weren't there for long when we got the word that it was time to head to Baghdad. It was April 3, 2003.

The 2nd BCT moved out, and we rolled out behind them until we got to the other side of the Euphrates. That would mark the third time I crossed the river. The 2nd BCT then proceeded to head west, and we moved out east along a narrow highway heading up to Baghdad.

Running up to Baghdad on the main road, we were stopped because of a stack-up of vehicles ahead. Airman Shopshire was in the vehicle in front of us and saw movement in the bushes on the side of the road. He jumped down and saw an Iraqi officer who at some point had been shot in the ass and was apparently looking to surrender.

Holding his rifle on the Iraqi, Shopshire gestured at him to walk toward us and then commanded him, *"Qif!"* We'd been told that *qif* meant "slowly," but what it actually means is "stop." The Iraqi stopped, and Shopshire gestured for him to keep on coming, and as soon as the guy took another step Shopshire said *"Qif!"* again. The Iraqi stopped. This happened over and over, and the Iraqi had no fucking idea what was going on; all he knew was that he didn't want to get shot again.

Shopshire yelled, "Why won't this bastard keep walking?" He was getting pissed off and started yelling at the Iraqi at the top of his lungs, *"Qif! Qif!"*

The Iraqi looked from Shopshire to the rest of us with an expression on his face like, "What the hell do you want from me?" Finally, the Iraqi was able to successfully surrender without getting shot.

I ended up being the lead vehicle for Crazy Horse, and to be honest, even though I like to lead from the front, that was not the place I wanted to be. We just knew Baghdad was going to be guarded by tanks, lots and lots of tanks. The whole U.S. Army was expecting a huge tank battle in the fight for Baghdad, and that road was only wide enough for one vehicle at a time. All it would take was one hit from a T-72, and not only would I and my whole crew be dead but everybody behind us would be stacked up like ducks in a shooting gallery.

We rolled as slowly as we could to make sure that Soprano could get a good look ahead of us. It was an urban area, with neighborhoods and commercial buildings everywhere. Our first contact came from a Toyota truck with six or seven guys in it with small arms. Soprano fired 25 mm at it. The first round landed just in front of the truck, and the next three rounds landed in the cab—that started and ended that fight. Not long after, I came upon an Iraqi fighting position dug in next to the road and we shot that up. Usually the troops in those little emplacements would try to hit us with RPGs.

"Soprano, Sully, you see anything that even looks like a fighting position, you light it up." I did not want to get hit with an RPG. I'd had quite enough of RPGs already.

"Copy that."

Dusk was approaching. We still had a long way to go and that meant I had to pick up the pace, because the last thing anybody wanted was another Ambush Alley. However, moving faster meant it would be harder to spot any Iraqis until we were right on top of them. It was a double-edged sword. Even though we owned the night with our superior night vision equipment, we all preferred to fight in the daylight.

Two miles from Baghdad I saw two 152 mm cannons aiming right at me. I slewed the turret to the first cannon and yelled, "Two guns, left one hundred meters, HE, fire!"

Soprano was on the ball and quick on the trigger. Five, then 10 rounds hit the two cannons. The ammo on one went up in a huge fireball, killing the three-man gun crew. The other gun crew scrambled out of their position and jumped into a big ammo truck. Soprano went to coax and fired a long 100-round burst into the cab as the truck was trying to drive away. Two men died in the truck and the third jumped out of the passenger side of the cab, but when he hit the ground, he fell under the back wheels of the truck and got rolled up. He ended up wedged between the wheels and the bed of the truck, bringing it to a stop on the side of the road. Broadhead let loose with his .50-cal, and the ammo in the back of the truck started going up.

We moved forward a short distance and came to an intersection where there were bunkers on both sides of the road. Soprano and Sully took out all the soldiers in them, then we started rolling out again.

Broadhead was looking back and thought the exploding ammo truck looked really neat. He stopped his tank and took a few pictures back down the row of our column, and when he got back to his radio, the profanity coming out of it—Broadhead had halted the column so that McCoy's tank was right next to the exploding ammo truck, and while he had been taking pictures, ordnance and pieces of exploding truck were whinging off the side of the Commander's tank. We thought it was funny as hell, but Captain McCoy sure didn't.

We got word that some 58 Delta scout helicopters had spotted armored vehicles at Saddam International Airport (which was later renamed Baghdad International Airport—BIAP), and we got the orders to head in that direction and destroy them. As we were rolling in, with the Carnivore in the lead, Broadhead in Camel Toe behind me, and Sergeant Wallace in his Bradley behind him, the fourth vehicle in the column slid partly off the road into a canal, blocking the road so that the rest of the troop couldn't pass. While they worked to clear the road, the three of us, two Brads and Broadhead in his M1, headed toward the airport.

We hadn't expected a fight in As Samawah and ended up in a two-day gun battle where we killed thousands of Iraqis. Rolling up toward An Najaf on a side road, in the rear to protect the supply train, we'd first rolled through the longest ambush in military history, then got stuck at the canal bridge at Objective Floyd and nearly died. We just knew Baghdad would be the site of a huge armor battle—but the fact is that while we spotted all sorts of T-72s and BMPs parked next to and in between buildings, we simply shot the hell out of them. I think most of them were unmanned; their crews had abandoned them.

Being at the front of the line, we knew to engage any armor we saw, but the troops coming behind us, sometimes days later, had some issues. Hitting a BMP or T-72 with a DU round kills it and everybody in it deader than dirt, but a lot of the time you can't tell it's been hit. DU kills with velocity—it punches holes but doesn't necessarily cause an explosion. After a few engagements with close calls, our armor developed a technique—hit the enemy armor with DU rounds so you know it's dead, then hit it with HE so everyone coming behind you can tell it's dead.

The objective was to get to Baghdad, but once we got to the area our troop didn't have any specific orders, such as hold this bridge or guard that intersection. I don't know if that was because we were making such fast progress or because the orders never filtered down from high command, but all we knew was to head up to the big city and kill anything and anyone that posed a threat and didn't surrender. Maybe they figured we'd be too busy fighting in an urban environment to worry about holding specific intersections.

After our three vehicles cleared out the area around the airport, we hooked up with the rest of the troop and continued toward our next checkpoint, which was an intersection near Abu Ghraib prison. Once there, I saw Iraqi infantry trying to dig in. Two of the soldiers got into a pickup truck and tried to drive away, and Soprano lit them up with 25 mm HE. The rounds exploded the truck and set it on fire.

As soon as we set up in a blocking position, more cars and trucks started coming down the road at us. The Carnivore was on the right side of the road and Camel Toe was on the left, with the rest of First and Second Platoons set up around and behind us. Civilian vehicles spotted us and usually did U-turns and did their best to get out of the area. From time to time we had a truck full of soldiers charge our position—I didn't know whether to admire their courage or marvel at their stupidity. Toyota pickups are not a good vehicular choice when doing battle with Bradleys and M1s.

Compared to what we'd already seen, there wasn't a lot of action happening in the outskirts of Baghdad. The headquarters platoon set up behind us with the supply vehicles, and that area became known as the new Crazy Horse Café.

Most of the action was happening elsewhere. "Contact! I have nine T-72s and have multiple dismounts ahead of me," I heard Sergeant Williams call in. The T-72s were dug in in a nearby palm grove. Apparently the Casanova was a tank magnet. He could also see more than 100 dismounts moving in front of him. The Troop Commander called someone higher up for help, which the air force was more than happy to provide.

"Keep your head down, you have air inbound," McCoy told him.

Williams moved the Casanova to a safer position as the Air Force came in fast and low. He watched as the A-10s headed straight at him, then roared over his head and dropped two 500-pound bombs into the palm grove right in front of him. The closest bomb hit just 100 meters from his Bradley, which was way too close. As the A-10s circled around to do another run, Captain McCoy got on the radio net and called off the remainder of the air strike.

"That's not going to work, friendlies are way too close, you're going to have to go in there and destroy them yourself," McCoy told Williams over the radio.

"Roger that," Williams told him, still seeing spots from the bomb blast.

Bradleys work in hunter-killer teams with M1s, and Williams's wingman was Staff Sergeant Crawford in Fourth Platoon. They engaged the T-72s and dismounts together. The A-10s had destroyed a lot of tanks, but there were still plenty of them in the palm grove showing no signs of damage.

With darkness closing in on them, Sergeant Williams took out the closest enemy tank with a TOW missile. It was a good hit, and there was no doubt everyone in the T-72 was dead, but the tank itself did not explode, although it was on fire. Williams engaged the second T-72 with his 25 mm main gun as the first tank burned in the palm grove, sending a big column of black smoke into the darkening sky.

Williams hit the second tank with one, two, then three rounds of DU, and with the third armor-piercing projectile the T-72 lost its turret in a huge fireball. Crawford in his M1 engaged the dismounts with his .50.

Williams's dismount, Specialist Clint Leon, was at the back of the Casanova engaging dismounts and watching the first T-72, the one they'd hit with the TOW missile, burn. In short order it exploded as well. His eyes were drawn to movement beyond the palm grove in the gathering gloom, and he saw 20 Iraqi troop transport trucks heading their way, headlights off.

"Shit!" There was too much noise to be heard, and he reached over and smacked the top of Williams's helmet where he was standing in the open hatch. When Williams turned around, all Leon had to do was point.

Williams immediately got on the line with his gunner, Sergeant Tom Hudgins. "Trucks right, four hundred, HE, FIRE!"

Hudgins was the squadron's Bradley top gun, and he had his first round off almost immediately. The first round missed, but he quickly adjusted his aim and fired a long burst. Three HE rounds hit the cab of the first truck in line, and four hit the bed. On fire and peeled open like a tin can at a shooting range, the truck lost most of its forward momentum and the second truck in line rammed into the back of it. Most of the soldiers in the back of the second truck went flying through the air.

Sergeant Crawford's gunner in the M1, Sergeant Christopher Sheridan, lit up the survivors of the second truck with the coax. While he was doing that, Williams slewed the Casanova's turret to the last truck in line.

"Last truck, HE, eight hundred, fire!" The last vehicle in the convoy was a fuel truck, and it disintegrated in a huge ball of fire when Hudgins put four rounds of HE into it. Flaming fuel ran all over the road and fields to either side, blocking the escape of the Iraqi soldiers from the remaining trucks as both the Bradley and the M1 began firing up the rest of the convoy. The burning fuel silhouetted the soldiers trying to run for cover.

The Casanova had moved to within 100 meters of the first truck when one of the nearby tanks Williams thought was destroyed backed up and turned at him. In a hurry he grabbed the Commander's override for the main gun, slewed his turret, and fired a long burst of 25 mm DU into the front of the T-72. How effective were the DU rounds? Those 25 mm rounds went *through* the T-72 and hit a truck behind the tank, destroying both of them.

There were only a handful of Iraqi soldiers left alive and they ripped off their uniforms and ran away naked. Williams let them run, as they were no longer a threat, but that close call with the T-72 he'd thought was dead had him worried. There were still half a dozen tanks in the now-dark palm grove, and he didn't know if they had been destroyed by the A-10 strike, were unmanned, or were just lying in wait. For the next two hours he worked his way through the palm grove and the middle of his sector, hitting any armor he found that wasn't already in pieces or on fire, just in case. Crawford's M1 pulled overwatch, and between the two of them they took care of the enemy armor and any dismounts crazy enough to attack American armor with AK-47s.

Between the intersection Broadhead and I were watching and Williams's palm grove, the rest of Crazy Horse Troop was seeing small groups of enemy dismounts attacking their positions. There was no shortage of concealment for soldiers who wanted to fight in an urban environment—ditches, walls, vehicles—but none of it provided cover for the soldiers when we started lighting them up with our heavy weapons. Whether they were on foot, in vehicles, or in sandbagged observation posts (OPs), we had the right medicine for the job. If 7.62 or .50-cal coax wasn't enough, we had 25 mm HE and DU. If that didn't do the trick, the M1's 120 mm HEAT rounds proved quite effective. When all else failed, or the distance was a bit much, it was only the matter of a few minutes to call in mortars.

Sergeant Christner, standing in the hatch of his Bradley early that evening, spotted an Iraqi OP (Observation Post) on a hilltop to our front. He couldn't tell if it was occupied, but he couldn't leave it alone. He called in a fire mission for Bennett's mortars, and after fifteen rounds the OP was no more.

I was on the command net when I heard a contact report of tanks moving on Apache Troop. It looked like they were in for the big tank battle we'd all been expecting since we started rolling on Baghdad. Iraqi armor was finally going to stand and fight. We could only listen on the radio, and while Apache had their work cut out for them, the engagement was almost completely one-sided.

The Iraqis had the numbers, and they had equipment enough to do us serious damage, but they didn't seem to have the skill or training to do battle with us. I don't know if a T-72 main gun round can get through an M1's armor, but it will sure as hell kill a Bradley. RPGs were flying around like mosquitoes during some of the

First Platoon, Crazy Horse, 3/7 Cavalry. On the eve of battle along the Iraq-Kuwait border, 2003.

Crazy Horse in Baghdad, 2005. Back row, left to right: Rodriguez, Dejesus, Cochran, and myself. Front row, left to right: Williams, Taylor, Liesbish, and Sowby. I'm carrying my M14 EBR, the rifle I used to take the 852 meter sniper kill, my longest shot. On the ground to my left is my Barrett M82, the weapon I used for most of my sniping. This photo would appear on the cover of *Soldier of Fortune* in August 2006.

Posing with the first AK and Iraqi flag I captured at As Samawah, where one of the bloodiest engagements of the invasion took place.

Riding around Iraq in the early days of the invasion, waiting for people to try to kill us. We usually didn't have to wait very long.

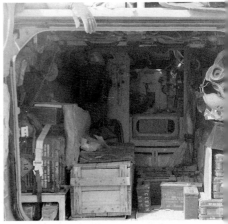

We counted the tanks, artillery pieces, and planes that we'd destroyed with the Carnivore and painted them on its side like a World War II fighter plane.

A peek inside the Carnivore. Look cramped? Well, this was shot before we began loading our ammo.

That's me with one of the thousands of AKs we took off dead Iraqi soldiers. This one had a folding stock, which made it very handy in the close confines of the Carnivore.

A shot of the Carnivore feeding on one of Saddam's personal armored Mercedeses (left) and an artillery piece (right).

If you look closely, you'll see "SSG J" spray-painted on the front of this Iraqi tank that was destroyed by the Carnivore.

An Iraqi MiG-23 on fire outside Al Asad Air Base. We had a lot of fun destroying Saddam's toys.

COUNTERCLOCKWISE FROM TOP:

Reporter Rita Leistner, Forest Geary, and me outside the oil refinery in Iraq where I ran the security for a short time.

Soprano with one of the lizards that were all over Kuwait. He named it Tara Reid.

Cochran gets a little sun with a new friend.

Jason Sperry, driver of the Carnivore in 2003.

The Carnivore and crew not too long after reaching Baghdad. I'm standing holding the .303 Mk III Lee-Enfield I took off the Iraqi sniper who was stomped by the bull. Soprano's smoking a cigarette and trying to look cool, Sully of course is lying down, and the kid in the helmet is Correa, another one of the many fine troopers we had in Crazy Horse. I used that same Enfield as a sniping weapon—it worked well for targets within a few hundred meters.

CLOCKWISE FROM TOP LEFT: My sniping spotter, Sergeant Jared Kennedy. | Here I am getting a Purple Heart (the result of an IED) pinned on me by the Commander of Task Force 6-26. | Captains McCoy (left) and Bair, relaxing in between missions. That's Sergeant Tony Broadhead (left) and Captain Burgoyne (right) in front, with Sergeants Leon (left) and Broussard in back.

Pulling guard duty on the bridge in Balad, we were on the lookout for weapons and large amounts of cash. Here I am listening to an Iraqi try to explain to me why he had a wheelbarrow's worth of money in his car trunk. Do I look like I believe him?

Guard duty can be boring—so I put on an Iraqi antiaircraft gunner's helmet over a gas mask, jumped out of the bushes next to cars stopped at our checkpoint, and spoke like Darth Vader. It scared the hell out of the Iraqis.

Back in Iraq in 2005, holding up just a couple of weapons we seized—a British Sterling submachine gun and an RPG warhead.

Sergeant Craig took this shot through his Bradley's gunsight while he was supporting our "naval" missions.

During my second tour in Iraq, the insurgency was in full swing. We came across this Hummer on patrol. It was crewed by multinational forces, and we medevaced out the wounded.

This is what happens when big IEDs go off near your Bradley—your idler wheels break and fall off.

Working as private contractors in Iraq, here we are securing a site after a bombing. We carried a lot more ammo on us than when I was in the Army because we were the backup.

With my beautiful wife, Amy.

My sons Jaycob (left) and Max, circa 2005.

This is me and Mark Schindel of Gerber Legendary Blades at the 3rd Infantry Division's Museum, at their small display of the things I brought back from Iraq. Visible is one of my uniforms, a sniper logbook, and the buttstock of the M16 I took out of Saddam's Water Palace. That's Geary's Bradley, Circus Freaks, firing a TOW missile during a training exercise at Fort Stewart.

fighting I saw, and a direct hit by one of them probably would have taken us out, but the Iraqis couldn't shoot worth a damn. Those 17 or so RPG warheads that did hit us directly didn't do much at all, because they hadn't been armed—the Iraqis firing them had forgotten to take the pins out. We fought an army in Iraq, but it wasn't a very professional or well-trained one.

CHAPTER 17

IRAQI BULLFIGHTING

White 4, let's check out the vehicle for intelligence," I said to Broadhead on the radio. The last troop truck we'd shot up on the road was still in good shape, and there was a chance we'd find some useful documents. We weren't any busier during the night than when the sun was out, but our night vision and thermal sights gave us a definite advantage.

"Copy that."

We moved up carefully, side by side, tank and Bradley, and just as we got to the truck, a guy inside jumped up and aimed an AK.

"Contact!" Broadhead yelled reflexively and shot him with his own AK. M4s work very well, but we never had any shortage of loaded AK magazines lying around. Broadhead and I had been just about out of ammo for our vehicles more times than we would care to remember, so it was good having at least one gun on board for which there was always a ready supply of ammunition.

There was nothing of intel value in the troop truck, so I saddled back up and we returned to our checkpoint. As soon as we got there, a round whinged off my turret.

"Sniper!" I called out and tried to spot him. Gunshots echo weirdly when there are walls for sound to bounce off, so it wasn't a simple thing to pinpoint even the direction from which the sound came. I looked across the road at Broadhead, but he just shook his head. With all the trees and houses in the area, it was going to be hard to find this guy. As I was scanning the area, looking for movement or a muzzle flash, trying to get my eye on him, another round cracked past my head and hit something very close. I turned to see that my matching unit was gone.

I could only stare. "You've got to be fucking kidding me."

That's right—I'd lost my radio antenna. Another one! How many did that make? I'd lost count. Now he had me pissed.

"Soprano! Get on the thermal and find me this fucker so I can kill him. He took out our matching unit. I'm gonna see if I can fix it." While I worked on the radio using an equal amount of tools and cursing, Soprano used the thermal sight to scan the area.

"Sergeant Jay, got a guy on foot walking toward us, about two hundred yards out. He's moving slow and creeping along."

"He armed?"

There was a pause, then Soprano was back. "I can't tell."

I sat and thought for a second, then got on the thermal sight myself. "Sperry," I said to my driver, "cut the engine."

As soon as the engine died the guy hit the ground. He was in a large field, cutting directly across it toward us.

"Yeah, that doesn't look suspicious at all." I got Broadhead on the radio. "White 4, I think I have the sniper on foot, moving toward us, but so far I haven't spotted a weapon." I gave him direction and distance.

The Iraqi stayed down until I had Sperry start up the engine again. Through the thermal sight I saw him get back up to his feet and start slowly walking our way. I smiled. "Sperry, kill it again."

When the engine died a second time, the Iraqi was about 100 yards out in the dark, and he immediately dropped to the ground again. I tried not to laugh. We waited for five minutes, but the soldier was patient.

"Okay, start 'er back up," I told Sperry.

This time, when the Iraqi climbed to his feet and started heading our way again, I could see that he had a rifle.

One man with a rifle, who probably couldn't even see us yet, wasn't an immediate threat, so I had the time to call Captain McCoy on the radio. "Sir, I have ID'd a man with a rifle, and he is working his way to me."

We weren't in the middle of nowhere, we were right outside Baghdad, so McCoy wanted to give the guy every opportunity to prove he was drunk, or lost, or planning to surrender if that's what his intention was. "Red 2, wait as long as you can before engaging him, to verify he has hostile intent."

"Roger that, sir."

Ten minutes later the Iraqi was within 40 meters of my position, and both Broadhead and I were watching him through our thermal sights. I watched him bring his rifle up and fire it at my Bradley. The clink of the bullet bouncing off the armor was barely audible over the sound of the engine.

Time to call McCoy back. "Sir, the dismount has just fired on my vehicle."

McCoy came over the radio net in a very tired voice. "Red 2, roger that. Take him out, quickly."

I called Broadhead. "White 4, I'm going to take this knucklehead out, you watch the rest of the area to make sure he didn't bring any friends to the party."

"Copy, Red 2, I'm tired of watching this show anyway, time to change the channel." By this time everybody in the platoon in view was watching this guy doing his best ninja-in-the-dark, you-can't-see-me impersonation. Hell, there was nothing else to watch.

With Broadhead providing overwatch, I gave Soprano the order. "Go to coax, range less than one hundred, and fire."

"Finally." Soprano fired a 10-round burst and the soldier hit the ground. There was nothing for two seconds, then the Iraqi climbed to his feet. He took one step toward us—gotta admire the balls or wonder at the lack of brains—and I was about to tell Soprano to give him another burst, when suddenly there was a smear of white (heat) across the thermals.

"What the hell was that?"

Charging from out of nowhere, a bull rammed the Iraqi at full speed and flipped him up in the air with his horns. The Iraqi landed hard. That was the second of the cattle-initiated ambushes I saw in Iraq.

"Holy crap. Did you see that?" I asked Broadhead.

The bull came nosing back to check out his handiwork as the soldier got unsteadily back to his feet, and when the bull came close enough he stabbed it. The bull ran off with a snort, and the Iraqi, using his rifle as a crutch, started heading for us again. He'd barely taken two quivering steps when the bull charged up again and hit him sideways, flipping him into the air like a rag doll. That bull was pissed off, and as soon as the Iraqi landed the bull proceeded to stomp him. Everybody in the troop was in hysterics, laughing all across the radio net.

The Iraqi started crawling toward us and the bull gored him, flipped him up, and carried him around on his horns for a while, until there was no doubt the man was dead. The bull then flipped him off his horns and stomped him again. I had tears running down my cheeks, I was laughing so hard. The bull kept at it for hours—it would stomp him and snort, then run around the field for a while, then come back and stomp him some more. Note to self: never stab a bull, it'll just piss him off.

The next morning that soldier was all of about three inches thick. Our medics were able to approach the bull and treat his stab wound, and for the rest of the time we were in that area we kept him around as a kind of mascot and protected him. We wouldn't let Iraqis or the other soldiers mess with him—he was an honorary member of Crazy Horse Troop. We gave him all the water we could and any vegetables we could find.

The rifle that soldier had been carrying was a really nice World War II–era .303 British Lee-Enfield, so I kept it for a while. The Lee-Enfield SMLE was the main battle rifle of British troops in World War II, a 10-shot bolt-action rifle that many experts thought was the best of its type. Later in the war I was shooting RPG guys at 200-plus meters with it. When that .303 bullet hit them they stayed down for good.

That morning Sully and Sperry were at each other's throats. I'd been watching it build for four or five days and kept intervening, hoping that they'd burn each other out. It didn't happen. Sully was a teenage smartass and Sperry was a bit of a punching bag, so Sully would always take jabs at him. The fact that we didn't have people trying to kill us every second meant that they had time to fight each other.

I got up to do my watch in the turret, and Sperry was up front where he was supposed to be. Sully decided to talk some shit to him and was walking around the front of the Bradley talking to him through the driver's hatch.

"Asshole."

"Fuck you, you're a piece of shit," Sperry shot back.

Well, Sully then decided to spit on him. I froze.

When Sully spit on him, Sperry went red, screaming and yelling, and climbed out of his hatch, ready to commit murder. I had to jump off the top of the vehicle and put my hand on Sperry's chest, push him back.

"Knock this bullshit off!" I told him, and shot a murderous look at Sully, too. "The two of you have to stop fucking fighting, you've got to depend on one another. We've got people out there trying to kill us. I don't have time for this schoolyard shit."

Sperry took a couple of deep breaths. "Okay, Sergeant Jay, I'm sorry, I lost my head, I just hate him sometimes." He was still shaking.

I said, "Relax, Sperry, it's not that bad."

So Sperry sat back in his hatch, and I got back on top of the turret. Sully walked by Sperry on the ground and said, "Good thing he stopped you, I was about to fuck you up, fat boy."

Sperry grabbed the hatch to the Bradley, started slamming it up and down as hard as he could, banging his head against the periscope, screaming at the top of his lungs.

Boys.

That afternoon First Sergeant Grigges called and ordered us to pull back to the Crazy Horse Café, our supply point. We didn't need much ammo at all, but we were low on fuel from idling our engines to power our vehicle. The first place we headed was the fuel truck. There we saw Sergeant John Williams and the Casanova; it was the first time I had a chance to talk to him in person since the war started.

Our two crews sat down under a palm tree and talked about home—what we missed and what we were going to do when we got back. The longer we talked, the more people showed up, sat down, and started reminiscing. Other than family, beer, and women, food was what everyone missed. MREs will keep you alive and aren't bad if you only eat one or two, but after months of nothing but MREs we hated the fucking things. We once went two days without eating the main courses, because all we had left were MREs with Chicken à la King entrées—and they were just horrible. The worst.

"What I miss is the Hooters in Savannah," Sully said with a smile. "I really miss those wings." He was the one who'd grabbed the Hooters flag for us to display proudly across the Carnivore in the photo taken at As Samawah.

"What you miss is Lulu," I told him. Lulu was one of the hotties working there that he'd mentioned more than once. "And it wasn't wings, I think it was breasts and thighs." That got a laugh.

My eatery of choice was Sonny's Bar-B-Q in Hinesville, Georgia, and their Big Deal, a pulled pork sandwich to die for. Several of the guys sitting around gave Sonny's raves.

"Y'all don't know what you're talking about," Sergeant Jason Raab told us. "The only place to go in Hinesville is Gilly's. Now *that's* a country bar."

"Any of you guys ever go to Doc Holliday's in Jesup?" John Williams asked us. "I want one of their big fat T-bones. That's real food."

Sergeant First Class Bennett wandered away from his mortar track long enough to join the conversation. "Food? Naw—all I want is to get back to the new Bass Pro Shop in Savannah," he told us. We passed as much time as we could, talking about home, good food, and loose women.

We actually got to bathe, then, for the first time since the war had started. There was a canal nearby, so we all stripped down and washed ourselves as best we could. Soprano ended up riding around on the shoulders of one of Christener's guys, both of them completely naked, blowing off steam like drunk frat boys. We tried to clean our uniforms a little, get the stink and dirt and sweat out of them, because when all the washing was over we were going to have to put back on the same uniforms we'd been wearing for a week straight. Why?

Remember how I mentioned that all of our duffel bags were strapped around the outside of the Carnivore's turret as we rolled into Iraq? Well, when the bullets and RPGs started flying in As Samawah, none of us ended up with a piece of spare clothing that didn't have 10 bullet holes in it. We wore the same uniforms for weeks, and seeing as my toiletries were also in my duffel bag, I didn't shave for three months.

Before long it was time to head back to our checkpoints. Williams would head back north and I would move south and set up with Broadhead again.

For two days Broadhead and I and our crews sat out in the sun and had only limited contact. Having to shoot up charging vehicles or dismounted soldiers several times a day was practically a vacation after what we'd been through. Most of the vehicles we saw, however, were civilians just trying to get from one part of Baghdad to another. Before we let them through our checkpoint, we would search their vehicle. I don't know whose idea it was, but before too long, to indicate that the vehicle had been searched and the occupants were okay, we began spray-painting Nowatay, our Indian-skull insignia, on their vehicles. That pissed off the Iraqis at first, but before long they stopped putting up a fuss. Turned out that our insignia on their vehicle saved them a lot of hassle at subsequent checkpoints, because the other units knew we didn't fuck around. If we spray-painted a vehicle, it was okay. Soon, we had Iraqis driving up in brand-new Mercedeses and BMWs, asking us to spray-paint Nowatay on them. I wonder if any of them are still driving around Baghdad.

We spent a while doing "blocking moves," setting up checkpoints in different spots around the city to control access. Command sent Broadhead and me out to an intersection one day, and as I rolled up toward the position we were supposed to secure I saw an Iraqi BMP with some dead guys hanging out of it. I could tell just by looking at them that they stunk, badly, and we scared away some dogs that were chewing on them.

When I had Sperry pull the Bradley up just far enough for Broadhead to do overwatch with me, Broadhead had to park next to the BMP.

"Red 2, you want to move forward, I've got some dead bodies over here stinking up the whole street," he called.

"Negative, sorry. I'm where I need to be in case anybody rolls up and we need to engage them."

It was a hot day, and it wasn't very long before he called me again on the radio. "Red 2, you need to move up, we can't sit here."

"White 4, Red 2, that's a negative. I'm in the right position. I cannot move forward."

The stench must have been incredible, because finally Broadhead sent out a couple of his guys. They pulled the bodies out of the BMP and buried them in shallow graves, covering them up with enough sand to cover the smell. I waited until they had them covered up, and then I moved forward. As I may have mentioned, sometimes I'm an asshole. But it was funny.

So I moved forward, and Broadhead moved up behind me. We were sitting off to one side of what would be an Iraqi freeway. There was a big truck sitting nearby, a tractor trailer with a sunroof and a flat nose. It had been shot up and disabled, and it wasn't going anywhere.

After a couple of hours, Sperry announced that he had to take a dump. The Bradley Fighting Vehicle does not have a toilet. We had an ammo can to use if we had to, but we hated to use it. Considering our cramped interior was already filled with sweaty, unwashed bodies, the last thing we needed was someone doing *that*. There weren't any convenient Porta-Johns, and I wasn't about to let him go inside a building, out of my sight. So he headed for the disabled truck.

Sperry climbed on top of the cab of the truck and took care of his business, which fell through the sun roof onto the driver's seat. He finished up, wiped himself with whatever he had at hand there, and walked back to the Bradley.

That afternoon, two Iraqi guys came walking up. "Mister, Mister," they called to us, and pointed to the truck.

"Yeah, sure, help yourself," I told them, waving them on. They walked over to the truck and started checking it out, seeing what was damaged, maybe what they could steal from it or strip off it. Baghdad was pretty much a free-for-all at that point and we were letting the locals do whatever they wanted to as long as they weren't trying to kill us. The two of them were wearing the traditional outfit a lot of Iraqi men wore. I'm sure there's an Arabic name for it, but I just called it the Iraqi man-dress. Usually white, it draped down to their shoes and looked like a baggy dress.

Iraqi #1 climbed up, opened the door, and sat in the driver's seat. It looked like he was trying to start the truck. After a few minutes, you could see him smell it. He looked around, smelling, looked around some more, did some more smelling, and then he stuck his hand in the seat behind him. He pulled his hand up, saw what he had on him, and was like, *"Aaaaaah."* He spat out a few choice words and got out of the truck. His white man-dress had a big smear of brown on the back of it. We were crying in the Bradley by that point, laughing as hard as can be.

About that time his buddy came down the back steps of the

truck. The guy who'd sat in the cab very sneakily pulled the smeared part of his man-dress up with his hand so his buddy couldn't see the smear and started talking, gesturing to the driver's seat. So the second guy climbed up into the driver's seat, tried a few things to see if the truck would start, and then saw his buddy fall down on the ground laughing.

Iraqi #2 was like, "What?" and the first guy showed him the smear on his man-dress. Iraqi #2 reached down, got it on his hand, jumped down from the cab, and started screaming and chasing his buddy, hitting him with his shoe. It was absolutely hilarious. We cried.

After a couple of days, command informed us we were to start doing patrols in addition to manning the checkpoints. Geary would be my wingman in his Bradley, as a lot of the roads and bridges in the area would not support tanks.

The first day out we rolled up on an abandoned Iraqi army post. Geary pulled overwatch as I checked it out for documents, weapons, whatever. Finding nothing inside, we moved out and headed down the road to another large building where I saw an Iraqi flag flying. Nobody shot at us, so I had Sperry take the flag down for our Troop Commander.

For a patrol in a combat zone we weren't seeing much action; it was more like a Sunday drive through Detroit. The Carnivore was in the lead on the way back when the road suddenly exploded next to my Bradley. I turned in the hatch and looked at Geary, thinking he'd fired his main gun at something next to me. That was when I saw four guys with RPGs fire a volley at him.

"Contact!" I ducked down inside the hatch and slewed the turret to more or less the right direction and yelled at Soprano to return fire as I got on the radio. As I called in a contact report to Captain McCoy, two RPG rounds hit the Carnivore. The first one hit my rear two road wheels, half-mooning them. The second one hit the driver's hatch but, luckily for Sperry, didn't go off. Thank God they rarely remembered to take the pins out of those warheads.

Soprano fired a burst of 25 mm, then another one. "RPG team is down!" he called out to me.

"Then where the hell is all that fire coming from?" Bullets were rattling off the hulls of both Bradleys, and more RPGs went whizzing by. "Geary, you see where they are?"

"Negative, negative!"

Our comm back and forth between the two vehicles was going across the net. Broadhead had been my wingman all the way through the war, and we'd taken care of each other when things got hairy, so it was killing him that I was in a firestorm and he could do nothing but listen to his radio. So he did what any good cavalryman would do: he got on his horse and charged to my aid.

The Camel Toe came roaring up the road, engine wide open. Let me tell you, that's a hell of a sight—60 tons of angry steel. Broadhead fired on the move and took out two guys in a building to my left with one 120 mm HEAT round. Hell, that one round took out the whole building. His gunner, Sergeant Hull, fired the coax 7.62 at a soldier running away, then Broadhead's tank got hit by an RPG round in his right-rear sprocket, knocking off part of one tooth. More AK rounds poured at us from nearby buildings.

"Red 2, White 4, you want to stand and fight?" Broadhead asked me.

"Fight for what? There's nothing here," I replied. There was no objective to protect or seize, we just had a bunch of assholes shooting at us from inside and in between buildings. Considering that was the heaviest fighting we'd seen in days, we moved back and called in indirect fire on that position. Actually, having indirect fire was a luxury we were hardly used to, and I hated to waste the opportunity.

Our 155 mm Howitzers have a range of 20 miles or so. For the next hour those poor bastards who decided we looked like an easy target got brutalized by our battery. The following day there wasn't much left of the buildings, much less the Iraqi soldiers who'd been shooting at us. I did get the sight off an RPG launcher for the museum at Fort Stewart.

The next day Geary, McAdams, and I went out on a reconnaissance mission to find out how the insurgents were getting into our sector. They weren't getting past us, and they weren't coming in through Sergeant Williams's area, but somehow they were getting in.

While we were driving around, Geary spotted a pontoon bridge built over the river. It was low in the water and looked like it was getting ready to sink at any time.

We had an engineer with us, and I turned to him. "Hey, you think you could help it along any?" He just smiled.

The engineer went out onto the center of the bridge while we covered him and he planted C4. When it blew, the top panel off one barge came flying over to where we were and almost hit McAdams's Bradley. McAdams was a flying-debris magnet—if anything was going to hit a vehicle, it was going to be McAdams's Bradley. He'd been rammed by a car and rammed by a bus, and now flying bridge pieces were whinging off his turret.

Apparently pontoon bridges are tough to kill, because even after the C4 blew, most of the pontoons were still floating. Insurgents would still be able to get across on foot and into our sector. So Geary and I backed up. He engaged the pontoons with TOW missiles and I used 25 mm HE until we sank it.

Just as soon as we returned to our position the Squadron Commander called Captain McCoy, who then called us.

"Red 2, he needs you to do a reconnaissance on a pontoon bridge, because the Colonel wants to use that bridge as a supply route for our vehicles." He gave me the coordinates of the bridge we'd just blown up.

"Uh, yes sir, however, there's no bridge floating there, it's sunk."

"Negative, Red 2, you must be mistaken, the squadron's recon aircraft flew over it this morning and it was still intact. He wants to take a look at the bridge himself and wants us over there to pull security."

"Yes sir, roger that." As soon as I got off the radio, I yelled, "Geary!"

Geary and I hauled ass over to that bridge. He grabbed his spent TOW launcher tubes and threw them into the river, and I frantically kicked my 25 mm cases in after them. Luckily for us a sandstorm rolled in and the Commander called off his visit, because that bridge did not look like it had died a natural death.

Early in April more special ops guys came roaring into our command center. They had a lead on where Saddam Hussein was. They had solid, verified intelligence as to his current location, not just the area, but which building, which house in Sadr City he was inside. They wanted armor to back them up, and they wanted me and Geary on the mission.

We broke out the maps and started planning the operation. Geary and I and our crews were ready to roll, just waiting for the go-ahead. Our Squadron Commander, however, wasn't completely sold on it. He got the Division Commander involved. They didn't really like the plan we'd worked out, going up there and making the raid with just two Brads, because they didn't think there would be enough support. They also didn't quite believe the intel, and then there was the matter of who would be in charge of the mission.

By the time command made a decision on what was going to happen and who was going to go, two days had gone by and Saddam had moved.

We weren't seeing a lot of action, but I know there were Army and Cavalry units all in and around Baghdad, some of them getting shot up quite frequently. The first few days after we pushed into Baghdad we took on whatever Iraqi army forces decided to fight. The rest of the time we did patrols or sat at checkpoints and waited to get shot at.

Around April 13, we got an order for change of mission. Another unit's HQ had been hit by a missile, killing their Sergeant Major, and they needed us to move to the east side of Baghdad to help out in their sector. We rolled out and arrived in the area at dusk. The first thing we saw was tanks, a hell of a lot of tanks, sitting just like new in the palm trees. We assumed they'd been shot up with DU by the unit we were helping out, but the not knowing for sure made for a long night.

The next morning I went out on patrol with McAdams and Broadhead—two tanks and a Brad. We were able to determine that the tanks we'd seen when we arrived had been shot up, but we rolled up on three T-72s that were still intact. Broadhead shot two of them, one with a HEAT round and the other with the M1's DU round, an armor-piercing sabot like we had, only bigger. If we'd had any doubt before about the T-72's armor, that was when we knew that it was real crap: the sabot round went in the front deck and right out the back. He shot the other tank in the side and the HEAT round popped the turret right off it in one big fireball. I killed the third.

We couldn't find any soldiers who wanted to fight. All we found was an amazing amount of abandoned equipment, all of which we were told to destroy. It was just insane—Broadhead destroyed more than 100 missiles and two ammo dumps. McAdams blew up more than 25 troop trucks. Soprano had a field day and shot the snot out of two MiG-23 jets, three fuel trucks, two MTLBs (Russian-made tracked APCs), and one large ammo bunker.

After being in the Army for more than 15 years and never getting enough ammo to shoot, I found myself in an unexpected position—tired of hearing the guns firing, tired of seeing stuff on fire; just plain tired.

CHAPTER 18

THE MAFIA HIT

While ambushes and snipers were a daily threat, there were no more big battles in Baghdad. What we settled into couldn't exactly be called routine, not with people shooting at us and trying to blow us up, but we had our jobs and we did them. Our time in Baghdad was mostly spent doing two things: running patrols and manning checkpoints, which were usually at intersections or bridges.

A short time after we arrived in Baghdad we were sent to Fallujah. Fallujah is about 60 kilometers west of Baghdad, and it took us two hours to drive there. Two Iraqi armored brigades had capitulated, and we had to drive there and meet with their Commander so he could officially surrender to us. There wasn't a lot more to it than that; he was basically promising they would play nice, in hopes of staying alive. While we were there we drove around to several of their motor pools and shot up a lot of T-72s—not on a whim, but following orders. If the tanks were broken, they couldn't be used against our troops. Then we returned to Baghdad and went back to running patrols and manning checkpoints.

We had enough time on our hands to get into trouble. Thinking to destroy more enemy matériel, I shot a 20,000-gallon fuel tank with HE when I was downslope from it. In hindsight? Bad call. I had a flaming barrel of fuel chasing me. Kind of like being on the bottom of a volcano with lava rolling toward you.

About a month after first roaring into Baghdad, we had settled in and were parked along a main thoroughfare. In addition to my regular crew of Soprano, Sully, and Sperry, we had a terp—an interpreter. He'd been with us for a week or so and was a big help. He'd saved us from having to shoot a lot of stupid and obstinate people.

A block down, a Suburban-sized vehicle turned onto the road and started heading toward us. It was white, with orange bumpers front and back—a Fedayeen vehicle, the kind that we'd first encountered in As Samawah.

"I got it!" Sully yelled out, and jumped on his M240. He fired a burst at the vehicle, which veered off the road and crunched into a ditch. The driver staggered out, Sully hit him with another burst, and he went down.

"Nice," I said.

There was a pause, and then our interpreter asked us, "Why you hate taxis?"

Wait, what?

Our interpreter had seen us shoot up at least a dozen such vehicles and just never understood it, so he finally asked the question. And that was when we found out that white vehicles with orange bumpers were taxis, not Fedayeen vehicles. The entire U.S. military had spent the last month destroying every white vehicle with orange bumpers that dared appear on the streets of Baghdad.

There were probably 50 such vehicles on fire in the city at that very moment. It was a simple mistake with huge consequences, all because during the first engagement of the war, at As Samawah, the Fedayeen took taxis into battle.

A short time later we were somewhere else in Baghdad, outside an ice cream factory, taking it easy. We'd picked up a 60 mm mortar and a bunch of illuminating rounds from somewhere and thought it would be cool to shoot them over the top of the ice cream factory. Like fireworks.

We thought Bravo Troop was inside the factory, but they'd been replaced by the 82nd Airborne. The change had been announced over the squadron net, but we didn't hear it. I started launching lume (illumination) mortar rounds over the top of them, and we were laughing our asses off—because it was fun and the lumes looked cool. They are flares, but they have 60 mm steel tubes around them that fall off so the flares can ignite and the parachute deploys. I'm not a mortarman, so I didn't know that I wasn't putting enough charges on them to get them high enough. The troops in the 82nd were getting bombarded by the falling steel canisters, and the lume rounds were exploding just overhead and hitting in the middle of their position, but we didn't know because we couldn't see. We launched about 20 rounds but finally gave up because there was no reaction from Bravo. We thought they'd left.

So, 20 minutes later we were sitting in the back of the Carnivore with the ramp down, bullshitting. We had the mortar tube sitting next to the ramp while we cooked a sheep—it was an enemy sheep—over a tanker's bar and a couple of 25 mm ammo cans we'd stacked up. If we'd had beer it would have been perfect. Suddenly all these guys from the 82nd maneuvered up on us, weapons out, until they saw we were Cav.

"Hey, what's up, dudes?"

They weren't in a friendly mood. "Have you seen anybody launching mortars?"

"Ummmmm, no, why?"

"Because we just got a Humvee damaged, and they just shot the shit out of our base, dropping all these incendiary rounds on us."

"What? Really?" I was pushing the mortar tube underneath the ramp of my Bradley with my toe. "What? We haven't heard anything."

"Are you sure? It sounded like it was over here. Maybe you can look around with your thermals and help us out." My crew was sitting there, afraid to say anything. I looked around and saw a mortar box here and a couple of mortar rounds there. I wiggled my eyes at Sully and cocked my head. He got up, went over, and sat on the box. After some grumbling, the 82nd guys maneuvered on, none the wiser. We gathered all the mortar stuff we had, dug a hole, and buried it. Oops. At least nobody got hurt.

Here's something you never want to do: SA-12s, the large Russian surface-to-air missiles that launch off a rail? You never want to destroy them by shooting them with coax, because you can ignite the rocket motor. The rocket doesn't take off, it breaks apart, and the engine flips and rolls and chases you like a dog after a squirrel. I was busy screaming, "Back up, driver, back up *now*!" Those rocket motors? They're about the size of a Volkswagen. Once is all it takes to learn that lesson.

More helpful advice from Iraq? Cornering a howler monkey and trying to pet it is a bad idea. We gave asylum to one that had been a prisoner in a zoo. If you chase the howler monkey down (it takes a while), get him caught in a corner where he's got no place to go, and reach in to pet him, he will bite down on your finger and dig the claws of his back feet into your forearm while he's trying to rip your finger off. I saw it happen. Try explaining that injury to a medic.

I've never been to Africa, but I've killed a lion. I actually killed several rare animals in Iraq, because in addition to his zoos Saddam had game preserves where he kept a lot of endangered species. We rolled into his Water Palace, which is outside the airport, not long after reaching Baghdad, and you wouldn't believe the cash and gold guns we found lying around. I found a full-auto M16 manufactured by Colt, which I kept in the Bradley as backup. There was a large game preserve at that palace, and all the animals were dying. We didn't have the resources to take care of them and we couldn't let them go, not that a starving lion running through the streets of Baghdad wouldn't have been entertaining. We were under orders to kill them, and that's what we did, but we didn't let them go to waste. In case you're wondering, gazelle tastes just like deer.

Now that the high-intensity combat was pretty much over with, media started to show up. When we were at the Water Palace a news crew interviewed me. I don't even remember what they asked or what I said, but they sent the segment to *Good Morning America*. Saddam had several armored Mercedes limos at the palace, and we entertained ourselves by driving over them in the Carnivore.

Bored out of our minds one day, we put 100 pounds of explosive all over a Toyota pickup, just to see what would happen. Well, not just to see what would happen: the driver had tried to smuggle weapons through our checkpoint, and our experiment was intended as an object lesson for any other would-be smugglers. It was very entertaining. It left a large black spot on the ground, and nobody else tried to sneak anything through. I don't want it to seem as if we weren't doing anything but getting into trouble, but the majority of our days consisted of waiting for somebody to try to kill us, either while we were manning a checkpoint or while we were patrolling. That can get damn stressful, and we got very imaginative when it came time to blow off steam.

Early on, we rolled up on an abandoned air base while on patrol east of Baghdad. It was one of the Iraqis' main bomber bases. There were a lot of buildings and the tarmac was covered with jets and trucks, helicopters and BMPs. We were under orders to destroy any Iraqi army ordnance or matériel, and one thing we spotted was an Iraqi army water truck. We were destroying all the vehicles we could find, so we shot the water truck with 25 mm. It was like shooting a beer can with a .22, one of the most awesome things I've ever seen. When you shoot a full beer can, it explodes and sprays everywhere. Now imagine that beer can was big enough for Godzilla to take a drink—that's how huge the explosion of water was.

The area had already been cleared of enemy combatants, so we weren't in any immediate danger, and we decided to search the buildings.

We found an Iraqi air force bunker full of 2,000-pound bombs. Standing orders were to dispose of enemy ordnance, so we decided we were going to blow the place up. We wired one of the bombs with a block of C4, put a five-minute time fuse on it, and drove as fast as the Carnivore could handle, which at that time wasn't very fast at all. Did I mention that there were fifteen hundred 2,000-pound bombs in that building? Not the best decision I've ever made in my life.

We were maybe half a mile away when it went off. It looked like a nuke, with a mushroom cloud and everything. I could see a purple pressure wave chasing us, flipping over BMPs like they were nothing.

"Faster, drive faster!" I yelled.

Sully was struggling with the back hatch and got it latched right before the blast wave hit us. It nearly flipped us over, probably would have if we'd been turned sideways to it. It blew windows out 23 miles away. There were Hind-Ds (large Soviet helicopters) on the airfield, and it destroyed them. We couldn't even find their rotors. MiG jet fighters were rolled 200 yards across the runways. All the buildings on the base were leveled, leaving just one giant crater the size of a big high school.

"What did we do?" Sully asked in awe, looking up at the giant mushroom cloud. "What did we do?" The shock wave from the explosion gave him two black eyes.

Minutes later several U.S. helicopters cautiously flew into the area, radiation detectors going. Command honestly thought a nuclear bomb had gone off. We couldn't exactly claim ignorance of what had happened, because there we were, one lone Bradley limping slowly away from the blast zone. There was so much debris in the air that command grounded all the helicopters in the area for a while.

Sergeant Christner was the first person from our unit to come roaring up, wondering what had happened and hoping nobody was injured by whatever had happened. He looked past us, at the mushroom cloud now a mile high, and then back at me. "What the hell was that?"

Since we were officially following orders, we didn't get into too much trouble, but after that a Corps-wide, theater-wide order went out for all of Iraq: troops were not to destroy any more munitions.

I did the math, in case you're wondering: fifteen hundred 2,000-pound bombs equals 3 million pounds of high explosives.

For two weeks or so I was in charge of security at the largest oil refinery in Iraq. It was just south of Baghdad, but when I was there it was more of a fuel distribution point than it was a refinery. It was supposed to be running 24/7, but the plant manager was having some problems. If the truck drivers arrived in the afternoon, coming in from Turkey and Syria and all sorts of places, they were refusing to drop off their loads until the next morning, and it was really jamming things up. I told them that I was going to start shooting them if they didn't unload their fuel when they arrived, and apparently they believed me, because they started unloading their fuel at night. The plant was able to keep operating 24 hours a day, and the plant manager absolutely loved me.

They were also having problems with employees stealing fuel. Their drivers would stop on the road and sell the fuel to civilians for a higher price instead of going to where they were supposed to drop it off. I would send patrols up and down the highway, and if we found any of the fuel trucks we would grab the drivers, threaten them, and send them off to the supply point. We would run over civilians' fuel cans in the Bradley. I don't know if the employees were doing that third-world steal-everything-that-isn't-nailed-down crap before the war, but I put a stop to it while I was there. When the Army pulled us out of there and replaced us with another unit, that plant manager actually cried.

The doctors did surgery on me when we were in Baghdad, trying to remove the bullet in my leg. They weren't able to get it out, and I ended up with a big hole in my leg for a while. I couldn't walk on it for a while, and at the time Crazy Horse was doing a lot of house clearings. Sully found a wheelchair somewhere, and I sat in it with an M4. While the rest of the troop would be kicking in the front door, Sully would push me in the wheelchair over to one side and say, "I think you can get a good shot at anybody coming out the back from over here, Sergeant Jay." It was funny as hell.

The 4th Infantry Division was up north of us in Balad, and they were getting hammered. They'd just arrived in Iraq and were trying a gentler, hearts-and-minds approach to combat or something, and it wasn't working. Not only were they getting beat up, they were hardly inflicting any casualties on the enemy. So command sent us up there.

Balad is about 90 kilometers northwest of Baghdad along the Tigris River. Balad is in the heart of the "Sunni Triangle," but most of its population is Shiite. In 1982, Balad hosted an assassination attempt on Saddam, and he came down hard on them. The Republican Guard killed hundreds, if not thousands, and Saddam installed Ba'ath Party loyalists in local government. We were based out of Balad Air Base and inherited a new Commanding Officer, Colonel Henry. The Colonel flat out said he didn't believe that we'd killed all the people we said we'd killed and ordered us to bring back the bodies the next time we were in an engagement. Our Troop Commander, Captain Brett Bair, thought that was a completely fucked-up order, and none of us had ever heard of such a thing—you counted bodies, you didn't bring them back.

We were on our first patrol in the area late one night at full blackout, and I was enjoying the scenery through the night vision. There were groves of date palms and vineyards, plus lots of canals and small villas. Pretty, yes, and every one of them a potential hiding place for insurgents. It was maybe 2 A.M. when Geary spotted some dismounts.

"Sir," he came over the radio, "I got people up here on the berm behind the irrigation canal. I got weapons. There's at least twenty of the fuckers."

Everybody slewed their turrets in that direction and we spotted them. There were about 15 or 20 of them on a small berm about 200 yards away. Through the thermal sight I could see they were dressed in typical Fedayeen attire: baggy pants, head scarves, and belts of ammo. They always had belts of ammo draped over their shoulders, whether there was a machine gun around to use it or not—I'm pretty sure they thought it made them look cool. They also had AKs and other weapons, and they were looking around. They could hear us, but they couldn't see us.

"Contact right!" Captain Bair called over the radio. We were waiting for the order to fire, but the captain had something a little more fun in mind. At his signal, everybody pivot-steered right and charged the dismounts, firing everything they had. Two whole scout platoons, 13 Bradleys in all, in line, firing 25 mm HE and coax at two dozen Fedayeen or insurgents or whoever they were. They never knew what hit them.

Standing in the hatch, I had a great time shooting on full auto the M16 I'd taken from Saddam's palace. I looked down inside the turret and saw that the Lieutenant was scanning back and forth inside the turret, holding the trigger down on the coax like he was shooting shit, but it was still on Safe. He heard my gun going off and thought he was shooting. I had to arm the gun for him to shoot, so he didn't get any guys when it first began.

Williams had a malfunction with the Casanova's main gun and announced over the net, "Switching to coax." A few seconds later he had a coax malfunction, and announced, "Switching to TOW."

He fired one TOW missile, which hit in the middle of the insurgents, throwing bodies everywhere. Then he fired another one. We threw enough ordnance downrange to dispirit an Iraqi battalion, which means it was complete overkill for two dozen dismounts. The engagement lasted a lot longer than it should have, because we kept pounding them.

The Iraqis had been positioned on a berm on the far side of a canal. When we finally stopped shooting—and were confident Williams was done launching missiles—all we could see through the thermals were a bunch of hotspots on the ground. As we arrived at the canal we turned on our headlights, dismounted, and searched for survivors—and bodies for the Colonel. I spotted someone still moving with an AK and shot him a couple of times. When we had finished clearing the area, Sully went looking for a body bag.

We'd never needed one before, so it took him a while to find it, but he finally brought out the one bag we had on board. Along with guys from a few other crews, we lifted a body into the bag and added as many assorted body parts as could fit. We ended up with parts from about seven guys in that bag, two left legs, five or six hands. It looked like Dr. Frankenstein's bag when we were done. We completely filled that bag, and it took about six of us to lift it onto the hood of my Bradley, where we strapped it down.

Once inside the base we rolled up to the squadron headquarters and I headed inside to track down the Duty Officer, who was Captain Kim. I knew Colonel Henry would already be in bed, but I needed to find out what to do with the body bag.

"I've got the bodies that the Colonel wanted. What should I do with them?"

Kim followed me out and took a look at the body bag. "You've got to take them to the morgue," he told me.

I said, "Look, I've been up for three fucking days, I'm not going to wherever the morgue is. You wanted the fucking bodies, they're here."

He just looked at me, said, "Take them to the morgue."

"Where the hell is it?" I had no idea.

"You go find it," he told me, and headed back inside. So I called the Troop Commander and told him the situation.

"Sir, what should I do?"

Captain Bair was more than a little pissed at us having to bring back bodies to prove we weren't inflating our BDA to begin with, and riding around with a body bag strapped to your hood doesn't do anything for troop morale. "Dump 'em," he told me.

"Roger that," I told him. I walked around to the front of the

Bradley and cut the straps, and the body bag fell right onto the steps of squadron headquarters. We drove over to our area and parked, and I lay right down and went to sleep because we had been up and moving for days. I lay down out in the open, because it was a zillion degrees out, and it seemed like only a few minutes later when I felt someone kicking my boot.

"Get up, Crazy Jay."

I cracked my eyes to see Sergeant Major Brahain, the Sergeant Major for the squadron, standing over me. He was just shaking his head. I sat up and tried to clear my head.

"Crazy Jay. Crazy, Crazy Jay. We *gotta* talk, Crazy Jay." He had a very interesting and entertaining speech pattern.

I said, "Hey, Sergeant Major, how's it going?"

He said, "Crazy Jay, y'all killed some people last night."

"Yeah, Sergeant Major, we killed a few people."

He said, "You put 'em in a bag."

"Yeah, Sergeant Major?"

"Crazy Jay. You done a lot for this squadron, you've killed lots of people, but you *cain't* be dropping dead guys off on the steps of squadron headquarters like it's a mafia hit. We just *cain't* have that happen. Ya understand what I'm saying, Crazy Jay?"

"I'm sorry, Sergeant Major, I was tired."

"I know, Crazy Jay, I know, but it cain't happen again! What *possessed* you to put dead people on my steps?"

I said, "Sergeant Major, I didn't want them here," indicating the Carnivore.

He looked at me for a while, then said, "That's a good damn answer. But I'm doing everything I can to keep the Colonel from court-martialing you."

Captain Bair came up then. "Sergeant Major, that was my idea. I had him do it."

The Sergeant Major looked at the Captain, then at me, and said, "Crazy Jay, you've got evabody pullin for ya, but you just cain't do that shit. You *gotta* get your shit together and think about what you're doing. Damn!" And he walked off. He was one hell of a good Sergeant Major.

The Commander did tell me to do it. He told me to drop them off on the steps of headquarters because the asshole Colonel wanted to see some fucking bodies. I just probably shouldn't have taken that order so literally.

That firefight and the body bag incident were written up by a reporter we had embedded with us at the time, Rita Leistner. She was a freelancer who had snuck into Iraq through Turkey and met up with the Cav while we were in Baghdad. She originally showed up as a photojournalist with the *Daily Mail* of London. She rode up to Balad with Crazy Horse and was in the back of Geary's Circus Freaks during the firefight after which we filled up the body bag. She liked the idea of having armor between her and the bad guys, and we liked her Iridium satellite phone, which we could use to call home. Her article on Crazy Horse, "The Burning Tip of the Spear," appeared in *The Walrus,* a Canadian magazine in early 2004. She thought Sully looked so young and innocent, she called him "Little Cow Eyes." Soprano actually ended up on the cover of the magazine, shirtless.*

Crazy Horse had gone into Iraq from Kuwait, and we didn't have much but the uniforms on our backs. Our mail hardly ever caught up with us, and we got shit for care packages. The 4th Infantry Division, on the other hand, came into Iraq straight from Germany, and they had their mail chain set up properly. A day or

---

* "The Burning Tip of the Spear," by Rita Leistner. *The Walrus,* February/March 2004.

two after the body bag incident I had a cute medic from the 4th ID walk up to me when I was sitting on the back of the Carnivore.

She said, "Sergeant Johnson, are you the one they call Crazy Jay?"

"Yes, ma'am," I told her. And she gave me a box.

The box was full of CDs, stuffed animals, and all sorts of candy, toothbrushes, toothpaste, and shaving cream and razors, which I instantly kicked underneath the ramp—I hadn't shaved in three months and wasn't about to start. Apparently I created a bit of a legend with the body bag stunt, and the 4th ID was very appreciative. They kept coming up to our guys and handing out extra candy and goodies from their care packages.

CHAPTER 19

STAGE 3

For five days in June, command had us guarding one end of a bridge over the Tigris in Balad. We were part of Operation Peninsula Strike, the biggest operation in the area since the fall of Tikrit in April. Our job was to check the cars for any weapons or large sums of cash, which might be used to support the guerrillas.

We had a small abandoned schoolhouse at our end of the bridge. The 82nd Airborne had the other end, and they were not happy. We'd been driving Bradleys everywhere, but they'd had to walk or ride like cattle in the back of deuce-and-a-halfs, in temperatures hotter than the sun. Those dudes hated everybody. People who came over to us from that side of the river were beat black and blue, and they had boot marks on their cars.

You'd think that with a war going on and armed, annoyed soldiers running roadblocks, the people who needed to cross the bridge would be polite and respectful. Shit.

Guys would curse us, spit at us, try to drive past us, refuse to get out of their cars, you name it. We couldn't hurt them, and we didn't have a jail to hold them, so we put them in time-out. That's what we called it. We'd make them stand in the corner, sit like the iron chair with their knees bent and back against the wall, put a book on their head and make them stand like that, or make them stand with their arms out and their palms up. That's all we could do to them, so we were doing stupid high school shit. For a very short while I gave the ones with bad attitudes shovels and sent them out back to dig holes, because that was how I always punished my crew. The first time I walked back there to watch them dig I saw the Iraqis crying and mumbling in Arabic as they worked the shovels.

"Why the fuck are these guys crying?" I asked someone.

I was told, "They think you're going to kill them and bury them. That's what Saddam did. They think they're digging their own graves."

Oops. Okay, lesson learned—no more digging holes for the Iraqis as punishment, although it turned out to be a pretty damned effective time-out technique. Those guys were damned polite after that.

One day a car came across the bridge with two drunk guys in it, one of whom kept saying, "I love Saddam!"

Forest Geary was working as my wingman that day. It was about 130 degrees in the shade, and Geary had about had his fill of idiots for the rest of his life. "Really, asshole? You love Saddam?"

The guy spit at Geary, so without thinking he reached into the car and grabbed the guy and shook him, and said, "Who do you love now, bitch?"

The guy said, "I love Saddam" again, and tried to roll the window up on Geary. He caught Geary's hand in the car and the car started moving forward. Oh fuck—so we rammed the car with the Carnivore, and when I say rammed it I mean we ran over the engine compartment.

Geary pulled the guy out of the car. He dragged him to the side of the road, pinned him down, and started hitting him. I pulled Geary off him and said, "That's enough! That's enough. You can only hit him so many times after he punks you out."

"He didn't punk me out! I'm punking him out!" Geary was still screaming at the guy, so we separated them and moved the guy down to a little schoolhouse. We were going to hold him in time-out. Geary probably could have used a time-out, too.

We called the medics to come over and look at the guy. All he'd suffered were a few bruises. There weren't any serious injuries because Geary is just a little wiry guy, and his punch was like a girl slap—or at least that's what I told Geary all the time. We loved to egg each other on.

After the medics looked him over, the guy was sitting at one of the wooden desks in the schoolhouse. He kept giving me this look of utter contempt. I said, "Why are you looking at me like that?"

He said in plain English, "Because you come over to my country and kill my fellow men because of our leadership. I hope you all die."

I walked over to him and said, "You hope *I* die?"

"Yes."

So I walked over and grabbed the front of his shirt and lifted him out of the chair. "Saddam's been torturing and executing people for thirty years, and you hate *me*?" Okay, maybe Geary wasn't the only person with a short fuse. The fact that it was so hot that it felt like our brains were being stewed in our skulls probably didn't help my temper any.

"Yes. I hate you all."

I threw him back in the chair and said, "You can stand up and do something about it. You don't have to sit there and take it." I wasn't going to punch him flat out, but if he took a swing first— hell, maybe I needed a time-out, too, or maybe it was just the heat.

There was an ice factory in Balad, and when we arrived the Iraqis were selling blocks of ice for 50 cents. After the Americans showed up, they decided they weren't making enough money and started price gouging. Blocks of ice went from 50 cents up to 5 dollars.

The heat was still insane, and Sergeant Wearnes got seriously pissed. He drove his Bradley up to the ice factory and blocked the door. He pulled a one-man blockade on the factory and sat there until all of their ice sitting on the trucks melted. He sat there in his Bradley until he came to an agreement with the guy running the factory—Americans got their ice blocks for 50 cents, and Wearnes got his for free.

The blocks of ice were three feet long. The guys laid on them, on their backs and their bellies, and it wasn't long before some, er, smartasses were sitting bare-assed naked on them. The blocks had three-inch holes running through the middle of them so they could be carried on poles, so you know what happened next.

"Bet you can't stick your dick in it!" someone shouted. Soprano took that bet and lasted seven minutes. The female reporter, Rita Leistner, was still with us, and she monitored the action very closely.

Since we'd been told to look out for expensive vehicles, we noticed when a new van rolled up to our checkpoint, driven by a guy who didn't necessarily look like he could afford a new van.

"Where'd you get the van?" I asked him. "You steal it?"

"No!" he told me. "George Bush give me."

"All right, get out."

I put him in time-out until he decided to start answering questions. He was as miserable in the heat as we were. We pulled the van over to the side, and in doing so we discovered something magical—the van had a working air conditioner. Trust me, you don't appreciate air-conditioning until you're wearing a combat load in triple-digit heat.

My guys rotated through the van in five-minute shifts until the gas ran out, then we made the guy walk back home. He was much more polite when he returned the next day with a gas can.

Every day outside our camp in Balad an Iraqi we called "Hamburger Guy" would show up and cook us some damn good hamburgers. I have no idea what was in them, probably sheep, but they tasted good. He would thin-slice cucumbers and do what he could to make them taste like pickles. Hamburger Guy really did a good job with what he had to work with. His food was one of the few things about being stuck in Balad that didn't suck.

One night Crazy Horse did a raid on a suspected insurgent compound and hit the jackpot—there were all sorts of guys in the house. We brought them back to our base and put them in a make-shift jail, and our intelligence people started talking to them one at a time, trying to get somebody to talk. That day, Hamburger Guy didn't show up. He didn't show up the next day either. So we went to where the prisoners were being kept.

"All right, which one of you bastards killed our Hamburger Guy?" we asked them. "We know you did it. You didn't like that he made food for us, right? So you killed him. You better tell us now, because if we find out . . ."

The colorful descriptions of hellfire and damnation continued. Finally, one of the prisoners raised his hand.

"You killed Hamburger Guy?"

"Uh, no, I . . . I am Hamburger Guy." We squinted at him. Son of a . . .

So we dragged him out of there. "I'm not an insurgent," he told us. "I love America. I love Americans. I was just sleeping there. I'm an honest businessman, just trying to make money."

Maybe he was lying, maybe he wasn't. The country was full of people who lied to us and tried to kill us, but this guy had something they didn't. He had a valuable skill set. He could cook.

"If we keep you locked up, you're going to get sent down to Baghdad and interrogated, and I don't know when you're going to get home," I told him. "They may send you to Abu Ghraib. If we let you go, you need to prove to us we didn't make a mistake."

So we got half-price hamburgers for the rest of the time we were stationed in Balad.

We were out one day on patrol, my head and shoulders sticking out of the hatch as usual, when I got shot by a sniper.

The bullet didn't hit me; it actually hit my vest and cut across the front of it from right to left, going in and out of the vest about seven times. The impact of the bullet—a 7.62x54R sniper round, equivalent to a .30-06—yanked my vest around, and I got a laceration on my neck.

The laceration wasn't a big deal as injuries go, but my neck started to swell up. The medic, Sergeant Cardone, was concerned because the laceration was near my jugular, so he sent me down to BIAP (Baghdad International Airport) for the doctors to look at it.

By the time I got in to see the doctors, my neck was purple and as big around as my head. I'm no doctor, but I didn't think that was good. They started asking me questions to try to figure out what was causing the swelling, assuming it was a massive infection. When the doctors heard that I still had a piece of a bullet in my leg and shrapnel in my arms and shoulders, they thought I had gangrene. They immediately put me on massive antibiotics and a lot of pain medicine and threw me on a big medevac. I officially left Iraq on August 26, 2003, and was transported straight to Walter Reed Army Medical Center in Washington, D.C.

I was in a lot of pain and had swollen glands all over my body. None of the antibiotics they were giving me were working, and doctor after doctor was asking me questions to try and figure out exactly what the problem was while they waited on the results of all the blood work. One day a doctor came into my room and informed me, "You don't have gangrene, you've got Stage Three cancer."

That's exactly how they do it, too. No "Hey, how you feelin', I've got some bad news for you" or "Um, do you have anybody you can call to be here with you?" before they break the news to you, they just walk up and say, "You've got Stage Three cancer, which means you're probably going to die. We give you a one in four chance of living. But, hey, it could be worse, it could be Stage Four." Fucking Army.

Further work on their part revealed that it was Hodgkin's lymphoma. After that, Army personnel from Aberdeen Proving Ground and Redstone Arsenal came to my room and started asking me all sorts of directed questions.

"Were you wearing your MOPP 4 gear while firing DU rounds in the Bradley's main gun?"

"Hell no. You know how hot that suit is? Plus, there's no room to move around when you're wearing it, and you can't see for shit with the mask on."

"Well, were you at least wearing the mask?"

"No, I told you, you can't see for shit with the NBC mask on."

"Sergeant, when you were engaging the enemy, was your Bradley buttoned up? All hatches and vents closed?"

"Seriously? No. I had my head and shoulders sticking out of the Commander's hatch most of the time."

"How many depleted uranium rounds did you actually fire while your head was outside of the hatch?"

I had to think about that one. "Maybe seven thousand."

The questions went round and round. *Did I have my NBC suit on, why not, you're supposed to have your NBC mask and protective gloves on when you handle that ammo,* on and on and on. When you shoot DU ammo, you're supposed to be fully closed up in the vehicle, with the mask on. That's a great theory, but it doesn't work so well when applied to the real world. Sort of like communism.

They kept trying to rule out the type of lymphoma with which I was eventually diagnosed, because doctors only ever saw that particular kind in guys who had worked in power plants and underneath power lines for 50 years. It's a radiation cancer, which means the only way you can get it is by exposure to radiation.

Depleted uranium is not radioactive. When you fire it, however, it's not depleted anymore; it becomes reactive from superheating. The Bradley's 25 mm main gun barrel generates particulate matter every time you fire a round. I was standing in the open Commander's hatch the whole time, getting the blowback from every round.

I wasn't joking about the one in four chance. I was given a 25 percent chance to live. They immediately put me on some sort of super-chemotherapy, but the only thing it did was make me wish I was dead. If you've never been through chemo, it's horrible. Basically, what it does is kill all your blood cells to try to get rid of the bad ones, so it takes you down until you have almost nothing left. You're too sick to eat. You're throwing up all the time. They give you shots of adrenaline, which are supposed to give you the energy to move around but don't. You're hyped up, heart racing, but you can't do anything. It's a horrible, horrible feeling, and I went through it alone.

Why alone? Amy had a job in Florida and was taking care of Jaycob with his cerebral palsy, and Max was still little, so she couldn't come visit me in Walter Reed. I was all by myself. Being alone in a situation like that was life changing. I guess it changed my persona in regards to how I look at life and how I accept things.

I'm a stocky guy, and that chemo got me down to 120 pounds. I looked dead. I think Amy didn't want to come up because she couldn't bear to look at me, I was in such bad shape.

At that point, in late 2003, Crazy Horse Troop was still in Iraq, and I hadn't had any contact with anybody in the unit. Command sent a few guys stateside to meet the Secretary of Defense at some fancy ball, since our unit had seen so much action. Broadhead was one of the guys who came back over, so he was one of the people who tracked me down and started motherfucking me, as in "Motherfucker, I can't believe you wrote that shit like you were the only one there."

I didn't know what the hell he was talking about, but I soon found out—the October 2003 issue of *Soldier of Fortune* magazine was on newsstands, and in it was an article about the battle of As Samawah that appeared to have been written by me. Broadhead was pissed because it seemed that in the article I was trying to take credit for most of the killing that happened at As Samawah, as if no one else had been there. Somebody at Walter Reed tracked down a copy of the magazine for me so I could figure out exactly what was going on. I hadn't written anything: I was too busy trying not to die from cancer.

The article, entitled "Bradley," was listed on the magazine's table of contents as being written by Anonymous, but my name was on the first page of the article. It was mostly a quick run-through of the events at As Samawah and immediately after, told solely from my point of view, with hardly a mention of any other troop. *SOF* wrote that the piece *passed through so many hands before it reached us, we have been yet unable to identify its author other than by name and rank as given. With the action recorded as taking place at Al Samawah, one might attempt to make assumptions regarding which American unit was involved, but we do not know for certain. In fact, we have been yet unable to further document this fragment of combat history other than by its own face. So we must leave the reader with a caveat: If this story is not true in every regard, it should be. If any reader has a POC (point of contact) for Staff Sergeant Johnson, we would appreciate it.*

[And there, right before the story itself, like a signature, was my name and rank.]

STAFF SERGEANT DILLARD J. JOHNSON, 19D

INCIDENT OF 23 MARCH 2003.*

A second quick read-through of the story was enough for me to figure out where and who it had come from, since I knew I hadn't written it. When Crazy Horse was still in Baghdad, high-ranking Army officers came through and interviewed everybody as to what we'd seen and done at As Samawah and afterward. These interviews weren't restricted to our unit, but were part of a huge effort to document the early days of the war. They were the basis for the book *On Point: The United States Army in Operation Iraqi Freedom,* the official Army narrative of the first five weeks or so of combat in Iraq.

---

* *Soldier of Fortune,* October 2003, p. 38.

As near as I could remember, the *Soldier of Fortune* story came straight from my interviews with those officers. In fact, several sections of the October 2003 article ostensibly written by me can be found in *On Point*, word for word.* One of the officers who interviewed me and the rest of Crazy Horse—we believe it was a lieutenant colonel or major—thought it was such a great story that he contacted *Soldier of Fortune* and passed along part of the report.

Soldier of Fortune of course jumped on it, because it *was* a great story. What was published, however, made it seem like I was taking credit for a lot of stuff I didn't do. I didn't mention other soldiers during the interviews because the officers were talking to all of us, and we were each telling our individual stories. While nothing in what *Soldier of Fortune* published was untrue, it was only a small part of the story and made me seem like a conceited asshole.

The story was a big success for *Soldier of Fortune* because it got them a lot of attention, both good and bad. A lot of people wrote into the magazine reaming them out for printing such obvious fiction. I tracked down the senior editor at the time, Don McLean, and asked him to print a retraction.

"Look," I told him, "you don't have it right. I didn't do it all myself, there were a bunch of people over there fighting and they need recognition."

"Sorry, the story stands as printed. We're not going to print a retraction. We'd be happy to print your side of the story, though."

Well, shit.

The first thing I did was contact the Public Affairs Office at Fort Stewart and talk to the Lieutenant there. He didn't see a

---

*On Point: The United States Army in Operation Iraqi Freedom, by Col. Gregory Fontenot, U.S. Army, Retired; LTC E. J. Degen, U.S. Army; and LTC David Tohn, U.S. Army. Office of the Chief of Staff, U.S. Army (2004), pp. 129–30.

problem with me setting things straight. The PAO looked at and approved everything I eventually wrote before it went out to the magazine. I couldn't eat or sleep and was too weak to do anything physical—I had nothing but time on my hands, which worked out well, because I am not a fast writer. The doctors couldn't give me any hopeful news, so maybe it was good that I found something with which to occupy myself. What I wrote for *Soldier of Fortune* was hugely long, but I did my best to mention everybody who was over there, everyone who played a part, and set the record straight. Crazy Horse was just starting to come back from Iraq at that time, and I wanted to give them their due. The magazine ended up running what I wrote for them as a six-part story, starting in the January 2004 issue and running through the June 2004 issue. A few guys from the unit, including John Williams, provided photos for me to submit with the articles.

So that was how I, suffering from cancer, a Kentucky kid with horrible dyslexia, ended up writing a six-part, 18,000-word feature for *Soldier of Fortune* magazine. To tell you the truth, Broadhead is still pissed at me about that. He saved my life more times than I can count, and I did the same for him, but when we weren't getting shot at, for some reason we just didn't get along. The whole *SOF* thing really put a nail in that coffin.

I don't know how long I underwent chemo. Four months, six months—forever. That was such a dark and lonely time that I'm just sad when I think back to the place I was at. It was so bad that I can't even say "At least it's better now," because when I do think about how things were it drags me down. It's shitty that it happened, but it happened, and that's all there is to that. Could I, should I, blame the military for the DU ammo? Hell, that ammo did a much better job saving my life than it did trying to end it. By the way, the military doctors would never come out and confirm it was the DU ammo that gave me cancer. Officially it is "Cause: unknown." I got another Purple Heart, number three, from the round hitting me in the vest and cutting my neck, so there's that.

Between the chemo and the super-chemo and the ultra-mega-chemo and surgery, eventually the doctors got the cancer under control. As I write this it is in remission. Hopefully it's still in remission when you're reading this, but there are no guarantees in life.

CHAPTER 20

EXCHANGING RPGS
FOR IEDS

Stage 3 cancer? Three Purple Hearts including part of a bullet still in my leg? That was more than enough to earn me a medical discharge, and who could have blamed me? At that point I'd been in the Army for 18 years, had seen more than my share of combat, and had a few medals to show for it. But, as I wrote before, ever since I was a little boy, I wanted to be a platoon sergeant. I wasn't going anywhere.

With the party still going on in Iraq, I knew it was only a matter of time before Crazy Horse went back over. In one of the *Soldier of Fortune* articles I had mentioned how I had dropped my Gerber Multi-Plier into a canal, conveniently forgetting to mention I had originally commandeered it from Soprano at As Samawah when I was trying to fix the matching unit for the radio. I ended up in contact with Mark Schindel at Gerber Legendary Blades, who hooked

up the whole unit with Gerber gear, including preproduction pro-
totypes of one of their new fixed-blade knives, the LMF II.

"We've got this knife you might be interested in," Mark told
me. "We haven't got it out yet, but we'll send you fifteen or twenty
and you guys see if you can break it. See what you can do with it."

"You got it," I told him.

Thanks to the articles, other companies tracked me down and
provided more gear for Crazy Horse, including Blackhawk and
Bushnell. Bushnell gave us several mil-dot Elite 4200 rifle scopes
and laser range finders, which would later come in very handy.

Things overseas weren't quite going the way the military had
expected, and the unrelentingly negative and biased news cover-
age wasn't making things any better for anyone. I wasn't surprised
when we got the word that we would be heading back to Iraq
sooner rather than later.

Crazy Horse Troop returned to Iraq in January 2005. I arrived
on January 22 and went right back to work. Since I'd been there
last, the situation had changed somewhat. The ground war with
the Iraqi army was long over, but the guerrilla and insurgent at-
tacks, the IEDs, and the bombings presented real and continuing
problems.

The nightly news in America was full of car bombs and snipings, all the bad things. They ignored all the good things the U.S.
military was doing with the power grid and the education system;
in fact, the U.S. news media seemed to forget that we were the good
guys. Some of them were still on the "no one can find any weapons of mass destruction" rant, conveniently forgetting that Saddam
proved to the world he had them when he used them on the Kurds,
long before the United States sent troops to the region. Hell, that's
how *Chemical* Ali got his nickname.

Back in Iraq, I was quick to see that most reporters hardly ever stepped outside of the Green Zone. Their news reports were videos after the fact, often provided by Al Jazeera, while they hid behind the fences, protected by the very military they despised. Did that make them willing stooges or simply propagandists?

I'd been to Iraq before and seen more combat than most combat vets. While Crazy Horse was heading back in-country with a number of experienced troops, we had a lot of fresh young faces as well. As the combat-seasoned veterans, it was our job to teach the new recruits and do as good a job as we could getting all of them back home in one piece. I was cocky and conceited before I'd gotten a Silver Star and three Purple Hearts, and beaten cancer, so I just knew that I was going to be better than the last guy. I can remember telling my soldiers how we were going to find all the IEDs and get the sons of bitches who had emplaced them. The battle-hardened Platoon Sergeant I was replacing wasn't impressed by my cockiness and told me not to worry about finding the IEDs—they would find us. No truer words have ever been spoken.

As the conflict had evolved into more of a guerrilla affair, the spec-ops and small-unit types were in their element—that was what they lived for. However, the last thing command wanted was another *Black Hawk Down* scenario, so for the first six months back in-country Crazy Horse was detailed to be the armor package for Joint Special Operations Command (JSOC) and Task Force 6-26. That was our Brigade Commander's decision. We were based out of Al Asad Air Base, which was run by the Marines. I wish I could tell you we were doing all sorts of high-speed ninja stuff with those elite troops, but the fact of the matter is we spent six months getting shot at and blown up, and even then most of the time it was boring. We hardly got to shoot at anybody, but even so I can't write about anything we did in any detail.

For the first part of my tour I was back in a Bradley, which I christened Carnivore II. Yeah, I know, not very creative—but why argue with success? We ended up going on 45 combat missions in Carnivore II and traveling over 25,000 miles, even though we later transitioned to up-armored Humvees, so it earned the name.

For one TF 6-26 mission we were outside of Fallujah in the town of Haditha. The mission was a cordon and search, with the armor doing the cordon part and the spec-ops guys doing the search. I had to cut down the side of a riverbank to cross over to an alley, and the riverbank gave out behind me. There was no way for me to go back; I had to go forward, but I found myself looking at an alley full of cars. The street was three cars wide, so with cars parked bumper to bumper on either side there was just barely enough room for someone to drive their car through. A car had plenty of room. My Bradley didn't.

I literally crushed 20 cars driving down the street. Cars on both sides of the road, all the way down the road, car alarms going off, the Iraqis standing there waving their arms at me and yelling the Arabic equivalent of "What the fuck?" I made canoes out of those cars, crushed them like bugs. Even though I felt bad that it happened, that was some funny shit.

I got my ass chewed by the Commander. "Why did you do that? What in God's name possessed you to do something so stupid? Do you have any idea what kind of public relations disaster I'm dealing with?" And so on. I explained that I had no choice. With the riverbank collapsing behind me, it was either go forward through the parked cars or abandon my vehicle. I couldn't do that, because the task force guys were in the middle of a major assault and I had to support them. Besides, there was no way I was giving up my vehicle. Letting it sit there would be no different from handing it over to the enemy.

The raid was a big success. They collected so many prisoners that they needed to use two Bradleys to take them back for questioning. We had them in the hell hole (the narrow slot behind the driver's seat), sitting on the turret floor, or standing up in the back of the Brad. When we raised the ramp it mashed them in so tightly they couldn't move. We had at least 20 people in the Carnivore II, which is designed to fit 7.

In early April 2005, we were working an escort mission for TF 6-26. Staff Sergeant David Miller was in the lead Bradley and I was at the rear, with four thin-skinned vehicles between us. We'd been out driving back and forth in 100-plus-degree heat for the better part of 12 hours, and we were burned out. With less than two miles left to base and no enemy contact, Miller and I rolled ahead of the other vehicles in our Bradleys so we could take out any threat that might lie ahead. It was almost 6 P.M. and I was glad my day was almost over.

I had a different crew in my Bradley this tour. Sergeant Sean Cochran was my gunner, and he was feeling a bit like a Thanksgiving turkey in the heat. He was a good guy and had the perfect build for riding around in armor all day—he was even shorter than me.

"Sergeant Jay, okay if I stand up and get some air? Aren't we about back?"

"Yeah, go ahead."

No sooner had I spoken than everything went black. The explosion was huge and rocked the whole Bradley. When the smoke from the IED cleared, I was happy to see we were still in one piece.

"Contact right!" Cochran yelled out. "Got a guy running into a building."

I tried to call Miller on the radio but got nothing.

"Shoot that guy!" I yelled at Cochran. There was no response, so I looked down into the turret to see what was taking him so long to fire. Smoke was coming out of the turret floor; apparently we weren't as undamaged as I'd thought. With the turret power out (which explained why Miller didn't answer: the radio was out with the power), Cochran was doing just as he had been trained, putting the 25 mm gun into manual operation.

Miller had been several hundred yards ahead of us but had heard the IED go off. As he was turning around to come help us out, Cochran, using the hand crank, fired half a dozen 25 mm HE rounds into the building after the fleeing insurgent.

With the thin-skinned vehicles we were escorting coming up fast, we couldn't press the attack. I shouted to Miller to call them and warn them of the danger ahead. While we were busy trying to get the Carnivore II back up, he found a bypass for the vehicles we were escorting.

We weren't having a lot of luck getting our power back up. Miller positioned his Bradley between the IED site and the bypass route, and he and his gunner, Staff Sergeant Jared Kennedy, kept overwatch on us until we could effect a repair. We finally realized we couldn't handle the job ourselves and put out a call for help. With the assistance of some very talented Marines, I had my Bradley up and running in no time at all. *Semper fi.*

That's how I got Purple Heart number four: flying debris from an IED. If it hadn't been for the Blackhawk tactical goggles I was wearing, I would have lost my eyesight. The goggles took most of the blast, saving my eyes, and all I suffered was a small cut on my face. I also had on body armor and Blackhawk's light assault gloves, and it's a good thing, because I got peppered with debris and shell fragments. The body armor took most of the shell fragments, but three pieces of metal went into my right wrist. The Blackhawk gloves did a damn good job of protecting my hands. We later found out that the IED was a hot-wired 155 mm artillery round, which packs a lot of explosive. That was the first but not the biggest or the last IED that Carnivore II would encounter. In my first tour it was RPGs; in the second, IEDs.

One afternoon we were coming back from a mission with TF 6-26 and rolled over a bridge to see a Humvee lighting a truck up with its roof gun. We slowed down to see what was happening, and as we got closer we saw that the Humvee was part of a convoy— one of our convoys, in fact. They were the support battalion for the 3rd ID.

Passing a convoy was just about number one on the list of ways to get guns pointed at you in Iraq at that time. Apparently when the truck was approaching, the troopers in the convoy had waved it off and tried to flag it away, but nothing was working. The truck started rolling past the convoy, and nothing the troopers were doing could get the driver to stop or slow down. At about the time the truck was getting ready to pass the lead vehicle in the convoy, somebody spotted what looked like an IED in the road ahead. Because the truck was ignoring all of their attempts to signal it, the Commander told the Humvee gunner to engage.

The vehicle was full of nothing but kids. Not one of them was over the age of fifteen, and they shot it with a .50-cal machine gun.

I immediately blocked the road so other traffic wouldn't get in the way, called squadron for assistance, and started doing first aid on anybody left alive. A lot of them were dead. I've seen horrible things, but that was just about the worst.

The Army did a full investigation to find out exactly what happened. They walked through everything, talked to witnesses, put the entire incident back together. Just prior to that incident two units had lost an M1 and a Bradley to IEDs. They were cata-strophic losses; the crews had burned inside the vehicles. Two days before the incident I'd lost a Humvee in almost the exact same place when an IED had gone off. Nobody had died, but the Humvee had burned down. So everybody in the convoy was on edge: a big ve-hicle refused to stop and started passing them, and up ahead was what everybody thought was an IED. Even EOD (Explosive Ord-nance Disposal), when they came out to defuse the bomb, thought the object was an IED, although it turned out to just be a muffler on the side of the road.

I understand exactly why it happened. There was a pile-up of extenuating circumstances, due mostly to escalating terrorist at-tacks in the area, and because of that a bunch of children died.

When the experts start talking about post-traumatic stress disorder, sometimes they don't know what they're talking about, sometimes they do. The gunner in that Humvee was fucking dev-astated. Thinking he was about to come under attack by terrorists, he machine-gunned a truckload of children.

For the first part of my second tour we had an interpreter who went by the name of George. He was the soldier at As Samawah who destroyed the Crazy Horse Café coffee box on the side of the Carnivore with an RPG. I decided to let bygones be bygones, be-cause I'd shot him four times and killed all of his friends—not that I ever told him that. The Iraqis working with us had their loyalty tested enough.

George was an excellent interpreter, but, like most of the Iraqis, he didn't know a lot about weapons handling. Sergeant Williams, George, and I were walking down a street on patrol in Salman Pak one day and George had what we in the business call a negligent discharge: he emptied an entire 30-round AK magazine on full auto into the ground between Williams and me. Since he was such a good interpreter and, honestly, not much worse with an AK than a lot of the Iraqis, all we did was take his rifle away. He wasn't supposed to have it anyway, but in a combat zone, one more good guy with a gun is never a bad idea. Well, almost never.

George also had this habit of stealing stuff out of every car we stopped. We tried to discourage it and kept a close watch on him, but he was persistent. Every time we raided a house, George came walking out with jewelry or money. I wish I could say he was unusual, but a lot of the Iraqis were like that. Whenever the Americans searched an area, like a neighborhood, looking for insurgents, we called it a "Cordon and Search." If any Iraqi troops were helping us out, we called it a "Cordon and Shoplift."

After surviving the Carnivore at As Samawah, George ended up dying young of a brain aneurysm. You never know when you're going to go.

Remember the trouble I had with the gate guard in Bosnia?

When I was working for TF 6-26 we were based out of Al Asad Air Base. It was a Marine base and a Marine sector. Normally when you left the base you were supposed to give the gate guards your unit, where you were going, how many people you had with you, and so on, because they were tracking everybody who was leaving and entering the base. We often had to roll out of the base at no notice to go support our task force, which was flying out on Blackhawks from different sites. The Marines at the gates were giving us a lot of problems, slowing us down, so we talked to the Base Commander. He gave us an All Access card to show to the guys at the gate.

When we showed them the card, they were supposed to write down the number on the card and then let us through without delaying us.

So one day our column rolled up to the gates, and there was a Marine Corporal there. I was the third vehicle in line, but ended up next to the guard vehicle.

The corporal asked, "Where you guys going?"

I showed him the card.

He glanced at it, then asked, "What unit are you?"

I said, "Read the card. It says 'Do not detain, let us leave immediately.' Just write down the number."

He frowned and said, "So how many people are going out?"

I said, "*Dude,* read the fucking card."

And he said, "Well, I've got to call this to higher."

Son of a . . . I got on the radio and called up ahead to Sergeant England in his M1. He was the lead vehicle. "This is Sergeant Johnson back here. Please crush that gate if you need to to get out of here. We need to support our elements."

Sergeant England's tank started to move forward, and I heard the Corporal say, "Hey, bring that gun around on him." There was a Humvee next to the gate, and the Marine in the roof turret swung a .50-cal machine gun around to bear on Sergeant England.

England stopped. There was a brief pause, then the turret on England's M1 started to rotate. England brought his 120 mm main gun tube around, it gently knocked the barrel of the Marine's .50 sideways, and the guy who was holding on to the .50 was now staring at the muzzle of an M1 Abrams main gun from six inches away.

Sergeant England yelled at the top of his voice, "Your move, fucker!"

So they raised the gate with no further issue. The guy in the Humvee hopped off it (probably to get away from the 120 mm muzzle) and opened it for us.

To add insult to injury, England ran over one of their concrete Jersey barriers and crushed it with the M1, and everybody rolling after him did the same thing. I got my ass chewed for that a little bit, but we told command that the checkpoint was too narrow and the M1 just needed to make some room to get through.

One fine day in Iraq we were going to do an entry into a house where we thought there were some bad guys. Some of my troops were going in the back, the rest of the guys were going in the front, and I was the last guy going in. I called it in on the radio, as we were doing two houses at the same time: "Breaching, breaching, breaching!"

They breached the front door, and everybody ran by this big guy in the front yard asleep on a mattress like he was a guard. This dude was big—Wilt Chamberlain/Shaquille O'Neal big. I ran by him, and just as I did the motherfucker jumped up and grabbed me and spun me around. He was so huge that he grabbed another one of my guys and was shaking him by his vest while I was riding on this guy's shoulders like a Chihuahua humping a Great Dane. I was trying to buttstroke him and trying to get off him, but he was just slinging me around, yelling incoherently. That's when I learned the value of quick release slings, because he had my rifle where I couldn't hit him or do anything with it. He had me about twisted in half by my own sling, all the while yelling, "Aaaaaah, aaaaaah!"

I finally got my pistol out and was about to put it to his head and drop him when his mother ran out of the house yelling, "Mister! Mister!" She was frantically twirling her finger around her temple to indicate that he wasn't right in the head.

"No shit!" I yelled at her. "Calm him the fuck down!" That dude was messing us up without even trying, but I learned something that day—apparently a finger spinning next to the head is the universal sign for crazy.

Something else I learned? Most of the time I was carrying an M4/203, an M4 carbine with an M203 40 mm under-barrel grenade launcher. Shooting at a door with a 40 mm grenade from 20 feet away? Bad idea. Some of the grenades don't arm until they've traveled a certain distance, but apparently 20 feet's good. You know, in the movies, it just knocks the door down. In reality, it knocks you down. It's really cool in the movies. In real life it's not so cool. I got a nice chunk of scrap metal in my leg from that self-administered IQ test.

Someone once asked me how good the TF 6-26 guys were at house clearing, since that's their specialty. Our platoon at one point was spending 16 hours a day doing nothing but house clearing, We were just as fast at it as the ultra-high-speed spec-ops guys, but every shot they fired hit exactly what they were aiming at. Those dudes could *shoot*.

The Iraqis had proven—to themselves and us—that they were no match for us in a straight-up fight, even when they had armor. In guerrilla warfare, however, even when you don't know what you're doing, you can cause a lot of problems. Some of the people we were going up against—whether they were Iraqis or Syrians or from wherever, in Iraq to participate in the jihad against America, the Great Satan—had smarts, talent, guts, or a combination of all three. Many of the IEDs we ran into weren't so damn improvised.

On a night in June we were doing another escort mission, protecting thin-skinned vehicles on their way to another base, then returning home. The route would be long—three hours each way—but easy, as the whole trip was on blacktop. Protecting the vehicles were me and my crew in the Carnivore II, and Staff Sergeant Sowby and his able Bradley crew.

When we were doing task force work, we usually had close air support. Considering they could pretty much get whatever they wanted, we either had Apache helicopters or an AC-130 Spectre gunship. When it comes to combat, the Spectre is a soldier's wet dream.

We were almost halfway there when the Spectre called on the radio.

"Hey, we're picking up a signal; somebody is trying to detonate on you guys. We're jamming the signal right now, but be advised this is a hot area."

Shit. "Roger."

We were behind the convoy, and the gunship was hovering near the front of it as we put on some speed to get out of the area. I don't know if the Spectre pulled farther away from us, or the range of their jammer wasn't too great, because it was only a few seconds later that a huge IED went off behind us. The blast was enormous and rocked the Brad, even though the detonation was more than 100 meters behind my vehicle. Sowby was a mile ahead of me and he felt the explosion.

We didn't see any insurgents, although we knew they were around. Even though we would have loved to stick around and see if we could draw some fire—and return it with interest—we had a job to do.

After making it to our destination without further incident and refueling, I checked out my Bradley. The suspension had been hit hard—we had a damaged right rear sprocket, right front sprocket, and idler wheel. We took rubber and a screw and beat it into the spall holes so it would hold oil until we got back, as we had a lot of oil leaks. Our two Bradley crews went to work using the battle damage repair kit (BDRK) that our troop XO, Bret Chastain, had gotten for us before we left for Iraq. In less than an hour we had the Bradley up and running. Since we weren't escorting anyone back, we left as soon as the Carnivore II was fixed.

On our way back to our base we came upon two Marine Corps Humvees that had been hit. It looked like they'd been caught in an ambush. One of them was just starting to burn, and the other one had been hit pretty good. We stopped and checked them out. Somebody had been wounded there; there was blood on the ground and signs of a firefight.

The Humvee that was on fire we just let burn, but the other one the Marines had unassed so quickly that they hadn't had time to pull all their sensitive items off it. So we removed a pair of NVGs and the Blue Force tracker (GPS unit), and disabled the .50-cal on top. We then watched the other Humvee burn to the ground. Not only didn't we want insurgents taking any gear out of it, but also we didn't want them taking any pictures of it to show on the Internet for bragging rights.

When we returned to Al Asad Air Base, we brought in the sensitive items we'd recovered to the Base Commander in the operations center. The battlefield in that area at that time was so confusing that they didn't even know which patrol had been hit. The Marines were escorting fuel trucks, water trucks, and ration trucks back and forth through the desert, and they were often out of radio contact.

So these young Marines doing the escort missions had almost no support, to the point where nobody knew which group had been hit, what had happened, or if there'd been any casualties. Nobody at the base knew anything. There was a big scramble after that; they sent out aircraft trying to find out who'd been hit, who was lost, whatever.

The next day we did a few more post-IED repairs and then took the Bradley out on a test drive. The left front drive sprocket immediately broke off and fell on the ground. Oops. Apparently the IED had done more damage than we'd guessed—and we were 100 meters away when it went off! We later found out that the IED had been made from two 500-pound aircraft bombs—1,000 pounds of explosive, detonating 100 meters away. No wonder the blast had seemed big—it was! Between the mortars, RPGs, and IEDs, I know I suffered a number of concussions during my two tours in Iraq, even though they were never diagnosed. Headaches? Take a handful of aspirin.

We got some new parts, and with the help of a Marine and his forklift we had the Carnivore II fixed in less than 72 hours. That mission was typical—six hours on the road, we got blown up, and we never saw anyone we could shoot. At least none of us were injured.

Working with Tier 1 units like JSOC can sometimes be really interesting. One afternoon I was hanging around the operations center and got to watch "Kill Cam"—the video from a Predator drone. Most of the time, unless there's some sort of ground action going on, it's boring, but as I was watching, a little smoke trail emerged from behind the Predator. Uh-oh. Then on the video screen—sky, ground, sky, ground, sky, ground, sky, ground, ground, ground spinning, ground spinning, ground spinning, static. The Predator had a mechanical problem and just burned right in.

As the officers were trying to make a decision about whether we were going to go out and recover the drone, the camera started working again. We saw feet and people picking parts off the drone, looking into the camera lens, and then the camera went dark when it was put inside a car trunk. In case you're wondering, the Predator was recovered.

Our six-month stint with JSOC ended without anyone dying—at least on our side.

Several things happened at the same time that year. We transitioned from using predominantly Bradleys to up-armored Humvees, and Crazy Horse took control of one of the major supply routes in eastern Baghdad. My platoon would be working with the 3rd POB (Public Order Brigade), Iraqis who wanted the best for their country and were willing to work hard and risk their lives to get it. Captain Burgoyne was our Troop Commander. He was tall and thin and reminded me of John Wayne in *The Sands of Iwo Jima*. We gave him the nickname Captain America for the way he always conducted his operations, just like the all-American soldier. Burgoyne called me into his office along with Sergeants Todd Young and Mark Madrey, the Platoon Sergeants from First and Fourth Platoons, to come up with ideas on how to take out the IED threat in our new zone in Baghdad. All four platoons spent two days doing recons of the area, and we knew it was going to be a tough job.

We came up with a great plan. Our mission was set and ready when Captain Burgoyne threw us a curveball and told us we were going to do a river assault on some islands in the Tigris. Insurgents were apparently hiding out there.

We laughed long and hard at that. "Yes sir! I'll go get my peg leg!"

Except he was serious. Long story short, Third and Fourth Platoons got the mission and, yes, it was down the Tigris River. The 318th Engineer Company, better known as Lightning Over Water Company, would be our ride across the river in their bridging boats. We'd joined the freshwater navy.

Before we could do the mission, we had to go through quick training. Our training consisted of jumping into an Iraqi swimming pool in full kit and taking it off without filling our lungs with water. They call it drownproofing. That pretty much sucked. When I was attached to the 82nd Airborne at Fort Bragg I had to do five parachute jumps. Jumping out of a perfectly good airplane made about as much sense to me as jumping into an Iraqi swimming pool in full kit, but you don't have to like it, you just have to do it.

The plan was to first take two boats upriver on a recon to check out if there were any sandbars that would screw up the bigger boats we'd use for the mission. We put the 318th's boats in the water downriver about 20 miles from the biggest island. The first boat held Captain Burgoyne, Lieutenant Cummings, Lieutenant Goulet, Staff Sergeant Ingleston, myself, and three members of the 318th.

The second boat was filled with members of the 318th who would provide cover and overwatch for us. Never ones to take half measures (or go anywhere without our Bradleys when we didn't have to), we positioned three Bradleys from my platoon in overwatch on the east side of the river, where they could follow our movements.

The boats had an elevated platform, like a flat-bottomed johnboat, and forward and aft of that was a deck actually under the waterline. Things almost never work out the way they're supposed to, and only 20 minutes into our mission the second boat had engine trouble and had to turn around. We still had three Bradleys and some Apaches to cover us, so we didn't feel vulnerable and kept moving north.

The weather was beautiful, and I was daydreaming about being back in Mosquito Lagoon in Florida with my buddy Mike Marple and my boys fishing for reds when the water around the boat started exploding. I looked to my right and saw insurgents firing from the west riverbank, about 150 yards away. Standing up on the elevated deck, I fired several magazines from my M4/203 at them.

Captain Burgoyne ordered the boat skipper to take us behind an island and out of the line of fire. As long as I could see them, I was going to keep shooting, and I fired six 40 mm grenades out of my M203. I loved shooting that thing. I packed it all that time, so for damn sure I wanted to shoot it when I got the chance. Realizing that I seemed rather alone in my work, I looked around inside the boat only to see that everyone had dropped below the waterline except me. I was on the engine deck, even with the top of the boat, while everybody else was lying on the decks below the waterline, shooting over the edges of the boat. The hell with hunkering down, I could still see them, and they were still shooting at us. I fired another 30 rounds from my M4, but it seemed that everybody who lived along the river had run to the shore with their AKs when they heard our engine. There were hundreds of people shooting at us along the shore.

"I'm out of ammo!" I said, and felt something along my leg. Always looking out for me, Burgoyne was holding up a magazine. I burned through that magazine, then another, then another— everybody in the boat who wasn't in a position to shoot was passing them up to me.

Burgoyne got on the radio net and talked the Bradleys onto the insurgents. Sergeant Craig opened up with his main gun, hitting the insurgents with more than 50 rounds of 25 mm high-explosive. Those who didn't die stopped firing and tried to get organized. I'll give them this—they were persistent. However, by that time, our attack air support was back overhead, and since I was the only one with eyes on target I called them in. Apaches kick ass—the AH-64D has a minigun and rocket pods and can take out tanks or infantry, whatever's on the menu.

"Max 26, Max 26, Crazy Blue 4, I'm in peril, I need you on my POS right now." I paused; I was trying to find my grid on the map and couldn't. Fuck it. "Okay, I'm the only boat in the river," I told him. "Repeat, only boat in the river."

I could see him coming in. He said, "You're the only boat in the river?"

I said, "Roger that, being engaged from the west side of the river."

He asked, "You are the Ground Commander?"

I looked down, and Burgoyne was still below the waterline. I said, "Yes I am, go ahead and engage." Max 26 went in and ripped those dudes up with his 30 mm chain gun and 2.75-inch rockets. It was beautiful. When we got back I wrote him up for a Flying Cross and it was approved. Later I gave him a big thank-you letter and a big bottle of scotch. He deserved it, because we were getting fucked up.

Going back down the river the way we'd come, we ran into yet another firefight. More insurgents on the far bank, peppering the water around us with their AKs. This time there was no delay on our part, and both Craig's Bradley and the Apache Max 26 hammered their position. We made ourselves useful and fired at them as well, and it was over pretty damn quick.

Even if we'd wanted to cruise the river looking for another fight, it was time to head back. I had fired all 10 of my 203 rounds, and we only had about 120 5.56 mm rounds left between the eight of us on the boat. I had to laugh at the ridiculousness of the situation, and laughed all the rest of the way downriver. Everyone in the boat was looking at me like I was crazy, but it wasn't me, it was what we were doing.

So when we got back, there was water leaking everywhere in the boat. There was an M249 light machine gun soft-mounted at the rear of the boat and an M240 mounted at the front of the boat, but nobody had touched them. All the way around that boat, everywhere above and at the waterline there were bullet holes, everywhere except for the 18 inches of hull where I was standing. That was just one of the many times when I should have died and didn't. I learned something new that day—I was seeing water splashes in front of me and thought the Iraqi incoming was falling short. However, when the water splashes at an angle, that means the bullet's still moving, they were skipping and hitting the boat all around me.

The Iraqis never could shoot worth shit. That whole "put the stock against your shoulder and look down the sights in the general direction of the target" thing seemed too tough for most of them. We called their shooting style "Iraqi Offhand"—hold the rifle up and forward, in the general direction of the target, and blow off a whole magazine on full auto. If they were aiming at you, you were pretty safe. As always, the bullets to watch out for were the ones addressed "To Whom It May Concern."

Captain Burgoyne just shook his head at me and said, "Crazy Jay, you are crazy."

"Why?"

"Everybody else was taking cover, and you were just standing up there returning fire."

I said, "Sir, where the fuck was I going to go? You were on my feet. You all act like I'm some kind of hero or some shit. I'm just *slow*. There was nowhere for me to go, because you were already there."

I had a real hatred for boats after that.

We'd gone out on a simple recon, gotten involved in two fire-fights, and nearly burned through all of our ammo. That had not been the plan at all, and I believe Burgoyne's exact words were, "Fuck this." After a quick rethink, command changed the plan. We would now assault the island from smaller RB-15s, which are seven-man rubber boats that can be put in the water almost any-where. I appreciated the fact that they could be put in anywhere, which added a level of surprise to the plan, but rubber isn't exactly known as great defense against bullets.

The day of our assault, I was number-one man and would be the first guy out of the boat. We put into the water without much fuss and headed into the river. Waiting for the first incoming round, the first splash of bullet hitting water, was nerve-racking, but we made it across to the target island without incident. As it turned out, none of the four islands even had insurgents on them. Well, hell, at least I got to play Navy for a few days, but then it was back to work.

CHAPTER 21

SNIPING IS AS SNIPING DOES

When you're riding around in armor, the way you usually find IEDs is when they blow up. That wasn't good enough for us. In addition to a number of action plans that we started implementing, we realized that having scout/sniper teams supporting us would be invaluable. Not only could they provide overwatch when the troop was static, it would be a good way to catch the insurgents as they were planting IEDs. We were also personally invested in killing every one of the bastards who was planting IEDs, as we'd just lost one of our own, Sergeant Lonnie Parson.

Iraqi insurgents were taking the rockets out of the pods of Hind-D helicopters to make their IEDs. They would set them up on the road and stick them in a PVC pipe or cut a half moon in the ditch to aim them. They'd hook up wires, command-detonate them, and hope they hit something. Sometimes they did, sometimes they didn't.

Lonnie Parson was the Platoon Sergeant of Bravo Troop, and he was hit by one of those Hind rocket IEDs. It hit him in the side, just under his body armor, and it did not explode, but the warhead went inside his chest cavity. It took EOD and the medics a while to get it out of him, and he didn't make it.

As happy as we would have been to send out a sniper team to kill every bad guy in the area, there weren't Army sniper teams just sitting around looking for something to do—if we wanted it done, we had to do it ourselves. The plan we drew up with Captain Burgoyne was simple. I had my platoon broken down into two sniper teams and a heavy support team of three Bradleys. Staff Sergeant John Williams was back in-country with Crazy Horse and would be in charge of one sniper team, while I would be in charge of the other. My new Lieutenant, David Dejesus, along with Sergeants Sowby and Craig, would be in the Bradleys.

Lieutenant Dejesus was a green Lieutenant, right out of the U.S. Army's new Lieutenant School. He was a smart, quiet kid from Puerto Rico, and I really liked him. He served well on his first tour in Iraq.

I could have backed off and rode around in the Bradley behind armor, but that's not how I operate. Lead from the front and look for a fight. I was the Platoon Sergeant, but I felt I was the only one in my platoon who had the skill to take on the task. I'd been in the Army almost as long as some of the new kids had been alive and was hunting for a decade before that. Also, I didn't mind killing people, and sniping can be quite different from heated combat. My spotter was Staff Sergeant Jared Kennedy, who was the Commander of his own Bradley before we decided to shake things up.

Kennedy was from Hawaii, of Hawaiian or Polynesian descent. He was slightly younger than me and a simply outstanding soldier. He was one of the finest NCOs I ever had the pleasure of working with. I could have chosen anybody as my spotter, and I chose him. He knew what he was doing and what needed to be done, and we worked well together.

In a sniper/spotter team, the sniper generally stays on the rifle, looking through the scope for or at a target. The spotter has a rifle as well, but his main job is to help direct the sniper onto the target—or targets, as the case may be. Traditionally, spotters tend to use binoculars more than they do rifles, but in Iraq, we rarely had only one target when it came time to shoot.

For those people to whom the term *sniper* has evil connotations, let me explain—the purpose of a sniper is to save lives. Cops don't shoot criminals for sport, they do it to prevent bad things from happening, and the same is true of snipers. Our role as snipers would primarily be to prevent IED emplacement, thus saving American lives. The fact that we hunker down and tend to ambush the bad guys from afar is just good tactics. In war, if you find yourself in a fair fight, your tactics suck.

In the military, if you haven't been officially trained as a sniper and don't have the certificate, you are not a sniper, even if you're sitting behind a scoped rifle shooting people at long range. If you're not a sniper, you don't get issued an Army sniper rifle, which is the M24. Only one guy in our unit had actually been to sniper school, a Private named Flint, and he had been issued his own M24. The rest of Crazy Horse had to make do with what we could find in the unit or scrounge.

We mostly used two rifles for sniping, a Barrett M82 and an accurized M14. Both rifles belonged to the unit. Although the M14 was assigned to me, while working as a sniper I mostly used the Barrett M82, which is a man-portable .50-caliber semiauto rifle. The Barrett is a big heavy beast (32 pounds) and fires a big heavy bullet. It fires the same round as the M2 .50-cal machine gun and was originally designed for shooting things (planes, helicopters, vehicles) rather than people. The Barrett isn't as accurate as most specialized sniper rifles, but then again most of the engagements we had would be considered short range for a sniper, since we worked in urban areas.

The second gun was an M14 EBR (enhanced battle rifle), which means they took a Vietnam-era M14 and put it in a new stock—not exactly a custom sniper rifle, but it hits harder than the M4 and is reliable. It chambers the 7.62x51 mm cartridge, the same one used in the M240 machine guns in the Bradley. The rifle wore one of the Elite 4200 mil-dot scopes donated to the unit by Bushnell, and both sniper teams had Bushnell laser range finders. The military does not issue Bushnell scopes, they issue Leupolds; the reason we had a Bushnell on the M14 is that we basically had to put the rifles together ourselves. The M14 was my rifle, and it was with me all the time. It was either in the back of my Humvee, in my Bradley, or somewhere close.

Sergeant John Williams's sniper rifle was a match-grade M16A2, basically the same rifle as my M4 carbine, only with a longer, more accurate barrel and a scope. With that rifle he was officially designated the squad's *marksman,* which is a military term essentially meaning "sniper lite." Williams was able to get hold of some match ammunition for it, and he and that rifle were a deadly combination.

Don't think we were just a bunch of good 'ol boys heading out to shoot some dudes with our rifles. Even though none of us (except for Flint) had been to sniper school, we'd all gone through mobile training. A lot of units just didn't have the money to send their people to sniper school, but that didn't mean they didn't need the training. As a work-around, the Army sniper school sent out MTTs (mobile training teams), who trained us up at Fort Stewart before we deployed. We were taught how to use laser range finders, dial in elevation, get on a distant target quickly—the basics of long-distance shooting. We weren't taught stalking or low-crawling through the underbrush, which is how many people envision snipers operating. Carlos Hathcock, the famous Marine sniper, did that in Vietnam, but Iraq was a completely different environment. In Afghanistan they were doing traditional sniping, sneaking and peeking and hitting skittish Taliban from way off, but our environment was a lot closer to what police snipers have to deal with.

Captain Burgoyne had all four platoons in zone at the same time. We would be working 14-hour missions outside the wire, putting pressure on the enemy. Our first night out, Williams spotted a would-be IED setter. He had the guy in his sights, but we were a bit new at this and wanted to make sure that we targeted the right people. Williams sat and waited and watched to make sure that the guy was actually out setting up an IED and not just taking a midnight stroll.

Once he was as sure as he could be, Williams called Captain Burgoyne and told him what he had. Burgoyne sent over Staff Sergeant Wyatt, our mortar Platoon Sergeant, who was acting as our light quick reaction force (LQRF) that night. When the guy saw the gun trucks coming at him he ran to his car.

Enemy armor and guys with guns are easy problems to solve, but an unarmed man running away? Williams was a bit conflicted as to what was the proper course of action. Why was this guy running? Should he kill him or let him go? Did the guy really emplace an IED? In the end, John Williams did the smartest thing he could. He looked through his Bushnell Elite 4200 rifle scope onto which was clamped a universal night sight, and at a range of more than 300 meters took out the passenger-side tires of the guy's car as soon as he started it up. The LQRF rolled up right then and grabbed him. Not only did Williams's quick thinking stop the guy and get him off the street, but we now could ask him questions and possibly gain intelligence about the people planting IEDs.

Our unit mostly worked along the main route near the Tigris River in Baghdad, quite often setting up on top of a flour mill that was 8 or 10 stories tall. From the top of that building you could see all the way up one way and down another, even across the river. We could spot snipers and direct the platoon to them. We always worked at night, and there was always something going on. We traded off on the sniper job, because there were other things that needed doing. The Barrett got passed around. Most of the time when I wasn't using it, Sergeant Anthony (Tony) Mitchell would run the .50 off the roof of the flour mill.

We would almost always set up on rooftops, because they gave a better view of the area. The guys we were looking out for were sniping, setting IEDs, running curfew lines, and trying to smuggle munitions. We didn't do any low-crawling through the weeds to get into our sniper hides, but we did our best to be as sneaky as the situation and environment allowed. For example, we would ride down the road in the back of a Bradley. The vehicle would make several turns and several stops. At the right point they would lower the ramp while making a turn, we would jump out of the back of the Bradley, and they would drive on. That's how we would infiltrate. The rest of the unit would go and set up in security or overwatch positions to support our mission. Most of the time we had an entire platoon in support. Sometimes they were right with us, other times they were positioned around the building we were in or surrounding the area. We always worked at night because the Iraqis didn't have any night vision, which was our biggest advantage.

Most of the Iraqis planting IEDs would walk in or get dropped from cars. We did not automatically engage everybody who had a rifle, because everybody had a rifle. We would have to see what they were up to. That said, we took out a lot of guys with AKs who were up to no good. Some nights we did a lot of shooting. Other times it was just a long-ass night of nothing.

One night we spotted two guys, one of whom had a rifle. They were acting very suspicious, skulking around buildings, and they got very close to the hide where Sergeant Williams and I were.

The two suspicious characters were right off the main route, and when we called them in, the brigade XO got involved and got everybody else involved. While Williams and I were going back and forth as to whether or not we should shoot the two guys, the brigade XO basically called down the entire troop to surround the area. We had a Falcon at our disposal, which is a small UAV (unmanned aerial vehicle) with a video camera in it and a Specialist trained to fly it. A Falcon is small—throw it in the air and it flies. It was in the air over our position, providing real-time video of the guys, and I was getting ready to take the shot, because these guys were obviously up to no good. Then we lost sight of the guy with the rifle moving through the underbrush.

Even though we lost sight of one of the guys, there was nowhere for them to go, because we had a whole platoon of Bradleys surrounding the area. I directed the section to the right place. Sergeant Kennedy brought them in and they tackled the one guy, and it turns out he was a chicken thief. Not an insurgent, not a terrorist, not an IED setter—a chicken thief. Sigh.

In July 2005, early on in the sniping phase of my second tour, Kennedy and I went up onto a rooftop in the area. We liked the spot, as it would give us a good view of potential IED sites. There were two guys sleeping up there. We didn't want them telling anybody we were there, so we took their cell phones and locked them up in a metal building on the roof. Kennedy and I stayed up there all night, and when morning rolled around we left. We liked the building and decided to come back there the next night and use it.

The next night, as we started heading up to the roof, Kennedy said, "Hey, it sounds like there's somebody in this building."

We'd locked the building from the outside. I stopped, looked up in the direction of the faint sounds, then back at Kennedy. "You didn't leave them fuckers in there, did you?"

He said, "I thought you were going to let them out."

Shit.

We'd locked two guys up in what was basically a metal sweat-box on the top of a roof in Baghdad in July for 24 hours. They were fine and, would you believe, very cooperative when we let them out. We gave them water, set them back in the building until we were done sniping that night, then released them.

For one straight week Kennedy and I did nothing but work as a sniper/spotter team and had absolutely nothing to show for it. It felt like we had been on every rooftop in town but hadn't seen one damn bad guy. Most of the time we went out at night, and when you hear people say that the desert gets cold at night because there's nothing to hold in the heat, they're not lying. We froze our asses off.

One night, finally, we spotted an insurgent. It was an easy shot, less than 100 meters, but just as I fired I realized there was movement all around us. I hit the target, but we were in a bit of a spot. The Iraqis weren't quite sure where we were, so we quietly slipped out of our position and moved into a compound. There was a big building with a parking lot around it. We figured out it used to be a car manufacturing facility. As soon as we got into the building we saw all sorts of movement around the perimeter, but they weren't moving toward us.

I got on the radio and contacted Lieutenant Dejesus.

"Sir, I took out a target, but we have unfriendlies all around our location. We're going to need an early pickup tonight." I gave him our coordinates and the proximity of the car plant to where we'd set up.

"Crazy Blue 4, roger that, but be advised we are fifteen minutes away." Crazy Blue 4 was my new call sign.

"Yes sir, that shouldn't be a problem."

The delay didn't worry me, because we were in a pretty good position—the building was dark, and they couldn't see us and didn't know for sure where we were. I eyeballed the front of the property and the gate, and Kennedy watched my back.

We owned the night, and it was dark as hell out there, so the situation was no big deal. With my night sight I had no problems counting the Iraqis out to my front, but they couldn't have seen me if I was standing up and doing jumping jacks. Then I heard the engine start on a generator and the compound lit up like a Walmart parking lot.

The night sight flared out on me and Kennedy and I hugged the inside wall even closer.

"You've gotta be fucking kidding me."

"Can you see the generator?" Kennedy asked me in a whisper. He was thinking we might be able to shoot it.

"No, I don't know where it is," I told Kennedy.

Emboldened by the lights, the Iraqis started actively hunting us. They moved around, spreading out, and shot into any shadow, any spot we could be hiding—rooftops, windows, you name it. We were screwed, because it was only a matter of time before they ran into us. I looked at Kennedy for ideas, and he was looking at me and pointing at the wall. I turned and saw the high-voltage power line running down the wall out into the compound, to the generator.

I nodded and pulled out the Gerber LMF II I'd received from

from Mark Schindel. I held it out to Kennedy. "You need to cut the line," I told him.

He looked at the knife, at the power line, and back to me. "Fuck you. You cut that line. That thing'll shock the piss out of me."

I vaguely remembered Mark telling me the handle of the knife was insulated against electric shock, or something like that. "Mark said it wouldn't, you can cut it safely."

"Fuck you, he told *you* that, he didn't tell me. You cut it."

We could tell from the sound of the engine that this was a serious generator, and we weren't looking at some thin electrical cord. The power lines were about two inches thick, including insulation, and had a lot of juice running through them. The LMF II had proven itself to everyone in the troop time and time again, because ever since we'd been in-country we'd been abusing the piss out of them. I actually used mine to get into and out of rooftop sniper hide positions; I would stab it into the cement walls that were everywhere and use it for a step. But nobody had used one to cut a hot wire.

I looked at the wire, at the knife in my hand, and at Kennedy. It was either cut the wire or engage a much larger force under stadium lighting conditions. "Well, fuck it," I said. "If this thing gets me fried, go kick Mark's ass for me."

The power line was high on the wall. After I scurried over to the wall I reached the knife above my head and stuck it in between the power line and the wall. Using my body weight I jumped and pulled down on the Gerber. There was a bright flash, and I felt heat in my hands, then it was dark again—or did I die? Nope. Holy shit, it actually worked!

With the lights off the Iraqis lost a lot of their courage, because they knew how good our night vision was, and they hauled ass out of the area. We were able to get out of the building without being spotted. A few minutes later Lieutenant Dejesus showed up in our Bradleys and we took the long ride back to our forward operating base (FOB).

There were a couple half-moons cut out of the knife blade by the current, but otherwise it was unharmed, and with a sharpening stone I was able to put a proper edge back on it. When I had a chance, I sent a thank-you letter to Mark Schindel at Gerber Legendary Blades, along with a photo of the knife.

Mark and the people at Gerber knew good press when they saw it, and they used my letter and a photo of the knife in some of their print advertising for the LMF II for a couple years. Several months later, after I was out of the Army, they flew me to Vegas for the SHOT (Shooting, Hunting, Outdoor Trade) Show and paid me to work their booths. A few months after that they flew me to Milwaukee to the NRA Annual Convention. Hotel, plane ticket, expense account, the whole nine yards. I have no problems representing a product that actually saved my life—and the damn knife isn't even expensive; they were 69 dollars when they were introduced!

While I was at the NRA convention, I presented an Iraqi flag that I'd captured to Wayne LaPierre, the Executive Vice President of the NRA. I was able to sit down and talk with him about guns and private contracting for about half an hour. It was very cool.

Our area of operations was right along the Tigris River in Baghdad, and a lot of my kills were across the river. It was about 600 yards to the far shore, and the 3rd Armored Cavalry Regiment was in charge of that side of the river. A lot of the rifles that "I" took off guys I killed were actually recovered by the 3rd ACR troops, and they would confirm the kill.

The Iraqis knew we were there, knew there was a curfew, knew we had night vision, and yet they still came out and tried to shoot us and set bombs. There's a technical term for that kind of person, and it rhymes with "dumbass."

Command had sent the word out that anybody crossing the river at nighttime was to be considered hostile. A large number of munitions, IEDs, and guns were coming across the river, and we were getting tired of being shot at and blown up. Putting bullet holes in boats won't sink them, not unless you're using a lot of full-auto fire, so we targeted the crews, not the boat hulls. I shot a lot of people making runs across the river at night.

Broadhead never got to see any action on his second tour because he was First Sergeant; all he did was bring chow and radios out to the guys and go on patrol every once in a while. He never really got to do anything fun. One night we were sitting up on top of the flour mill and suddenly we got a call on the radio—vehicles were running up the road toward us, big trucks. Tractors and trailers, hauling ass into Baghdad after the curfew. All of us were thinking they were big bomb trucks, because we'd had a lot of those going off in the area.

Broadhead was all jazzed because he was finally going to see some action. He got in his vehicle and started flying toward the trucks. His gunner opened up on one of the tractor trailers, which were just hauling ass, doing about 50 miles an hour.

I had Sergeant Rodriguez, one of the other kids who'd been through mobile training, on a rooftop nearby with the M14 (actually, he was on the roof where Kennedy and I accidentally locked the two guys up for a day). Rodriguez lit the first truck up and put about 20 rounds into the radiator because they were heading right for him. He pounded an entire magazine into the front of that vehicle. When he was done, the radiator was going crazy, the engine was messed up, and the driver was freaking out, because Rodriguez put a couple in the windshield too, just for good measure. So the lead driver stopped, and the other three trucks behind him stopped as well.

Everybody started racing up to their position, and Broadhead's gunner was still lighting up the back of the first truck. He finally stopped shooting when we got there and we all got out. There were four semi trucks, and maybe eight guys, all completely frazzled but unharmed. They had no clue what was going on, they just drove up from Basra. We did a quick check of the trucks and discovered that they were filled with tobacco.

Everybody knew there was a curfew, but some guys were just assholes and acted like they didn't know. Most of the time if you ran the curfew you would just get stopped, but this time, they didn't just get stopped, they got accosted.

The first truck was in the way, blocking the road. It was overheating, and steam was coming out of it. We had a pretty good idea that the truck was going to die. We didn't want the guy to get back in the truck, because he might try to drive off or ram something, so I hopped in the truck to drive it off the road. I can drive just about anything, or at least get it into gear. I stopped the tractor trailer on a steep incline, almost a 45-degree slope, so steep the truck almost tipped over. The ground was so slanted that it was hard for me to push the door open to get out.

We searched the other trucks, tearing through the boxes, and all we found was tobacco and more tobacco. After about an hour we gave up on it and realized that these guys weren't insurgents, they were just stupid. So we gave up on it and left them there to load the tobacco back into the trucks. Well, about 20 minutes later we were up on the rooftop, watching, and I saw the driver get back into the first truck. He put it into gear to drive off, and the truck turned over as soon as it started to move, landing with a big thump. Oops. Well, he did it, I didn't.

Apart from the incident at the car plant, Kennedy and I never got attacked while we were set up in a sniping position. After we shot, they were either trying to get away or confused as to exactly where we were. Williams, on the other hand, had an exciting night when somebody tossed a grenade into his position. He was fine, but there's nothing like a live grenade to get your heart beating fast. He was the Section Sergeant, but I was the Platoon Sergeant and Platoon Leader, so I had other missions and responsibilities. Williams did nothing but go out on sniper missions every night. He was by far a better shot than me and took out more guys than I did.

Private Flint, the only member of our unit who had attended sniper school, got his first kill with a sniper rifle one night when I was with him. I wasn't spotting for him, I was up there with my M14 working in tandem, but I verified and confirmed the kill for him through my scope. The shot was about 600 yards. I actually just ran into Flint a few months ago, at the SHOT Show in Vegas. He was still in the Army and in fact had joined the Special Forces.

In late October 2005, my platoon was set up in two overwatch positions on the Tigris. Staff Sergeants Sowby and Craig were to the south of my location on top of an old pool house, and we were on the roof of a big old house that allowed me to see the other side of the river. Gilbert, my new Iraqi interpreter, had told me about the spot, and it was perfect.

After setting up on the roof, a new guy, Private First Class Patty Turnbull, told me he had movement on the other side of the river. It was a long way away, and other than movement he couldn't pick out any detail. Then we heard a mortar being fired from the other side of the river, at the 3rd POB headquarters. They were firing from behind a wall in some trees; we knew exactly where they were but couldn't actually see them. I called my Commander for air support—Apaches—and was told it would be a little bit before they could get there.

The Bushnell laser range finder told me it was over 500 meters to the mortar position. I didn't want to wait for air support; those bastards were mortaring my guys. But what to do? Then I had an idea.

I pulled out four 40 mm HEDP rounds and told Turnbull to do the same, then called to two other nearby soldiers who also had M4/203s. One of them was Specialist Gillespie, whom we called Gummy Bear. Gummy Bear got his nickname at Fort Irwin NTC when he ate an entire 10-pound bag of gummy bears by himself.

"Follow my lead, aim like I do, and shoot after me in one-second intervals," I told them.

I'd put a lot of 40 mm grenade rounds downrange that tour and was getting pretty good with the thing. While the under-barrel launcher could throw the grenade round a lot farther than anyone could throw a hand grenade, the 40 mm grenades still had a pronounced rainbow trajectory. I fired the first round, Turnbull fired the second round, and we did a round robin. In total we fired 12 HEDP rounds. Gummy Bear shot the last one.

The M203 and its 40 mm round isn't the most accurate weapon in the world, but the HEDP round is damn effective and has a good blast radius. We were able to curve them over the top of the wall. I watched the first round hit almost on top of the mortar team and 11 more hit that same area in just as many seconds. By the time the Apaches got there the mortar was silent. The chopper pilot could see hot spots on the ground but couldn't tell if they were bodies.

It would be almost a week before we found out that we had taken out an enemy 81 mm mortar team with our improvised mortar barrage, killing three insurgents.

I was minding my own business one day when one of the Iraqi cops with the 3rd POB came up to me and said, "I've found an IED."

"Cool," I told him. "Let's go." Cochran and I grabbed our rifles.

We jumped into a Humvee and drove down the road a while until he told me to stop. We got out and walked a short distance, Cochran watching our backs. I was expecting the Iraqi cop to stop, point down the road a good distance, and say, "There it is, over there."

After a short walk, he stopped, pointed at his feet, and said, "Here it is, right there." Next to his foot was a hole, and visible inside the hole was the top of what I recognized to be an IED.

"Motherfucker, are you kidding me?" I yelled at him. Actually, I didn't yell, because you never know what might set those things off, but I cursed him up one side and down the other as we beat feet away from the bomb.

I backed the Humvee up until we were a safe distance away and called in EOD. EOD—Explosive Ordnance Disposal—handled most of the IEDs we encountered. They were usually able to defuse them, but from time to time they had to blow them in place. Talk about a job I would not want to have—bomb disposal was number one on that list. The EOD tech showed up with his little remote-controlled bomb robot, Johnny 5. He drove Johnny 5 over to where the hole was.

"I can't see any IED," the EOD tech told me, looking at his video monitor.

I looked at the screen. "Some of the dirt's fallen into the hole and covered it," I told him. "It's there."

"I don't see it," he insisted.

"Dude, there's an IED in the hole, just put the C4 on it and blow it up," I told him.

"I can't do that without confirming that there's an IED there," he told me obstinately.

"I'm confirming it," I growled, starting to get a little pissed.

He shook his head. "I need to see it or something."

"So take Johnny 5's little robot arm and dig out some of the dirt or something," I told him. "Seriously, what the hell's the problem?"

"Fine," he said. Very carefully manipulating the controls, he started working the robot's arm. As soon as he touched the dirt over the top of it, the IED went off with a huge blast. Dirt and little robot pieces rained down all over the road.

I laughed hard and long. "Looks like you need another Johnny 5," I told him.

He turned to me, rage in his eyes, and grabbed me by the front of my vest. He almost lifted me off the ground. I said quickly, "Dude, dude, relax, I was just making a joke." I held up my hands. Nobody had been hurt by the blast, and nothing had been destroyed, so I wasn't sure why me being a smartass had made him so upset.

"You don't understand," he told me, angry and sad all at the same time. He sagged and let me go. "That was my last robot. Now I've got to go look at the IEDs myself."

With the year winding down, the weather wasn't getting any warmer. I'd been cold in September lying on a roof all night, and October wasn't any better. November and December were just as brutal. I called Amy, my wife, and told her to go to Walmart and buy a Thermos to send to me, because I was freezing my ass off at night. Every night it was bone-chillingly cold. I described to her what I needed, how it was insulated and would keep soup or coffee hot for hours.

Package delivery, depending on how it was mailed, isn't as slow as you might think to Iraq, but after a week and no Thermos I called Amy again. "Hey, babe, when you sent that Thermos, how did you send it? Because it's still not here."

"Oh. Well, I didn't get it yet," she told me. I understood, she was busy, she had the kids to deal with, and her job, but I was in the business of killing people before they killed me.

"Okay," I told her. "You need to go get that Thermos and send it to me, because it's cold."

I waited for almost another week, and still no Thermos, so I called her again. "Did you get that Thermos?"

"No, I'm sorry, I've just been so busy . . ."

I don't have the best patience when I'm in a good mood, but at that point it had been close to three weeks. It was just me and Kennedy up on the roofs and I was practically freezing to death. At night it only got down to 31 or 32 degrees, but if you're sitting and not moving for hours and hours, that is really damn cold. It was 80 degrees in the daytime, and we had to dress for that, too. When you're in a sniper position, you might have to E&E (escape and evade) in a hurry, so you don't want to be weighted down with anything more than you need.

I'd see an insurgent 100 yards out, which is practically point-blank range for a sniper rifle, and I'd shoot at the center of his chest and hit him in the shoulder, or his hip. I was shaking so bad I couldn't hold on to the damn gun. We'd gotten so cold, Kennedy and I, that we were hugging on the roof and shaking, just a poncho liner wrapped around the two of us. When the sun finally came up, we didn't care about insurgents or targets, we were just trying to get into direct sunlight, get warm, like a snake on a rock.

"You need to go get that damn Thermos!" I yelled at my wife, and hung up the phone. Not my best moment, I admit.

Amy left work right then, went out and bought a Thermos, and mailed it to me. I was waiting, and waiting, and then I had to wait some more, because she sent it regular mail. It took two weeks to get to Iraq. When it finally did arrive, I opened up the box and saw that she'd sent me a coffee cup with a screw-on lid. It wasn't a Thermos at all.

I picked up the phone without a pause, dialed her number, and when she answered, yelled, "What the hell were you thinking?"

"Excuse me?"

I said, "I tell you to send me a Thermos over here, I'm freezing my ass off, and not only does it take you four weeks to get one over here, you send me a fucking coffee cup?!"

I finally got one in the mail three days before I left the country.

That's the closest we've ever come to getting a divorce, over a stupid Thermos. And it's still a sore point between the two of us. Say "Thermos" to Amy and she gets murder in her eyes. When you're in a combat zone half a world away, having instant telephone or Internet access to your loved ones can be a wonderful thing, but it's a double-edged sword.

CHAPTER 22

THE LION'S MOUTH

We hadn't been stationed in Baghdad during our second tour but rather had been moved all over, wherever we were needed. Late in 2005 they were having problems with insurgents planting IEDs outside of Salman Pak, so Kennedy and I headed over there to see if we could help out.

Salman Pak is 15 miles south of Baghdad along the Tigris River, and most Iraqis know it as a historical and recreational area. It's the site of the Arch of Ctesiphon, in the remains of the ancient Persian capital, and is named after Salman the Persian, who was a companion to Muhammad and is buried there. Before the war it was a common day-trip destination for residents of Baghdad and even featured a floating casino. Under Saddam, however, Salman Pak became better known to U.S. forces as a center of chemical weapons production and secret police training.

We did a lot of patrols along the river, usually south of Salman Pak. There was a mosque there with a minaret, and we were pretty sure the insurgents, after planting IEDs, would stand in the mosque so they had a good view up and down the road as they waited for U.S. troops to drive by. Then they'd detonate. Ironically, there was a Pepsi factory right next to the mosque, which is not something you see every day.

One night Sowby, Kennedy, and I were on patrol in that area when an IED blew up between Kennedy's Bradley and mine. The Carnivore II took all the shrapnel, but the blast itself really rattled me—I know I got a concussion, as I had a little bit of fluid coming out of both of my ears.

Kennedy saw movement, hopped down inside the turret of his Bradley, and told his gunner to engage.

"My optics are out!" the gunner said. Kennedy and I had been rolling down the road pretty close together, and the blast had blown out his ISU (integrated sight unit).

Kennedy called me on the radio. "I can't identify, my optics are out."

I couldn't engage them because Kennedy was between us. "Shoot from the hip, shoot from the hip!" I told him.

Kennedy saw several guys running in front of the Pepsi factory. He grabbed the Commander's override and opened up the 25 mm with HE rounds on high rate, trying to hit the fleeing insurgents. He started off really high, because you never know where the barrel's going to hit—you shoot and you adjust from that—and he worked his way down and across the front of the building, chasing the guys with about 70 rounds of high-explosive. It just destroyed the front of the factory, chunks flying everywhere, and looked like a scene from an action movie.

The insurgents made it to the riverbank, and Sergeant Sowby, who was behind me, finally had the angle and opened up his 25 mm. He pounded the guys in the bushes right before they got to the river.

Our original mission was to head to a small town south of Salman Pak and try to locate a known terrorist. The plan was to head to his house in the middle of the night just to see if we could catch him at home. Even though we'd been a bit rattled, none of our vehicles were damaged, and we continued on our patrol. Since Kennedy's ISU was out I put him in the middle of our small column, with Sowby in front and me in the rear, because I was still really rattled from that IED. We called the Apaches in and one came into the area and covered us as we rolled—our old friend Max 26. When we got to a point in the road where we needed to make a turn, we slowed down, and an IED went off in front of me.

Honestly, we were lucky that the IEDs we were dealing with were just rewired bombs. Insurgents would plant them in the ground and blow them up when the Americans drove by. If we weren't right on top of them, usually all we got was blast. Other troops were having to deal with insurgents planting EFP (explosively formed penetrator) bombs—these were charges that would rip through just about any armor we had.

The second IED of the night rattled me as well. Max 26 was on station but radioed us that he couldn't see anything or find anyone for us to kill. We were too far south to call all the way to base, so I called Sergeant Wyatt of the mortar platoon at Salman Pak. "Hey, please relay back to the Commander that this is a wash. We've already been hit with two IEDs. No real damage to the vehicles, no injuries. We're coming back up to Salman Pak."

"Roger that."

Max 26 was low on fuel and handed off to Gunslinger 24, which was on station overhead as we started rolling back. The Apaches we used were aviation assets with the 101st Airborne, and they were great. They saved our asses more times than I can count.

Our column was almost all the way back to Salman Pak in

a little village when we got hit with another IED. This time it caught the rear of Kennedy's vehicle and the front of Sowby's vehicle. That's when I'd had about enough. We stopped. I left the gunners and drivers in the vehicles, but the Commanders and our dismounts got out and went kicking in every door in that village looking for somebody, anybody, whose ass we could kick. Finally we found the sheik in the town. I grabbed my interpreter and had a very intense conversation with that sheik in the front yard of his house.

"Make this very clear to him," I told my interpreter. "If we or any of our forces get hit by another IED on this road, I'm going to come back here and drive my Bradley through his house. Crush his house. Make sure he understands me." I stuck a thumb over my shoulder at the Carnivore, which had rolled up.

The interpreter relayed my message. The sheik, through the interpreter, told me, "There's nothing I can do, I am very sorry."

"There better be something you can do," I told him, motioning my driver to pull forward.

He kept saying, "There's nothing I can do," and I kept motioning for my driver to pull forward. My driver kept pulling forward until the Carnivore hit and ran over the wall around the guy's yard and was creeping toward his house. The Bradley was in his front yard, inches away from his front door, before the sheik told me in English, "Okay, I understand, I understand."

"You understand?"

"Yes," he said. "But I have people coming here. I can't keep the people who are doing this out, they're coming from the river. They're coming from the other side, I can't stop them."

Okay, now we were having a conversation. "What do you need to stop them?" I asked. "Do you need the police here?"

"No, the police are worse than the people crossing the river."

"So what do you need?"

"I need guns and ammo."

"How much guns and ammo?" I asked him.

"A lot."

I smiled. "Okay. We'll give you AK-47s and ammo." We always had AKs and mags in our Bradleys, taken off the insurgents that we'd killed. I gave him four AKs and magazines, then told the interpreter, "You tell this guy to handle his shit or I'm going to come back and raze his village. Do you understand me?"

The interpreter passed it along. The sheik looked at me for clarification. "What?"

"I'm going to burn it to the ground and crush every fucking thing in here. If anybody gets shot at while we're driving down this road or if another IED goes off."

We never had another problem on that road again.

That sheik took care of his business, and he gained a lot of respect from the people in that area because he handled it himself. Because of that, he got his village back, and we actually developed a good relationship with him and his people. It wasn't uncommon for us to be driving through that area on patrol and have somebody run out and flag us down. Through our interpreter we'd hear that the sheik wanted to honor us with chai (tea). So we'd stop and have chai and talk with him.

For several nights Kennedy and I had been in the same location, a building that Alexander the Great built—or at least, had someone build. That's how old it was. Our sniper position was on the roof, and there weren't stairs to get up there. We had to climb piles of rocks and collapsed columns to make the ascent. Hollywood could have filmed *David and Goliath* in that place.

During the day there were sheepherders all over, and they weren't traveling far at night. Not only did Kennedy and I have to infil and exfil very covertly, to keep our position secret, we had to stay low on the roof all night to avoid being spotted. I was on the Barrett .50 and Kennedy was working as my spotter behind the M14. There was a lot of enemy activity in the area, plus we had a convoy scheduled to roll through, so we knew we'd probably see some action there. It was only a matter of time.

Through the thermal sight I watched a donkey come strolling down the road into view, with two guys riding it. They rode up close to us, dismounted, and proceed to place an IED. There was no doubt about what they were doing, and I called Sergeant Wyatt on the radio, talking as quietly as I could.

"I've got two of them, and they're definitely emplacing an IED. I want to take them out."

"Crazy Blue 4, wait," he told me. "Watch and see where they go, we want to get their cache."

I wasn't necessarily happy about that. "Okay, but get EOD on standby. I'm going to need them to come down here and get that IED before the convoy comes through."

"Roger that, Crazy Blue 4."

The two insurgents finished planting the IED and moved out, walking beside the donkey. They moved down the road and kept going and going. I got back on the radio with Wyatt. "Hey, they're still going, and I'm going to lose them on the curve." There were no other troops in the area, and Kennedy and I weren't about to try sneaking after them on foot.

"Okay, take the shot."

I was back on the radio in a second. "Wait, they're coming back." The two of them walked partway back to the IED location and stopped on the side of the road in some long grass. I don't know if they were talking or sightseeing or waiting for someone, but they were out there forever, just standing there next to the donkey.

"What the fuck are they doing?" Kennedy finally said. "They on a date?" He was getting as impatient as I was.

I got back on the radio with Wyatt, and by extension Burgoyne. "They've been out there forever, they're not going anywhere. I'm going to take the shot."

"Roger that, go ahead."

"Okay, I'm going to shoot the guy in front," I told Kennedy, "and when I do, you shoot the guy in back."

"Gotcha."

I centered the scope on the center of the man's chest, took a breath, held it, and squeezed the trigger. The Barrett jumped with the earth-shattering KABOOM like it always did, so I lost the view through the scope. When I got back on target, I couldn't see anything. I looked at Kennedy.

"You fucker, why didn't you shoot?"

" 'Cause they were gone," he told me.

"What do you mean they were gone?"

"They disappeared when you shot," he told me.

"My ass. There's no way I missed him, I was right on the guy, it's only a hundred yards!"

My spotter was insistent. "I'm telling you, they were gone, that donkey hauled ass." Yep, that's what he said.

What the fuck? I called the troop on the radio again. "Call in EOD, the site's clear."

"Crazy Blue 4, what about the insurgents?" they asked me.

"Um, I think I hit one," I told them, sounding like an idiot. "I can see a hot spot on the ground, but I can't really tell because of the grass."

"All right, we'll have EOD check it out."

EOD didn't arrive until the next morning. They rolled up in their Humvee and went to the shooting site. I could see one of them looking at something, then he walked back to the vehicle and got on the radio.

"Crazy Blue 4, Engineer 4, I don't know what kind of sick games y'all are playing, but we don't have an EOD incident out here, and we don't appreciate coming out here to look at the live-stock you've killed."

He was broadcasting across the whole squadron net. I jumped on the radio right quick.

"Engineer 4, Crazy Blue 4, negative, negative. EOD site is another fifty meters. You've stopped short."

"Oh, roger."

They proceeded to the IED location and spent a couple minutes looking it over. "This is Engineer 4," they called over the radio. "Be advised we have identified the object as a threat, and we're going to have to detonate it in place." While they were setting up to do that, I got back on the radio with Wyatt, as the EOD guy had just called me out in front of everyone.

"I don't know what they were talking about at the first site, so I'm going to go down and talk to him."

"Copy that. Don't take too long, that convoy is on its way."

Kennedy and I climbed down the rickety, 2,000-year-old structure and got out of the building without killing ourselves, then walked over to the EOD team. The guy in charge was the operator of the late bomb robot, Johnny 5. When he saw me he started shaking his head.

"I should have fucking known," he spat.

"What? What the hell's going on?" I asked him. "What did you see?" He told me.

That donkey had been in front of both of the men and raised his head just as I shot. As he did that, the man in back apparently caught up to the other guy. I hit the donkey right between the eyes. You could see the bottom part of his sockets, and the top of his head was still on. That big .50-caliber bullet kept going, hitting the guy behind the donkey in the chest; his collarbone was gone. The bullet deflected up and the guy behind *him* caught the bullet in his face. The top half of his head was gone. One bullet from a Barrett killed two guys and a donkey, so instantly that Kennedy couldn't get a shot off. The Barrett, remember, was designed for destroying big things, and its heavy bullet has a hell of a lot of momentum.

The EOD guy stared me straight in the face and said, "I'm never getting another bomb for you, ever, in my life. Don't even fucking call."

Outside of Salman Pak, the Iraqi police forces went out and captured a whole small town because there had been an IED set off on a police truck. They brought the whole town in and were beating them with sticks—even the kids. One of the kids was maybe 10 years old and had lumps the size of goose eggs on him. I was so offended by how badly they beat him that I called my squadron XO and told him that we needed to get down there and stop that shit. While waiting for orders I made a command decision—my platoon pulled some of the kids they were beating away from the Iraqis at the police station. We pulled them into a different room and were pretty much in an armed standoff with the police. There was a whole Sunni-versus-Shiite backstory going on there, but we didn't care. If you're beating children you're in the wrong.

In 1981, the Israelis bombed the Osirak nuclear reactor in Iraq. The reactor was built with the help of the French and was nearly completed when it was bombed. It was located 18 miles south of Baghdad, and the Israelis believed it was going to be used to build nuclear weapons. The facility was far enough along that there'd been radioactive material in place. Bombs and nuclear reactors are never a good combination—a lot of people on that side of the river had birth defects due to the radiation.

There was a small village in the area, and the head of the village was the local imam. He had a grandson he was very proud of, but his grandson had a lot of health problems. The little boy had severe cerebral palsy, and with my boy having CP, I had a special place in my heart for him. We would frequently stop at the village, and I would have my medic go in and check on the grandson and we would do whatever else we could for them. I had a good relationship with the imam.

When we stopped we would have chai with him and his family, and they would always serve us homemade pita bread. It was really good bread. In the summer, we met with him in his house, but now that it was cooler, we were outside in the sun. His daughter was just a few feet away, making the bread. My medic was checking on the boy, seeing if he was all right, while Kennedy, Cochran, and I were just sitting there getting ready to eat some bread.

The daughter pulled a blob of dough out, kneaded it with her hands, and threw it inside their mud brick oven. Then she squatted down on the ground, grabbed a cow patty, and threw the cow patty into the fire under the bread. I've learned since then that dried dung is a common fire fuel in a lot of parts of the world, but not when cooking food (or at least, I hope not). Anyway, with those same hands she rolled out some more dough and threw it in the oven as well. No hand washing for any of it.

Needless to say, I ate very little bread that day, but I did drink the chai. About the time we were ready to head out I watched the daughter take the chai cups down to the Euphrates River. She dipped the cups in, wiped them out with her dirty dress, brought them back up, and put them on the serving tray, which she then took back into the house. I think I would have rather eaten the cow patties than drunk Euphrates River water, after seeing everything that was dumped into it. So there I was, eating cow shit and drinking piss for about six months, just so I could help out that little boy.

December had arrived, and as we were scheduled to rotate home in January we were all looking ahead to what we'd been missing. I wanted to spend time with Amy, and most of the other guys were thinking about women as well. The Iraqi elections were coming up quickly, and they were a big deal. They were the first elections in post-Saddam Iraq. You probably remember seeing photos of smiling Iraqis holding up their ink-stained fingers to show they'd voted. Well, we assumed that the insurgents would pull out all the stops to disrupt the elections, so we were working 18-hour days.

We'd put 25,000 miles on the Carnivore II and done 10 major repairs to it. After traveling as far west as Ar Rummanh, on the Jordan border, as far south as Karbala, and as far north as the city of Balad, we finally got to rejoin the rest of our squadron at Camp Rustamiyah on the southeast side of Baghdad. Captain Burgoyne was more than happy to have his troop intact again. With the upcoming change of responsibility we would have to patrol south to Haji Ali Ash Shahim, a small town that had been handed over to the Iraqi army. Considering that the last time we'd been there we'd been ambushed by IEDs on our way in and out, I wasn't exactly looking forward to the trip. The Salman Pak River Road followed the Tigris River south, and that would turn out to be our last trip down it.

Our job was to check all the polling sites in our zone for the upcoming elections. My platoon would send out three gun trucks, up-armored Humvees designated M1114s. Staff Sergeants Sowby and Williams would be in the lead vehicle, Lieutenants Cummings and Harris would be in the second truck, and I would bring up the rear with my crew.

Most of the ride went without a problem, and at 1 A.M. we were just two miles to the turnaround point. I'd been doing patrols long enough to feel that something wasn't quite right, however. Even at that time of the morning, there should have been other vehicles on the road, even a donkey cart, but nothing was moving. I had our vehicles change speed and spacing. Less than a mile from the turn-around point, there was a hairpin turn, and we had to close up the distance between vehicles.

Just then there was a bright flash and a blast, and dust and rocks danced on the hood of my Humvee. I was on the radio before the rattling rain stopped. "Contact! All vehicles stop and call in your status!" I ordered.

The first two vehicles had already passed the IED when it went off. It detonated behind the second Humvee, just in front of mine. Luckily the thick armor on the M1114s worked, and nobody was injured. We knew it had to be command detonated, which meant there was someone nearby we could go after. All vehicles stayed where they were while we scanned the area.

Lieutenant Cummings took charge and had me dismount with a small team to try and catch the insurgents who had emplaced the IED. I jumped out with Sergeant Cochran, one of my team leaders, and Private First Class Turnbull. We moved carefully toward the blast site. The bomb had blown a big hole in the road on the side closest to the river. Command detonated meant wires. I was looking for the wires, because I wanted to find them and follow them back.

"I got movement out there!" Cochran called out, pointing. I loaded a flare round into my 203 and fired it into the air. When the parachute deployed we could see at least one man running toward the river across a big field. I opened fire on him and started chasing after him, yelling for Cochran to follow me. The Iraqi was running like a deer through the Tennessee hills, firing his AK-47 wildly over his shoulder. I could hear the rounds snapping around my head as I fired back at him on three-round burst. I tripped and fell in a ditch, and after Cochran helped me up, I took off running again. At a dead run I fired until I emptied my magazine.

I saw the Iraqi go down and I was pretty sure I'd hit him. I stopped and did a quick reload, and moved closer to where the Iraqi had fallen. Right before I reached the spot I checked behind me. Cochran was way back there. He had his flashlight on his rifle and it was waving everywhere. I could hear him yelling and equipment going everywhere as he took a tumble into another ditch. Running in the dark is generally a bad idea even where there isn't anybody shooting at you, and we were running across uneven ground covered with elephant grass.

Right where I expected the Iraqi to be lying on the ground, bleeding out, I stumbled onto the bank of the Tigris River. I hadn't hit the guy at all; he'd just jumped down the bank and was now clambering up into a small boat. There were two other Iraqis in the boat as well, and we saw one another at the same time. Their eyes got huge, but nobody had a gun in hand; they were lying in the boat.

As they went for their rifles, I raised my M4, pulled the trigger, and nothing. Instead of performing an immediate action drill—which is what you're supposed to do when your weapon doesn't go off—I took the rifle off my shoulder, turned it sideways, and looked at it stupidly. As I was doing that, however, one of the guys in the boat went for his AK.

Without thinking I just reached forward and fired my M203 40 mm grenade launcher at the boat. In slow motion I watched the 40 mm round smash into the rifle carrier's hip, ricochet into the back of the boat, and detonate on the chest of the other soldier. The three of them were blown back into the river. The buttstock of my rifle came back and hit me in the chin, and I fell back onto my ass.

I slid down the steep and muddy riverbank until I was knee-deep in the cold Tigris. It has a fast current and steep banks, and I had to hold on to the cattails to keep from being swept away. Cochran finally showed up, panting. I'm short, but he's two inches from midget and all of that is torso, so it's no wonder he couldn't keep up with me.

"Fuck, fuck!" Cochran said, looking at the sinking boat and the bodies.

"Fuck nothing, come here and help me!" I yelled at him.

He helped me up the bank. We could just make out the outline of the boat as it sank into the river, the bob of a body or two.

Just as we were getting up, Specialist Jeff Sund, the Lieutenant's gunner, spotted one insurgent on the other side of the river, shooting at us. Sund was the best M240B gunner we had in the troop. At a range of more than 400 meters, he fired across the river at the insurgent. By his second short burst he was on target. He then opened up with a long 75-round burst that ate up the insurgent and the riverbank, just in case there was anybody else lurking about. Max 26, our friendly Apache gunship, showed up then and shadowed us overhead until our vehicles got back to base.

Why did my gun jam? Turns out that I shoved a bunch of elephant grass into my mag well when I reloaded, which bound the bolt carrier up. I learned several valuable lessons from that incident: (1) a scared guy can run faster than a mad guy; (2) never chase a bad guy with someone you can outrun; (3) 20 feet is not really a safe distance to be firing a grenade launcher at someone; and (4) don't load weeds into your rifle.

Almost our whole platoon had been involved in a big counterinsurgency sniper operation on the river. We were on our way back and dragging tail, as we'd been up for 36 hours. Right outside Salman Pak we ran into an MP (Military Police) company, which had found some artillery rounds. Those rounds would certainly have ended up as an IED somewhere, and our squadron XO told us to secure the area while the MPs took care of business.

By the time we were finished with that task we'd been up for 40 hours, and we were just trashed. We were so tired that on the way back one of my gunners fell asleep in the turret and lost his rifle. It fell off the Humvee. He realized he'd dropped it, but whether that was three seconds or three minutes after it happened I couldn't say, and neither could he. We turned around and looked for it but couldn't find it, so we headed back to base and reported it. What did they tell us to do? Go look for it again.

So we went back out and searched the route again, but no rifle. By the time we straggled back in through the gate we'd been up for something like 42 or 43 hours and could hardly see straight.

As we were pulling into the base, Sergeant Anthony Mitchell was heading out in his M1. Tony and I had traded off on the Barrett regularly, and he was a good guy and a good soldier. One of his crew had to secure something on his tank, so our two vehicles paused beside each other just inside the gate. "Hey brother, take care of yourself out there," I called to him.

Tony just gave me a shit-eating grin and said, "I got this shit."

We passed ways, Tony went out the gate, and he hadn't gone 500 yards down the road when he saw fuel cans sitting by the side of the road. Seeing them as a hazard, Tony used the front of his tank to push them out of the way. There was an IED planted in among the fuel cans, and it went off and killed him instantly.

Crazy Horse was a tightly knit group. We were all family, in some ways more than others—Tony was in one of our tank platoons, and his brother was in the other. We heard the IED go off, and when the word went out across the radio that Tony had been killed, the entire troop was crushed. Everybody liked Tony, and both he and his brother had a lot of friends.

The Troop Commander came over to us as we were just sitting there, not knowing what to do, and he said, "I need you to take your guys back out there. We have to control that sector. The tank platoon is devastated—hell, both tank platoons are devastated, but we have to go back out. I don't want to have to order you to go out there."

I said, "Not a problem, sir, we'll go out there."

When we went back outside the gate, it was very hard controlling my troopers, keeping them from shooting every Iraqi who was out there. We left the gate with tears in our eyes and heavy hearts, but we were professional and dedicated. We went back out into the lion's mouth, and my platoon of Crazy Horse troopers swallowed their feelings of revenge and did their jobs. Nobody even fired a warning shot. Tony Mitchell was the only casualty we had in our troop while I was there, and yet we went right back out, did a patrol, and didn't participate in any abuse or revenge killing or anything else. That's one of the hardest things to do in war—after losing a friend, to immediately go back out there with those same hostiles and not let your anger overtake you.

We did another eight-hour patrol of the section until we could get another unit to cover for us. When we finally made it back to base we'd been up for more than 50 hours.

I feel somewhat responsible for Mitchell's death. My crew and I had driven up and down that route three times right before he went out, which means we missed those fuel cans, missed the guy planting the IED, missed something.

CHAPTER 23

SYRIA VS. KENTUCKY

On December 14, 2005, the day before the Iraqi elections, we were set up at the 3rd POB headquarters on the Tigris River. We'd been working 18-hour days for close to two months, and everybody was exhausted. We had four Bradleys with us and an MP with his bomb-sniffing dog. Everybody was chilling, and I was hanging out with Cochran and Kennedy and the MP just outside the old hotel in the 3rd POB's compound.

That morning we were just sitting in the sun like lizards, relaxing, enjoying the quiet time before something else exploded or somebody started shooting. I looked at Kennedy, then over at the MP.

"Hey, the Commander wanted to see you at the front of the compound," I told the MP.

"Yeah? About what?"

"How the hell should I know?"

"Okay, I'll be back," he told me, and left the dog with us. He was barely out of sight when that dog crawled into my lap and I started feeding him some muffins I had left over from breakfast. That dog loved me and hated his owner, in part because I was always feeding him good food instead of crappy dog chow. I'd give him muffins and ham slices and whatever else I had every chance I could, because he was too damn skinny. That MP, he never could figure out why that dog liked me so much, or why I kept sending him on so many useless errands.

At about 10 that morning the 3rd POB guys opened up from the roof of the hotel with their big 14.5 mm antiaircraft guns. We hardly paid it any attention, because the truth of the matter was that the Iraqis loved those damn guns and used any excuse they could find to shoot them. They were shooting across the river at something—again—and we just ignored the noise and continued chilling. Until one of them came running down from the roof to us.

"Sergeant Jay, Sergeant Jay, sniper!" he told me, panting.

"What?"

He pointed up at the top of the old hotel. "Sniper, sniper! We have hurt, wounded, and need some help. The sniper is on the other side of the river."

"Shit." I looked at Cochran and said, "Call the CO and tell him we've been asked to help the POB as they're under fire and they've got wounded, and we'll keep him informed."

"Kennedy, go wake everybody up, tell them to head to the roof," I told him, and he trotted off. The hotel was 14 floors, which meant from where we were sitting we'd have 13 flights of stairs to climb. Working elevator? Ha. I looked over at the ramp of the Bradley, where our rifles were sitting, my Barrett (32 pounds) and Kennedy's M14 (14 pounds). After another glance at the top of the hotel, I walked over to the Brad, grabbed the M14, and jogged toward the door of the hotel. I heard Kennedy coming up behind me. He grabbed the Barrett and followed me into the stairwell.

"Sarge, you've got my gun," he called up after me as we moved up the stairs as fast as we could. "Sarge, you've got my gun. Sarge . . . (pant) . . . you've got . . . my gun. Sarge . . . (pant) . . . you've . . . (pant) . . . got . . ." Pretty soon it was just heavy breathing behind me, drawing farther and farther back. Hey, I may be old, but I'm not dumb. I had quite a lead on him when I got to the roof.

My Iraqis were ducking and bobbing at the edge of the roof, firing their AKs in the general direction of the river.

"Anybody see him or know where he is?" I yelled over the noise. They were right, he had to be on the far side of the river, but that encompassed a big swath of countryside.

"No," several of them told me.

"Then what the hell are you shooting at? Get off the roof," I told them, and moved forward toward the low wall around the edge of the roof. As I moved forward, they moved back, still firing their AKs—and one of my Iraqis shot me dead center in the back from six feet away.

I spun around, murder in my eyes, and his eyes went as wide as dinner plates. I grabbed the AK out of his hands, threw it off the roof, and put a boot to his chest. He went flying backward down the stairs just as Kennedy came chugging up. Kennedy didn't even ask, he just avoided the tumbling body.

Fuck, did that hurt. The AK round hit me right in the center of my SAPI (small arms protective insert) plate. If I hadn't been wearing my armor plate that would have been it for me, I'd've been killed. As it was, I still have back problems because of the blunt force trauma to my spine. That dude's lucky I didn't throw him off the roof after his rifle.

In pain, and now seriously pissed, I duckwalked to the edge of the roof, Kennedy at my elbow. I heard the rest of the platoon thudding up the stairs behind us as we got into position. A round hit the wall near us, causing both of us to flinch. Kennedy and I scanned back and forth, back and forth through our rifle scopes. I was so pissed, I never wanted to shoot someone in the face as much as I did at that moment.

"You see him?"

"No, I don't see shit," Kennedy told me.

I was just getting the M14 set up and in a solid position when a round hit the wall right next to my face, spraying me with dust. Getting shot in the back had pissed me off—now I was furious.

"I need this fucker," I growled at Kennedy. The insurgent sniper hit the wall again, six inches to the other side of my face. He was all over us, and we still hadn't even spotted him. We ducked down, moved, and popped back up, still searching for him.

"I think I have something," Kennedy told me. He talked me into the spot, which was a long way off. "Just in front of the tree line, I think I saw some dust, maybe from him firing." I used the Bushnell laser range finder to get the range. It was 852 meters, a hell of a long shot. I called the range out. And were there two of them? I looked through the scope again. If that was a guy, he was laying down, and all I had was a head shot. But off to the side, was that another guy?

"I think he's got a spotter with him, off to the side. You see him?"

"Yeah. Shit, eight fifty-two?" I knew what he was thinking. We hadn't zeroed either rifle in weeks. That wasn't a big deal when we were only shooting out to 100 or 200 yards, but 852 meters? That was over 930 yards, well over half a mile.

"Yep." I cranked the elevation knobs on the scope. "I'll take the one on the left, you take the one on the right, and fire after I do."

I put the crosshairs on the tiny little smudge and slowly, carefully, squeezed the trigger.

My shot was on line, but 10 meters short—I saw the dust kick up. "I'm short," I told Kennedy before he fired. I gave him the range adjustment.

Through the scope I watched as my smudge stood up—it was a man. He calmly dusted off his pants, picked up his rifle, collapsed the bipod, and started walking away. Well, shit, I had the windage right for the first shot, and while I'd been low, now I had a standing target—much more forgiving when it came to elevation. I held high, fired three more shots, and hit the sniper in the hip or leg. Injured but not down, he started limping to make his escape. I emptied the rest of the 20-round magazine at him. He was on the ground by my fourth round, but I still emptied the magazine. Fuck finesse.

As I was firing on the first sniper, Kennedy finished adjusting the elevation on his Leupold scope and engaged the spotter. The insurgent must have fired just as Kennedy did, because as the Barrett was coming down out of recoil a bullet zipped up Kennedy's sleeve, grazing his arm. Kennedy hit the man in the head with his first round—a hell of a shot, especially considering he'd never fired the Barrett before.

"Shit! I'm hit!" Kennedy said, grabbing his arm. He didn't know how bad it was at first, but the round had barely broken his skin and only made a red mark on his arm.

With the sniper and his spotter down, the woods behind them emptied out, and we saw half a dozen guys with weapons running to a white truck. By this time the rest of my platoon was on the roof, with their M4s.

"Everybody fire at the truck, just a couple rounds," I told them.

The truck had to be close to 1,000 yards out and started pulling away with guys in the bed. My platoon fired en masse, and we could see the bullets come down on the far side of the river. The bullets hitting the ground looked like a small rain cloud kicking up dust, but they hit short of the truck.

"Adjust up and empty your mags!" I told them.

Everybody fired again, and I watched as the truck swerved suddenly and went into a ditch, flinging guys out of the bed. I don't know how long it had been since the U.S. Army used volley fire in combat, but we did it that day, and it worked.

I called up Burgoyne and told him what had happened. He said he would be by in about 10 minutes and wanted to see where the bad guys were. That gave us enough time to get down off the roof.

Our 3rd ACR owned that side of the river. When they approached the white truck they saw a few guys still moving in the ditch and shot them before getting close. The truck had been so far away that most of the bullets from the M4s had just dented the sheet metal and not penetrated. At least one had gone through the driver's window, though, hitting him in the arm, which had caused him to swerve into the ditch. The accident had caused more death and injuries than our bullets did.

Both the sniper and the spotter were armed with Romanian PSLs, what most Americans who know about guns think of as Dragunov sniper rifles. They are stretched, accurized versions of the AK design firing the 7.62x54R cartridge, very similar in ballistics to our .30-06. Romanian rifles had very good quality control compared to some guns from Eastern bloc countries, and Romanian AKs were highly prized by anybody who could get their hands on them. The standard scopes on PSLs weren't that good compared to what we were used to, but a good shooter could do a lot of damage with one. The scope on the sniper's rifle was a commercial German model, even better for sniping than the standard-issue 4x scope.

That sniper was a better shot than me. He was hitting within inches of my head, from half a mile away, before I ever saw him. I just got lucky. I was later told that he wasn't Iraqi, but Syrian, and was believed to be the same sniper who had killed upwards of 20 American soldiers with some damned good shooting. Some of those kills had been filmed, with the footage put on the Internet or sent to Al Jazeera. Whether he was that guy or not, the sniping stopped after I killed him. They wrote up the incident in *Stars and Stripes* with a photo of me and Kennedy,* and I got the Bronze Star for killing the sniper, but I didn't know who he was at the time. All I knew was that he pissed me off.

My sniper logbook is in the 3rd ID museum at Fort Stewart along with a few other things I brought back, including an RPG-7 sight and the Iraqi flag we pulled out of As Samawah. In all, I got credit for 121 kills with a sniper rifle during my second tour. As I mentioned before, the Army wasn't big on "confirmed kills" in Iraq, so that number isn't a guess Kennedy and I came up with looking through binoculars. I took 121 rifles off dead guys whom I'd shot. I didn't know it at the time, but that's more kills than any U.S. sniper had during the Vietnam War. However, I think that's a bit like comparing apples and oranges. Most of the time I was engaging two or three guys at once, at relatively short distances. We had a target-rich environment.

It was only a few short weeks later that Crazy Horse went home. I officially left Iraq on January 10, 2006.

When I went to Iraq in 2003 I was an E6—Staff Sergeant. When I returned in 2005 I was an E7—Sergeant First Class.

---

* "Four Terrorists Killed in Separate Incidents," *Stars and Stripes,* January 4, 2006.

Adjusting to a stateside routine is always difficult after being in combat, and I had very little tolerance for bullshit to begin with. One Friday afternoon, the Sergeant Major told me to go have my guys jump into the Dumpster to retrieve aluminum cans. My first reaction was "Are you out of your mind?"

His reply was, "Look, Sergeant Johnson, I don't care if you've been to combat or not. We're back here in the garrison world, and I'll get my chance at combat. Until then, get your troops over there and make them clean that Dumpster out. We're not going to be the embarrassment of Fort Stewart."

So I retired.

While I loved the Army and had made a career out of it, I didn't have much interest in riding desks. I didn't go into the Army to sit on my ass, especially not when there was still a war on. I officially retired on July 31, 2006, after 20 years, 4 months, and 25 days in the U.S. Army. In that time, I spent almost 10 years working overseas (one tour in Bosnia and three in Iraq, starting with Desert Storm in 1991). Once I got out, I went right back to work—for Blackwater.

Thanks to the American media, even people who don't know anything about the military or modern private contracting have heard the name Blackwater, and to most of them it probably has a negative connotation. The simple fact of the matter is that we worked for the U.S. State Department and the Chief of Missions there, but because we weren't encumbered by miles of red tape we could do things much more efficiently and quickly than the military. Not only that, they paid a hell of a lot better.

I'd seen and interacted with contractors while I was in-country with Crazy Horse, and I have to admit the job appealed to me. I had a military pension, but it wasn't going to make me rich. Even though I was only in my mid-forties, there was no guarantee how long I'd be able to earn a living for my kids. My Hodgkins lymphoma could jump out of remission at any time. Jaycob's cerebral palsy wasn't going to go away.

So, I could go back to work in a country I knew very well, doing pretty much the same thing I'd been doing for the U.S. military, only for a hell of a lot more money. Not one of the toughest decisions I'd ever had to make.

CHAPTER 24

BLOOD, SWEAT, AND TEARS

There was a real need for private contractors in Iraq thanks to a number of different factors.

The first was just the size of our peacetime military. Compared to how many troops we'd had in the field during World War II, Vietnam, even during the Cold War, we were small. Fighting battles is one thing, but policing a country filled with insurgents, with more of them flooding in from half the countries in the Middle East every day, takes a lot of bodies.

The second reason the U.S. government liked contractors was that we operated under what are known in the trade as Big Boy Rules. What's that? The U.S. military, in all its wisdom, hardly trusts its soldiers with loaded weapons except when they're on the front line. Americans died at the consulate in Libya because the Marines there weren't allowed to carry any live ammo in their weapons. That wasn't the first time that had happened, and unfortunately it probably won't be the last. If a convoy is attacked or a helicopter goes down, and 90 percent of your weapons are secured in the armory, it's going to take you a lot of time to get geared up and on-site. Private contractors didn't have those same restrictions. We were all vets and were deemed adult enough to be responsible for our own weapons. We were all armed, and since we were on call 24/7, all of our guns were loaded. If a helicopter went down our reaction time out of the gate was one-tenth what the military's was, so we went out and secured the scene until the Army or Marines showed up with the armor and heavy weapons. We were professional soldiers working for the U.S. government; we just had a middleman. Even though we would have had no problem getting alcohol shipped in, we had a dry facility. Supervising a bunch of A-type personalities with guns was tough enough—the last thing I needed was alcohol thrown into the mix.

One of the reasons the Blackwater name is so well known is because of the incident where some of its contractors shot some civilians who had shot at them first. Oh, you didn't hear that part on the news, about the "civilians" shooting at our guys first? Didn't think so. That incident, ultimately, was what cost Blackwater its Iraq contract with the State Department. The PSD (Protection Security Detail) team involved in that incident was Raven 23, and afterward the management at Blackwater made me the shift leader of the team to make sure there weren't any more problems. There weren't, but it was too late for the company, although it took some time for the giant to fall. When Blackwater left, all of their contracts transferred to another company, and I and everybody else went right back to work for them, doing the same job for 50 dollars more a day. At one point I was supervising 128 people, but I was still going out beyond the fence, because I've always believed in leading from the front. Not only was I in charge of all the teams, I led a team. I never asked anybody to do anything I wasn't willing to do.

Except for the occasional screw-ups (and they're the only things that seem to make the news back home), the people I supervised were professionals and acted like it. We weren't running our own war or running wild, we were doing a job. Any time we fired a shot we had to write up an incident report, and that report was reviewed by an agent of the State Department. We couldn't go back out until he'd cleared us.

While we operated under fewer inane rules than the U.S. military, we still had them. Not too long into my contracting life, we were told by the powers that be that the guys working on PSDs couldn't have any optics on their weapons with higher than a 1.5x magnification. Whoever made this decision apparently concluded that anything higher than 1.5x was an "offensive" sight, and we were only supposed to be operating defensively. The inexperience and ignorance, if not outright stupidity, of this decision was the kind of thing we dealt with every day

It just so happens that my favorite optic that I used while contracting in Iraq was a 1.5x Trijicon mini-ACOG, so the optics restriction didn't excessively piss me off. The extra little bit of magnification over a nonmagnified red-dot sight was sometimes just what I needed to get the job done. I beat the snot out of that thing and it never let me down. In fact, I still have it.

Contracting isn't easy—that's why it pays so well. You're risking your life every day in a high-stress environment. Standard rotation was three months in-country, one month home, and I did that for five years. Most of the time I was in Iraq, but I spent a little time contracting in Afghanistan, too. Even if nothing happened, riding around in 100-plus-degree heat for hours on end waiting to get shot at or blown up by an IED is as stressful as hell. Waiting for hours in the trucks was also boring, and the practical jokes we played on each other were brutal.

We would make MRE bombs with hot sauce—you take the chemical heater from the meal, fill it up with hot sauce, add water, seal it, and drop it down inside a vehicle, then block the doors so the guys inside couldn't get out. The vehicle would fill up with improvised OC gas—pepper spray. Or you could drop it inside a water bottle and leave it there until it exploded. Guys would like to see who was quicker with knives, as well, so the medics would always be stitching them up in the back of the trucks.

I spent a lot of time in the TSTs (tactical support teams). One of the guys I supervised was named Oatridge, but we didn't call him that for very long. The daughter of one of the other guys on the team, Jackson, had sent him a five-pound bag of frosted animal crackers. Jackson had it in the vehicle with us when we were on standby at a checkpoint one day.

"Jackson, can I have some of your cookies?" Oatridge asked.

"Sure, dude." Oatridge stayed in the vehicle while Jackson and I were nearby. After two hours it was time to get back in the vehicle and head out.

"Lemme have the cookies," Jackson said to Oatridge. Oatridge handed over the box, and Jackson reached inside. There was one cookie left.

"Motherfucker, are you kidding me? I said you could have some of the cookies, not all of them! My daughter sent me those."

"There's some left," Oatridge said defensively.

"There's *one* left!" Jackson roared.

"You ate five pounds of cookies?" I said in disbelief.

After that, Oatridge was forever known as Cookie.

I did my best to keep in shape, both for self-preservation and to burn off stress, and ran regularly on the treadmill we had in our compound. At one point I was running five miles in half an hour, which was close to an 800-calorie workout—and I was still chunky. What the hell, distance running breeds cowardice anyway, right? If you can't run far, you have to stay and fight.

While contracting I wrote several more articles for *Soldier of Fortune* detailing Crazy Horse's second tour in Iraq. The editors actually chose one of the photos I submitted for the cover of the August 2006 issue, inside of which was my write-up of my brief adventure in the freshwater navy.* It was a group "hero" shot of some of the troop, including Lieutenant Dejesus, Sergeants Cochran, Sowby, and Williams, and me, posing with our weapons.

After five years of contracting, I'd had enough. Forty-eight was still too young to retire, though, so in addition to getting to spend time with my wife and sons I started doing firearms training at a facility called the Big 3 Training Center outside of Daytona Beach, Florida. After the war it seemed like everybody who'd ever worn a uniform or heard a shot fired in combat started up a training school. Some of them were good, some of them not so much, but after a quarter of a century as a professional soldier I've learned a couple of things.

When I went to Iraq the first time, in 1991, I shouldered my rifle like a lot of old-school trap and skeet shooters—with my right elbow way up and out there. However, on that first visit to Iraq I took a round in the elbow. It went through the sleeve of my shirt and took a little piece of skin off the underside of my elbow when it was up in the air, but that was enough to teach me—tuck your wings in. This was long before trainers started teaching people to tuck in their elbows during CBQ (close-quarters battle). The fact

---

* "3/7 Cavalry: Fighting the Good Fight, Part 2," by SFC Dillard J. Johnson, *Soldier of Fortune*, August 2006, p. 22.

that keeping your arms tucked in while house clearing prevents you from banging your elbows against doorframes is a bonus.

I have been reading about how unreliable the M16 is for years. Stoppages are a big problem, you have to keep it spotless for it to work, blah, blah, blah. In 20 years of active duty and 5 years of contracting I had only three—yes, three—issues with M16s and M4s. One was with an old M16A1 that had had tons of rounds fired through it, so it was due for a new ejection spring anyway. The second was when the M4 I was using at As Samawah was disabled by the airburst mortar round. (Hell, before it was disabled, I emptied 14 magazines through that M4 on three-round burst as fast as I could load them. That was after 238 miles of desert sand and cold rain.) The third was when I stuffed elephant grass into the mag well of my M4, late in my second tour.

Once, while contracting, we headed out to secure the crash site of a downed helicopter. Our M249 SAW (a light belt-fed machine gun) was out of operation, so I grabbed an M4 and a five-gallon bucket full of 30-round magazines. I took a position on a rooftop overlooking the crash site and almost immediately had to deal with a number of insurgents on the roof of an apartment building opposite me. They were slightly above me and protected by a wall, and it was my job to keep them from shooting at the wreck until the cavalry arrived. I put 500 rounds of ammo through that M4 on full auto as fast as I could fire and reload. The barrel turned orange from the heat, but the rifle never stopped working.

I have been asked about M16 barrel failures, but I have never seen one; they are sort of like Bigfoot to me. I just don't think an M4 barrel will fail without sticking it full of mud. Did we use some sort of secret, high-tech lube on our M4s? Nope. I used 15W40 motor oil for lube during both tours in Iraq with Crazy Horse. Ask the insurgents how it worked.

Another common complaint about the M16 is the caliber. It is a small-caliber (.22) round, albeit a high-velocity one. Lots of people have referred to the rifle as a "poodle shooter" because the bullet is so small, and that was before the Army started issuing the SS109 green-tip armor-piercing ammunition that doesn't expand and rarely tumbles. How well did SS109 ammo work for me? It worked just fine—it kills bad guys dead. However, I don't belong to the same school of thought as the "magic bullet" people, always looking for the rifle or cartridge that will give them the mythic "one-shot stop." I shot people until they were dead. How many rounds that took depended on what I was using. The most effective weapon I ever utilized was a B-1B bomber.

The Beretta M9, on the other hand, I fucking hated. I can't even remember how many times it tried to kill me. Several times during the battle at As Samawah it jammed on me, but I can't really lay all the blame for that on the pistol—politics are to blame as well. In 1994 Congress passed a bill banning the sale to civilians of magazines that hold more than 10 rounds. The only new full-capacity magazines being manufactured in any bulk after that time were going to fulfill military contracts, where I suspect the manufacturers thought oversight was pretty much nil. So they put out magazines that seemed to only meet the bare minimum requirements, maybe. If the magazines we were issued sucked and we had the inclination to buy some of our own, we couldn't afford any because the prices went through the roof on those few pre-ban magazines still for sale. I wasn't the only soldier having problems with substandard Beretta magazines, either; I heard it was quite a widespread problem.

That magazine ban expired in 2004, and since then our soldiers have been able to get what they need, thank God, even if they had to buy it themselves, with their own money.

The problem, however, wasn't just the magazines. I shot several Iraqis half a dozen times with the Beretta, and the 9 mm full-metal-jacket ammo just didn't put them down. On my second tour in Iraq, as soon as I had the opportunity, I ditched my Beretta for a Browning Hi-Power. It was still a 9 mm, but at least I didn't have to worry about it jamming on me. You want to know how much I hated the Beretta? I can tell you exactly when and where I replaced it with the Hi-Power: March 23, 2005, in Salawa, Iraq.

There seems to be a bit of an argument within the "sniping community" as to whether the traditional bolt-action sniper rifle is outdated. Yes, bolt-action rifles are inherently more accurate than semiautos such as the M14 and Barrett, but having to physically work the bolt doesn't allow for quick follow-up shots. In Iraq, quite frequently we had more than one person to shoot at when the time came to pull the trigger.

How many of the 121 confirmed kills I had as a sniper were taken with a bolt-action rifle? None. That should pretty much make my opinion on the subject clear. After leaving the Army I often used an AR-10 pattern rifle when working overwatch. The AR-10 is an upsized AR-15 chambered for the larger .308 round, the same round that the M14 fires. AR-10s tend to be more finicky about ammunition but are also (generally) more accurate.

This is not just a book about me. It is about young men who deserve your respect, and because I was there I can write about them. They fought for their country and their friends, and will forever be changed.

Where is everyone now? To be honest, I've lost track of too

many of them. Broadhead was a career man and was still in the Army the last time I checked. Sergeant Major Brahain just recently retired. Soprano got out of the Army and went back to school. Sully stayed in Crazy Horse for a while, but we lost touch. Jason Sperry, my driver, got out of the Army after 2003 and headed for parts unknown. He did all that was asked of him, but now he wants the past to be the past. I stayed friends with Captain Burgoyne, who is still in the Army and is now a Major. Captain Bair is now a Major as well. Captain McCoy received the Silver Star for his actions in and around An Najaf and got promoted out of the field. Lieutenant David Dejesus was well on his way to becoming a fine officer but was tragically killed in a non-service-related accident after his return to the States.

There were too many troopers in Crazy Horse to mention everybody, but one soldier I did want to credit was Jerrod Fields. Early in 2005, when I was in-country, he got the lower part of his left leg blown off when an IED hit his Bradley. He was so concerned with getting his crew out of the kill zone that he continued to drive even though he'd lost his leg, for which he received a Bronze Star. Jerrod went back and got a prosthetic and stayed in the Army. In fact, he was reenlisted by Vice President Dick Cheney. Not just that, he'd always been a great athlete, and he continued with that, ending up in the Army's World Class Athlete Program. He was featured on the cover of the April 23, 2008, issue of *ESPN The Magazine*. Jerrod is still a Bradley gunner, a Crazy Horse trooper through and through.

*C*arnivore is my story. Maybe 5,000 soldiers saw direct combat in the first few months of the war, and every one of them has a story. This is what I saw and did. There were a lot of things that went on that aren't in the book, but this is what I felt was important to show the effect that armor had on the war.

I can't speak for what anyone else saw and did. I know I was just a small part of a huge effort—and also lucky as hell. My nickname should be Lucky Jay, not Crazy Jay, because I should have died a dozen times over. That's how I know there has to be somebody up there looking out for me. I was blown up—or almost blown up—so many times that a lot of my memories of the war are jumbled or completely gone. I don't know how many concussions I received, because I never had the time to get them diagnosed, much less treated—I was too busy shooting back. I don't think the super-ultra-mega-chemo did anything positive for my brain cells, either. A spoken word or something I'll see will jog my brain, and all of a sudden I'll remember something that happened in Iraq that I'd completely forgotten about.

Right about the time I finished this book I found out that my cancer was back. There have been a lot of medical advancements in the almost nine years since I last beat it, and I'm confident I can beat it again. It's not going to be fun or pleasant, but chemo is better than the alternative.

Large numbers of soldiers and Marines have gone to combat, but only a small number have stepped into the mouth of hell, shed blood, and experienced the loss of friends. The fighting men and women of this country put everything in their lives on hold for the freedom of another people and some have given their lives for this true and just cause. We must never let our fallen friends be forgotten. Going to Iraq I think has made our military stronger and made our country stronger. Far too many of our citizens have forgotten that freedom isn't free. I lost good friends. The old saying that what does not kill you makes you stronger is not true. What does not kill you leaves you in pain for the rest of your life.

Contrary to what a lot of people who have never been to Iraq think, I believe it was a good thing for the United States to go over there. From what I personally observed, I feel that the Iraqi people are better off now than before. There has been no change of heart on my part, even after all I've been through.

For those who lost a loved one in Iraq, know that they died winning freedom for the Iraqis. I am truly sorry for your loss and hope that you are not bitter about it. Your loved one has done the greatest thing any human can do in their lifetime, and there is a very good chance that he or she changed someone's life for the better.

As for myself, all the combat I've seen has changed me. You can't go through what I and my crew went through and not be changed in some way. I've seen too much death, caused too much death.

I try to remember the good things, the brave things, the funny things, but I have a lot of memories that aren't so great. At As Samawah, the second day, when the Commander told us to go back across the bridge and hold it, I was stopped next to the little guard shack. That shack was the first thing Broadhead and I had shot up, and there were 15- and 16-year-old kids going inside the building and stealing Iraqi weapons. The Lieutenant's gunner was right next to me, and he opened up on the guard shack with HE rounds. They passed right in front of my face, and he killed or maimed those kids as they were coming out. I don't think they were getting the rifles to fight, I think they were just going to sell them, but he saw them as weapon carriers on a battlefield and thus fair game.

Iraqis from the village came out, crying and screaming, and a woman holding one of the boys ripped her clothes, showing us her breast, signaling to us that he was her kid. I got out and was trying to put pressure dressings on them—we didn't have tourniquets back then—whatever I could use out of my vehicle's combat life-saving kit, trying to help those kids.

That was a horrible thing for me to see, because I'm a father of three boys. I try not to think about it, and the memory fades over time. But it still happened.

Before heading to Iraq in 2003 I hunted a lot in Kentucky. Now, when I hear guys talking about going deer hunting or bagging a big buck, I just sort of snort. How hard is it to kill a deer? Did he have an AK or an RPG? Was he shooting back? I don't really hunt anymore, because I get nothing out of it. Something Ernest Hemingway wrote I have found to be completely true for me: "Certainly there is no hunting like the hunting of man and those who have hunted armed men long enough and liked it, never really care for anything else thereafter. You will meet them doing various things with resolve, but their interest rarely holds because after the other thing ordinary life is as flat as the taste of wine when the taste buds have been burned off your tongue." It takes a lot to get my adrenaline going.

We went over as liberators, not conquerors, but it's like when a bully has kids under control on a playground. When you take that bully out, all of a sudden you have 30 little bullies instead of that 1 big bully. That was what happened in Iraq. We took out the big bully, Saddam, and then we had a bunch of little groups to deal with who didn't respect us. They thought we were weak because we were helping them, so they were particularly brutal to us. I wasn't the "hearts and minds" guy, because I realized early on that the only way we'd be able to do our mission and survive was for us to be brutal right back. So I was brutal.

Some people may ask, why did you and your men drag that guy out of the car and smack him around? Because we never had a problem with that guy again. Why did you blow that truck up with

10 pounds of plastic explosives? Because we never had a problem at that checkpoint again. I protected those who needed protecting, I gave medical treatment to those who needed to be treated, and I punished those who needed to be punished. I did not rob, I did not rape, and I did not pillage, and neither did anyone under my command. I took care of my men and my unit, up front and to the utmost. I brought every one of my soldiers home from every tour.

It has taken a long time to put my story down in ink. After years of combat and one too many traumatic brain injuries, I find it hard to remember some things now. I still get flashbacks and try to write them down when I can. For some things in here, I had to rely on the book *On Point* and friends who were there, as some of my memories are still fuzzy. We are all a product of the choices we have made, however, and I wouldn't do anything differently. I did what needed to be done, and because I was there and made the tough decisions that had to be made, my men went home to their wives and their children.

ACKNOWLEDGMENTS

I have many people to thank for this, and so will proceed in chronological order:

First, Robert "Buffy" Ellison, for showing me what a true war hero looks like. Silver Star, two Bronze Stars, three Purple Hearts, three tours in Vietnam—and no one reading this book has ever heard of him, because after medically retiring from the Army he went home, lived his life, and raised his kids, like most combat veterans.

To Patrick Sweeney, prolific book author and Handguns Editor for *Guns & Ammo* magazine, for seeing something in me and getting me into the professional writing world. This couldn't have happened without you. Also, for introducing me to Dave Fortier. I can still remember us sitting around the table in Las Vegas, three skinny white guys with goatees. Right after that meeting, they both shaved theirs off. Mine just keeps getting grayer.

To David Fortier, fellow writer, my conscience and rabbi in the professional gun writing business, who told all his editors they should use me and got me into the TV side of the industry. Some debts can never be repaid. Also, for introducing me to Dillard "CJ" Johnson. My first exposure to CJ was a three-hour ride from the Kansas City airport to Dave's house with CJ and his three boys in a rented POS Mercury Marquis. You learn a lot about people on long car trips, especially if there are kids present. I learned CJ was a good father. Everything else is secondary.

To Jill Fenech, who helped transcribe some of my early phone interviews with CJ while he was still contracting in Iraq. She struggled valiantly with some of the military acronyms, doing her own research so she could get things right. And for not once complaining about CJ's regular use of the term *assclown*.

To Richard Venola, former editor of *Guns & Ammo* and perhaps the Most Interesting Man in the World, for reading through the rough draft of *Carnivore* and providing numerous helpful insights and comments, all of which made this a better book.

To Peter Hubbard, my editor at HarperCollins, for reading that first unsolicited query and giving CJ's story an audience.

And to Andrea, for believing.

James Tarr